Contents

THINGS IN
THE DRIVER'S
SEAT

Things are in the saddle,
And ride mankind.

— Ralph Waldo Emerson
"Ode to W. H. Channing"

THINGS IN THE DRIVER'S SEAT:

Readings in Popular Culture

Harry Russell Huebel

Texas A & I University

Rand McNally College Publishing Company • Chicago

Current Printing (last digit)
15 14 13 12 11 10 9 8 7 6 5 4

INTRODUCTION: 1865–1945

William Holmes McGuffey's school readers ("God will love the child that's gentle, / And who tries to do no wrong; / You must learn then to be careful, / Now while you are very young"); denunciations of "gaudy shows, gambling devices, organ-grinding, conjuring, mountebankism" at state fairs; intense village baseball rivalries; church "socials" ("supper was served and all sorts of games and music helped to make the time pass quickly away")—items from a world that urbanization swept away. For students of popular culture the urban movement has a special relevance because it brought about an intensification of the commercial element within American culture. Rural America had not been innocent of the pecuniary spirit; however, most of the recreational activities of rural life were based upon kindred, religious, and community ties. Urban life weakened those bonds and professionals stepped in to provide amusement. The end result, in Foster Rhea Dulles's crisp phrasing in *America Learns to Play,* was that recreation became "passive, commercialized, and cheap."

Illustrative of the commercialization of the culture was one of the most compelling themes of late nineteenth-century songs, plays, and fiction—the tribulations of the country girl who moved to the city. Sentimental versions of this story concluded with the preservation of her innocence and her values. But, alas, it is more likely that Theodore Dreiser's novel *Sister Carrie* told the real tale. Carrie Meeber was seduced by a city man and city values. More shocking, she did not die diseased and impoverished for her sins, but won material success. Carrie's rejection of the old culture was signified in the political system by the failure of William Jennings Bryan in his bids for the presidency in 1896, 1900, and 1908. To be sure, Bryan represented farmers who worried about the price of crops, but he also articulated the frustrations of men who found that they were characterized as "hayseeds" and "clodhoppers" by the urban masses. Vachel Lindsay captured the essence of Bryan's cathartic appeal when he intoned: "Prairie avenger, mountain lion, / Bryan, Bryan, Bryan, Bryan."

Rapid technological advances accelerated the formation of a commercial culture. Thomas Edison invented the phonograph in 1877; comic strips and primitive movies became common in the 1890s; and Henry Ford devised his first automobile in 1896 (the Model T was marketed in 1908). Guglielmo Marconi's experiments in the nineties and Lee De Forest's invention of the Audion tube in 1906 opened the way for radio. But it was not until the 1920s that these new industrial products became essential components of American popular culture.

Spectator sports enjoyed a tremendous boom in the twenties (the American Professional Football League was organized in 1920); jazz was commercialized for white audiences; the first regular radio broadcast (KDKA, Pittsburgh) took place in 1920; and, most significantly, movies and automobiles became vital experiences for people of all classes and geographic regions. Attempting to depict America's fantasies in the twenties, Henry Miller wrote in *Tropic of Capricorn:* "To walk in money through the night crowd, protected by money, lulled by money, dulled by money, the crowd itself a money, the breath money, no least object anywhere that is not money, money, money everywhere and still not enough, ..." With some exaggeration, popular culture after 1920 might be defined as the expenditure of money. Even in the "free" medium of radio, aside from purchasing a receiving set, the audience was expected to heed commercial messages. (A classic joke attributed to Red Skelton went: "The longest word in the English language is 'and now a word from our sponsor.'") Automobile ownership made possible the ultimate step in commercializing American life—loafing became "taking a ride."

Commercialism resulted in the bolstering of the established power structure within the United States. Dependence of the culture upon industrial products transformed it into a powerful agent of conservatism. The popular arts ignored, muffled, or misrepresented demands for fundamental reforms. Audiences were offered comedy and what Pauline Kael has succinctly labeled *Kiss Kiss Bang Bang.* Radio produced a genteel version of this fare because of the nature of its listeners. As Gordon Allport and Hadley Cantril explained in *The Psychology of Radio:* "The radio is a modern substitute for the hearthside, and a family seated before it is obedient to its own conventional habits and taboos. The radio dares not violate those attitudes fundamental in the great American home." Radio programmers proved what many critics of American culture maintained: violence was acceptable "in the great American home," sex was not.

Radio did an efficient job of policing itself, but the movie industry had difficulties from its birth. The cash value of Clara Bow, Jean Harlow, and Mae West was obvious. When Mae West said "come up and see me sometime" or "it's not the men in my life that count—it's the life in my men" and acted accordingly on the screen, profits were assured. Church organizations eventually pressured moviemakers to adopt self-censorship. The consequent code was ridiculous. Needless to say it did not eliminate sex in films, but it did impede the realistic portrayal of life and made moral endings obligatory.

When the popular arts dealt with problems, they were usually depicted as individual in nature. Criminals foiled by Batman and the Shadow were victims of their own evil genius, not of poverty. Amos and Andy got themselves into fantastic predicaments not because of the inherent plight involved in being black in a racist society but because of their bumbling life-style. Soap operas presented troubles in a local context wherein hard work and character could be marshalled up to resolve them. Can a woman of thirty-five or older find romantic happiness, asked "Helen Trent." The answer was yes; in fact, *Life Begins at Forty,* Walter B. Pitkin assured Americans in the best seller of 1933–1934.

It would be unfair to leave the impression that popular culture was devoted entirely to escapism and defense of the status quo. Movie producers occasionally delved into social criticism. Stark portrayals of the depression in the United States such as John Ford's film of John Steinbeck's *The Grapes of Wrath* questioned the viability of capitalism. Charlie Chaplin's *Modern Times* castigated the entire industrial process in 1936. Other deviations were less obvious. Humphrey Bogart and W. C. Fields were subversive of accepted truths by their very existence, whatever the overt content of the movie. In like manner, the Marx brothers held a mirror to the anarchy of the world in all their films. Although comic books appeared to uphold law, order, freedom, and opportunity, in *The Great Comic Book Heroes,* Jules Feiffer declares that the popularity of the super hero "was a bizarre comeuppance for the American dream.... Here was fantasy with a cynically realistic base: once the odds were appraised honestly it was apparent you had to be super to get on in this world." Despite these (and numerous other) exceptions, the overwhelming bent of the popular culture was conservative. Consider this: when Jack Armstrong "the All-American Boy" grew to manhood, he became an agent for the Scientific Bureau of Investigation (SBI)!

Conservative intellectuals assaulted popular culture during this period with the argument that any art form popular with the masses was necessarily mediocre. Leftist intellectuals also opposed the culture saying that it did not respond to the genuine needs of the people but was simply a tool of the capitalists who used it to exploit people by creating artificial desires for products and to dupe them by misconstruing social issues. Beginning with *The Seven Lively Arts* in 1924, Gilbert Seldes (almost alone in the intellectual community in this matter) insisted that popular culture could potentially enrich the lives of Americans. Naturally, the people ignored the entire debate. They were intent upon listening to Bing Crosby trade insults with Jack Benny, watching Clark Gable seduce a movie queen, cheering Dizzy Dean, or checking the mailbox to see if the Captain Midnight Code-o-graph had arrived.

Currier and Ives:
A Content Analysis

Morton Cronin

Critics of American culture often decry the lack of interest in art among ordinary Americans, yet when the people do exhibit a liking for a particular artist or school of art their taste is usually deplored by those same critics. An excellent case in point was the expert's disdain for the Currier and Ives prints of the late nineteenth century, which were quite popular then and remain so today. The prints were consciously produced for the masses and sold for a modest price; they could be compared to the poster prints of the 1960s.

Like the posters of the sixties, the Currier and Ives lithographs presented a selective view of American life. Morton Cronin details their portrayal of America and indirectly comments upon the comfortable, romanticized self-image of Americans found in the prints. Currier and Ives's preservation of the agrarian myth through the use of the industrial process is one of many pronounced ironies within the article. Compare Currier and Ives's treatment of Negroes with the discussion of Uncle Remus by Bernard Wolfe in this book. For additional information students may wish to consult Harry T. Peters, Currier and Ives, Printmakers to the American People *or* Currier and Ives' America, *edited by Colin Simkin.*

Between 1835 and 1907, Nathaniel Currier and the succeeding firm of Currier and Ives, a partnership formed in 1857, published at least 6,879 different titles representing a great variety of subjects. I have had available for inspection the reproductions that have appeared in books of 543 of these, or roughly 8 per cent of the number that have been discovered so far. If we assume that this sample has not, insofar as the categories employed in the present study are concerned, been seriously distorted by the desire of editors to please living Americans, then we may regard it as sufficiently numerous to be fairly representative. My particular study, however, does not utilize the entire sample, for I have directed my attention only to those prints which bear upon three important matters in American history. This narrowing of my focus, although it reduces the number of references to 205, should not shrink the percentage of pictures in any of the three categories. In any event, the reader will discover that the character of the prints is so consistent that it does not seem probable that any expansion of the sample would alter my conclusions. But I must frankly admit that this study is not based upon the best conceivable sample, but only the best available outside whatever collections of a more representative character may exist in museums or in private hands.

I have selected for analysis those prints of Currier and Ives which depict farm life, industry, and two minority groups in America—the Negro and the Indian. My purpose is to determine, by examining the content of such pictures, the attitudes which they express toward these aspects of American life. I shall not reveal any attitudes that were not previously known to exist in America, but I shall demonstrate the manner in which they were embodied in a medium that has not heretofore been studied for that purpose, at least in any systematic way. Those who have discussed the prints of Currier and Ives in books and articles often insist upon the significance which these prints have for the student of American history, but none of them have anything in particular to say as to just what that significance is. My guess is that this neglect is attributable to the absence of any well-known method whereby pictorial symbols can be subjected to a sociological analysis and interpretation. The quantitative approach of that recently developed discipline called *content analysis* provides at least the beginning of such a method, and that is the approach which I shall use in this paper.

Our sample furnishes us with twenty-three prints which exhibit farm life in the East. I have excluded from their company any prints whose titles indicate that they represent rural scenes in the West. Since pictures depicting the Western farmer and pioneer comprised a definite category

From *American Quarterly*, 4 (4), Winter 1952, 317–330. Reprinted by permission of the author and the *American Quarterly* of the University of Pennsylvania. Copyright 1952 by Trustees of the University of Pennsylvania. (Footnotes and illustrations have been omitted.)

among the "stock prints" of Currier and Ives, it is reasonable to assume that those which do not have such titles were inspired by Eastern farm life, an assumption which the topography, buildings, and other items in most of our twenty-three pictures support. Thus, whatever conclusions I reach regarding the conception of farm life embodied in these prints, I shall not have to disentangle attitudes inspired by farming in itself from those inspired by farming in conjunction with the great adventure of winning the West.

If we were to make, Brueghel-fashion, a great composite picture of these twenty-three prints, we would find in it thirty-eight horses, thirty-three cows or oxen, fifteen dogs, and a number of chickens, ducks, turkeys, sheep, and hogs. The horses, without exception, would be excellent specimens—sleek, plump and, where they appear in pairs, well matched. The cows would be uniformly fat, and all of the oxen big and powerful-looking. Nowhere would a scrawny beast appear. There would be numerous chickens; ducks and turkeys in smaller number; one group of sheep; and one pair of hogs. The great decline in sheep raising which occurred in the East after 1840 may explain the scarcity of those animals, but I suspect an esthetic prejudice behind the poor representation given the hog. Although not as numerous as in the Corn Belt, hogs rooted about many a New England farm. The dog meets with much acceptance, but not as much as the number fifteen suggests, for six—a bitch surrounded by five puppies—appear in one picture. Nine other prints present one dog each.

When it comes to human figures, we find that our prints contain sixty-nine men, twenty-five women, and eighty-six children. The men, whenever their figures are large enough to be inspected, are strong and healthy, decently dressed, and often expressive of quiet dignity. The women are plump, mild featured, and good looking. None of the men or women bear any resemblance, physical or spiritual, to the couple in Grant Wood's "American Gothic."

Not only does the large number of children harmonize with the popular belief in a connection between rural life and large families, but their treatment in these prints strongly suggests that country life affords a paradise for them. In the majority of prints in which children appear—and they appear in all but five—they are seen in attitudes of play or inactivity: skating, sledding, fishing through the ice, riding in a wagon, standing close to their mothers, leaning on the knee of a grandfather, playing in the yard. In those cases where they are working, we find them leading an ox, holding a horse, or gathering apples. In one instance only, a small figure in the background of the print stands beside something which looks suspiciously like a woodpile. But whether working or playing, they look healthy, well fed, and happy.

I have divided the farmhouses depicted in these prints into two classes—large ones and small ones. A large farmhouse I have arbitrarily defined as one possessing two storeys or more, plus at least one capacious wing. Nine of the pictures display such habitations. In eleven of the prints, the houses fall below this standard, but almost all of them are of two storeys. It is evident that our collection of pictures favors the dwelling of the prosperous farmer. The concept of the rural slum finds no place in them.

I have also divided the prints as a whole into two classes—those dominated by scenes of recreation, and those which emphasize episodes of labor. By the first, I mean those prints in which the foreground is occupied by figures engaged in skating, sledding, receiving visitors, or riding in a sleigh, buggy, or wagon for purposes other than work. Twelve of the prints are of this character, although in their backgrounds one often finds figures at work: a man plowing, a woman standing in a doorway with a basket in hand, a farmer on his way to the barn, etc. As the titles of our twenty-three prints indicate, winter scenes are especially popular—there are twelve of them—and the fact that winter is the season of sport and relative leisure among farmers is probably one of the reasons for this popularity, although the pictorial value of snow, especially for black and white prints, may be a factor of even greater weight.

In the eleven remaining prints, the accent is on labor. But it is important to understand the manner in which the labor is depicted. The figure of no man is ever expressive of vigorous exertion, much less fatigue, even when he is behind the plow. In the winter scenes, he never looks cold. When his figure in a picture is sufficiently large to convey the impression, he often radiates composure, mild dignity, even nobility. It is a question, however, as to how much the absence of strenuous expression in the figures and faces of farmers can be attributed to the artists' attitude toward country life in particular. The absence of such expression was a convention of the time in serious pictures of all types. Thus, the lovers in Currier and Ives are masters of poker-faced ardor, and even prize fighters pose like undressed statesmen.

But the effect of pleasant and leisurely effort which the work pictures provide is also the result of other factors, one of which is that, although one or two figures in such a picture may be working, others in the same picture, sometimes equally prominent, are not. In "Husking," for instance, a farmer stands in a barn with a basket of corn on his shoulder. But at his left a young man and woman are sitting on a pile of husks, absorbed in conversation. At his right an old man is braiding ears of corn. But the old man wears a coat, vest, and plug hat, and a child leans against his knee. In "American Forest Scene—Maple Sugaring," which I also classified as a work picture, a man is emptying a pail into a barrel, and a woman is feeding a child. There are, however, fifteen other figures in the picture: four are sitting in one group, talking to one another. Three other groups consist of two individuals each, also talking to one another. One man leans against a pole. In the background, four figures stand beside a yoke of oxen. These last may or may not be working.

Work as casual as this, if not more so, is characteristic of six of the eleven prints portraying scenes of country labor. In four of the remainder, all hands are occupied. In the last, "Winter in the Country—Getting Ice," three men are working, one is looking on, and four in the background are skating.

Women appear in six of the work pictures, performing the following tasks: feeding a child, lifting a basket, gathering apples, sitting in a barn, carrying a hamper, feeding chickens. No woman is seen washing clothes, fetching wood, milking cows, hoeing in a garden, or carrying water.

Judging from those I have seen, most of the prints of Currier and Ives which depict scenes in the West are devoted to the life of the trapper, the hunter, or the Indian. Our sample provides twelve, however, whose subject is the Western farmer, farmstead, or farm community. The most obvious manner in which they differ from depictions of rural life in the East consists in their greater concentration upon scenery and a correspondingly smaller emphasis upon human figures and habitations. Often panoramic in scope, all of them exhibit a plenitude of trees, eight of them include mountains, and nine display water in one form or another—a river, a lake, a pond, or a waterfall. The dry and treeless prairie is obviously not emphasized in these pictures. In those in which the cultivated prairie appears, there is nothing to indicate that it is anything but abundantly fertile. What evidence we have, therefore, suggests that Currier and Ives added their voice to that chorus which sang the praises of the West as a veritable garden, ignoring the serpent of aridity in that garden, together with all its consequences.

These pictures, in short, reveal as idealized a conception of farm life as do those whose locale is the East. Half of them exhibit substantial frame houses, the other half log cabins. A description of three of the former will suffice to provide the reader with an idea of their character. "The Western Farmer's Home" shows a settlement of large houses, some of them estate-size, surrounded by neat wooden fences. Stretching into the background is the open prairie, plowed in precise furrows. In the foreground, a man and woman are chatting by the side of a road; there is a figure on horseback, and one in a wagon. In "A Frontier Settlement" the foreground is taken up by a lake on which there are a sailboat and two rowboats occupied by figures in the attitudes of a boating party. The background exhibits substantial New England-type houses, surrounded by mountains and trees. "The Mountaineer's Home" provides us with a gabled house with such details clearly apparent as clapboard siding, shingled roof, and a trellised doorway overhung with flowers. In the front yard, which is on the edge of a waterfall, a mother is surrounded by six happy children. The pastoral effect is enhanced by the presence of a few sheep nearby.

The six prints which contain log cabins do not, despite the more primitive character of such dwellings, differ essentially from those I have just discussed. The total effect which they convey is snug, pleasant, and romantic. Thus, "The Pioneer's Home" shows a mother and child standing in the doorway of their cabin, while two other children, prettily dressed, are running to meet two men who are carrying a pole on their shoulders from which hang a deer and five fowl. Chickens, two goats, a stand of wheat, a woodpile, and a haystack complete the impression of abundance and good cheer, however primitive. In "A Home in the Wilderness" we find a wife, a child by her side, feeding chickens, her husband and another child returning from a hunting expedition, and a third youngster skating or sliding on a frozen pond. "Across the Continent" shows a village of log cabins, but the largest of these is a public school, in front of which a group of children are happily playing.

The accent is on work in only four of the twelve prints. But even in these there is scarcely a hint of grinding labor or strenuous effort. The nature of the work depicted may be understood by rereading my descriptions of "The Pioneer's Home" and "A Home in the Wilderness," which represent two of the four work pictures. Even less work seems to be done in the West than in the East, although this impression may be simply the result of the greater emphasis, referred to earlier, on the West's spectacular scenery. In any event, this stress on scenery is itself significant as another symptom of that nature worship which has played such an important part in American culture. Farming, family life, and living close to nature—these constitute the outstanding items in the formula for the good life that has been implied by the prints I have considered so far.

The copyright dates for most of these thirty-five pictures have been established. They range from 1849 to 1878. During this period an important ingredient in the political ideology of this country was the notion that the American farmer, owning and tilling his own land, was an ideal citizen, possessed of dignity, inferior in no essential manner to anyone, and fulfilling in his person and way of life the democratic principle in general. Mr. Henry Nash Smith has contrasted the flourishing career which this idea enjoyed in politics with the great resistance it encountered in imaginative literature during the nineteenth century. In the prints of Currier and Ives, however, we find an artistic medium which accepted the idea relatively early and expressed it consistently and wholeheartedly. In the pictures we have examined no farmer is depicted as a boor, a comic, or a quaint rustic. There is no suggestion that the agrarian population consists of a squirearchy on the one hand, and a peasantry on the other. And, finally, we encounter no indication that farmers are inferior to city folk. Whatever tribute these prints pay to the traditional idea of an aristocracy resides only in the fact that they give the farmer some of the traditional characteristics of an aristocrat. Let us turn now to those prints which, in their various ways, express the Industrial Revolution.

Our sample provides forty-two pictures which exhibit railroad scenes. The production of Currier and Ives prints coincided with the early development of the railroad in America, and as a result they offer an opportunity to examine one kind of evidence concerning the popular attitude toward this new phenomenon. The substantial number of prints devoted to the subject is in itself interesting, for it suggests the extent to which the people's imagination was stirred by the railroad, even to the point of considering it, in an artistically conservative era, a fit subject for artistic representation. Many years before the advent of Constructivism, Purism, Futurism, or any other machine-inspired esthetic, Currier and Ives, presumably in simple response to public interest, had discovered material for art in at least certain aspects of the mechanization of America.

Fourteen of the railroad prints are of a humorous character, and I shall consider these separately. Of the remainder, eleven are completely dominated by one or more trains—that is to say, there is little or no landscape in them. In eleven others, trains are the featured subject, but the pictures include considerable landscape. And in six, scenery is dominant and the trains, usually in the background, are incidental.

This classification provides us with the basis for certain conclusions. First, it is apparent that trains alone, with all their parts reproduced with meticulous accuracy, were considered, if not exactly things of beauty, at least objects of commanding interest, worthy of an artist's exclusive attention, and capable of decorating walls without the companionship of any of the traditional subject matter of art. On the other hand, it is also evident that the public of Currier and Ives did not find it difficult to reconcile this symbol of industrialism with nature. Not only is it frequently surrounded by an abundance of scenery, but apparently no incongruity was felt when it was thrown in as an incidental portion of a landscape picture.

In short, these railroad prints express no consciousness of that conflict between industry on the one hand, and agrarianism or nature on the other, which was in process of developing large proportions in America. Trains are depicted in as handsome and approving a manner as are landscapes or scenes from rural life. It is perhaps significant that, except for the humorous prints, our collection does not present a single example of a train wreck, despite the fact that disasters, seriously depicted, were a popular subject of Currier and Ives.

The fourteen humorous prints involving railroads are chiefly of two types. The first type involves the collision between trains and farm animals, thus providing us with our only instances of an awareness of any conflict between industrialism and farm life. There are four of these cartoons. The second type of humorous picture involves the conflict between trains and human beings. The conflict takes such forms as an individual finding himself wrapped around the engine of an oncoming train; or rushing from a station dining room, napkin still in hand, in order to board a departing train; or falling victim to various sleeping-car embarrassments. There are seven cartoons of this kind. If we accept certain theories of humor, we may toy with the idea that these comic prints are evidence of misgivings, on some level of consciousness, in respect to the new mode of life which the railroad represented.

The Industrial Revolution, however, is represented in the prints of Currier and Ives by the steamboat no less than it is by the railroad. Our collection provides forty-four pictures which include steamboats. In twenty-five of them, they are the featured subject. In the remainder, they are often conspicuous but they share honors with other items, usually scenery. The popular interest in this other symbol of the machine age is indicated by the fact that fourteen of the prints are of specific ships, and sometimes the margins of such pictures are filled with statistical descriptions of them. Unlike our sample of railroad prints, however, these are sometimes associated with disaster. Our collection reveals seven examples of steamships about to retire to the depths.

Five of the prints exhibit steamboats in the harbor of New York, four show them on the Hudson River, but the locale for twelve of them is the Mississippi, thus suggesting the extent to which the steamboat had become identified with that particular river. In fact, our total collection of prints provides only one view of the Mississippi which does not include a steamboat, and that one involves an Indian village on the upper reaches of the river.

America was industrialized chiefly by means of the steamboat, the railroad, and the factory. As we have seen, Currier and Ives did ample justice to the railroad and the steamboat, but my inspection of over five hundred prints did not reveal the depiction of a factory, or of life in a factory, even once. As was true of other artists of the day, those who worked for Currier and Ives were apparently not urged either by their employers, by the public at large, or by their own impulses to exploit this phase of our national development. With some exceptions, the life of the workingman—as distinguished from that of the farmer—did not, evidently, appeal to the imagination. The exceptions are interesting, however, because they indicate the kind of manual labor which did stimulate the public's fancy in some measure.

Our total collection of prints provides fourteen which exhibit workingmen at their tasks. Four of them are devoted to firemen. Their titles alone ... suggest the obvious drama which made them appealing. Two prints, although they contain steamboats and much scenery, accord conspicuous space in their foregrounds to Mississippi raftsmen who are romantically conceived as dancing and making merry in general as they float down the river. One print exhibits men mining gold in California, another shows a dandified barber attending a woman of fashion, and a third reveals a blacksmith at his forge, although in this last the stress is on the horses. Four prints, three of which are humorous, involve railroad workers, but the emphasis is either on the passengers or on the trains themselves. Finally, a unique composite picture presents a telegraph operator at his desk and, in the background, a group of printers operating a steam press.

One other group of prints is connected with the workingman—those which preach a temperance sermon. There are eight of these. Four of them, each bearing the same title, constitute a series, amply annotated, which tells the story of a mechanic's downfall through drink and his subsequent reformation. Three of the remainder also involve workingmen. Only one of the eight pictures presents its hero in the well-dressed aspect of an upper-class member of society. These prints are significant because they suggest a popular identification between laborers and hard drinking, because they indicate that it was chiefly the workingman's drinking habits which aroused concern, and because they add a link to our chain of knowledge in respect to the history of the Prohibition movement.

We may now consider the depiction by Currier and Ives of two minority groups in America, the Negro and the Indian. Negroes appear in thirty of our prints. Seven of these are serious pictures. The rest are humorous cartoons—an important fact in itself, for it indicates that the Negro was thought of primarily in terms of comedy. Eleven of these cartoons present Negroes performing actions that are more or less normal for ordinary folk—riding in a train, pulling a mule up a hill, playing baseball, operating a fire brigade, etc. The humor here consists of the ludicrously inept manner in which these commonplace activities are performed, the suggestion clearly being that the Negro cannot execute the simplest maneuvers of everyday life without making himself ridiculous. The rest of the cartoons—twelve of them—exhibit the Negro in situations of a different kind: those in which he displays an absurd propensity for putting on airs and presuming above his true station in life. The comedy, of course, resides in the incongruity between the presumption and the Negro's actual situation, which the cartoon is careful to demonstrate beyond any possibility of doubt. Thus, in "The Darktown Hunt—The Meet" the Negroes are depicted in attitudes of extravagant pretension, but they are mounted on broken-down nags and adorned with ridiculous costumes. In "The Aesthetic Craze" a Negro is shown, sunflower in hand, in the pose associated with Oscar Wilde. But the locale is a backyard occupied by a washerwoman at her tub. In short, the situation changes from one cartoon to another, but the humor is created by applying the same principle in each.

Of the serious prints which include Negroes, three of them exhibit Negroes dancing. A fourth—"Catching a Trout"—shows a Negro netting a fish that is being reeled in by one of the two white men that occupy the boat with him. The subtitle reads, "We hab you now, sar." The three pictures that remain are the only ones which do not exhibit the Negro in a spirit of humor or jollity. One of them, dating from 1845, depicts the branding of slaves on the coast of Africa. Another is a highly sentimental picture of Little Eva hanging a wreath of flowers around the neck of Uncle Tom. The third is a political cartoon which shows a drowning Southerner refusing the outstretched hand of a Negro, while President Grant stands nearby and chides the Southerner for not swallowing his pride.

Finally, we may note that in the prints of Currier and Ives the Negro works even less than the white man. A few of the humorous cartoons show him in situations that would normally be associated with work, but the comedy abolishes that suggestion. In only one of the serious prints— "On the Mississippi—Loading Cotton"—do we find him toiling, and even here he is represented in that activity by tiny figures in the background of the picture only, while the foreground is occupied by Negro children dancing.

Our sample includes thirty-two prints which depict the Indian. Only two of these are humorous, and in neither is the joke upon the red man.

Eleven of the serious pictures show him in conflict with white men. Although in none of them is he permitted to triumph over his adversaries, he is invariably depicted with respect—the white man's foe, but a dangerous and worthy one. In one of the pictures, for instance, a mounted white man looms over a dying Indian stretched on the ground, but the latter gives forth with a last defiant war whoop. Nor does the Indian appear in any of these prints in the character of the treacherous redskin. In his struggles with the white man he is never shown fighting less fairly than his opponent. These prints provide one example of deception and cunning, but it is the whites who display these qualities.

The rest of the Indian prints—nineteen of them—exhibit the Indian in peaceful pursuits, which suggests the extent to which his life appealed to the public's imagination even when it did not conflict with the white man. Eight of these show the Indian as a hunter, his quarry being the buffalo in five of them. Four depict him in various ritual dances. Two show him playing games, two others present family scenes, and a third pair provide views of Indian villages. The one remaining picture exhibits him looking on in a benign and friendly manner as a wagon train invades the West. This is the only example of whites and Indians depicted in the same print without menacing one another.

The degree to which the various aspects of the Indian's life were covered in the prints of Currier and Ives, although not exhaustive, is impressive. The Indian was recognized as a dignified human being, with a legitimate life of his own, to a far greater extent than was the Negro. Above all, he was taken seriously. Whether fighting the white man, hunting animals, performing his rituals, or living with his family, he is presented in a spirit which, when it descends from admiration, goes down only to respectful curiosity.

In their heyday, Currier and Ives prints adorned the walls of barrooms, firehouses, barbershops, hotels, and thousands of homes. Dealers and collectors have found them in every section of the country. Sometimes selling for five to twenty-five cents each, and never for more than three dollars, they were aimed at the masses and the middle classes, a market which it was difficult to impress with the names of artists. Indeed, on a majority of prints no artist's name appears. The pictures were calculated to sell themselves as much as possible by virtue of the innate salability of their subject matter and of the fashion in which it was presented. If we assume that people prefer pictures which harmonize with their preconceptions of the proper nature of things, then the fact that Currier and Ives were primarily interested in selling as many prints as possible suggests that the ideas embodied in those prints reflected the dominant views of the American community. On the other hand, it is possible that Currier and Ives did not accurately apprehend the popular ideology, or that they were not able to prevent the artists whom they employed from expressing relatively unique ideas of their own. If either of these situations was the case, then the prints of Currier and Ives represent a minority report, one that contains ideas and emphases which were not dominant in the American community.

To what degree Currier and Ives prints represented public opinion in nineteenth-century America cannot be determined here, much less the extent to which they can be held responsible for the currency in our culture of the ideas which they express. My objective has been reached if I have simply indicated what these ideas are, if I have demonstrated the manner of their embodiment in pictorial symbols, and if I have suggested the kind of influence—assuming they have had any positive influence whatever— these symbols must have exerted, and continue to exert.

Uncle Remus and The Malevolent Rabbit

"Takes a Limber-Toe Gemmun fer ter Jump Jim Crow"

Bernard Wolfe

Uncle Remus, the storyteller created by Joel Chandler Harris, is usually pictured as an Uncle Tom, a nice old "darky" who spins tales for small children. Bernard Wolfe refutes that image by uncovering the meanings of the stories Uncle Remus tells. In doing so, Wolfe clarifies the conflicts over sex and power between blacks and whites in the late nineteenth-century South, and obliquely contributes to an understanding of the forces that led to segregation.

From the Amos and Andy radio show to Bill Cosby and his (white) nightclub audiences, the interaction of Uncle Remus and the young white boy has been repeated throughout the twentieth century. A revealing article about the Negro attempt to conceal their attitudes toward whites is Hortense Powdermaker's "The Channeling of Negro Aggression by the Cultural Process." For a savage depiction of the consequences of this behavior see "The Allegory of the Black Eunuchs" in Eldridge Cleaver's Soul On Ice.

Joel Chandler Harris's collection and reshaping of the Uncle Remus tales is an excellent example of the use of folk materials in popular culture. The alteration of jazz and folk music by commercial musicians also illustrates the same process.

Aunt Jemima, Beulah, the Gold Dust Twins, "George" the Pullman-ad porter, Uncle Remus. . . . We like to picture the Negro as grinning at us. In Jack de Capitator, the bottle opener that looks like a gaping minstrel face, the grin is a kitchen utensil. At Mammy's Shack, the Seattle roadside inn built in the shape of a minstrel's head, you walk into the neon grin to get your hamburger. . . . And always the image of the Negro—as we create it—signifies some bounty—for us. Eternally the Negro gives—but (as they say in the theater) *really gives*—grinning from ear to ear.

Gifts without end, according to the billboards, movie screens, food labels, soap operas, magazine ads, singing commercials. Our daily bread: Cream O' Wheat, Uncle Ben's Rice, Wilson Ham ("The Ham What Am!"), those "happifyin'" Aunt Jemima pancakes for our "temptilatin'" break-fasts. Our daily drink, too: Carioca Puerto Rican Rum, Hiram Walker whiskey, Ballantine's Ale. Through McCallum and Propper, the Negro gives milady the new "dark Creole shades" in her sheer nylons; through the House of Vigny, her "grotesque," "fuzzy-wuzzy" bottles of Golliwogg colognes and perfumes. Shoeshines, snow-white laundry, comfortable lower berths, efficient handling of luggage; jazz, jive, jitterbugging, zoot, comedy, and the wonderful tales of Brer Rabbit to entrance the kiddies. Service with a smile. . . .

"The Negroes," writes Geoffrey Gorer, "are kept in their subservient position by the ultimate sanctions of fear and force, and this is well known to whites and Negroes alike. Nevertheless, the whites demand that the Negroes shall appear smiling, eager, and friendly in all their dealings with them."

But if the grin is extracted by force, may not the smiling face be a falseface—and just underneath is there not something else, often only half-hidden?

Uncle Remus—a kind of blackface Will Rogers, complete with standard minstrel dialect and plantation shuffle—has had remarkable staying power in our popular culture, much more than Daddy Long Legs, say, or even Uncle Tom. Within the past two years alone he has inspired a full-length Disney feature, three Hit Parade songs, a widely circulated album of recorded dialect stories, a best-selling juvenile picture book, a syndicated comic strip. And the wily hero of his animal fables, Brer Rabbit —to whom Bugs Bunny and perhaps even Harvey owe more than a little— is today a much bigger headliner than Bambi or Black Beauty, outclassing even Donald Duck.

For almost seventy years, Uncle Remus has been the prototype of the Negro grinner-giver. Nothing ever clouds the "beaming countenance" of the "venerable old darky"; nothing ever interrupts the flow of his

From *Commentary*, July 1949, 31–41. Reprinted by permission of the publisher and the Harold Matson Company, Inc.; copyright © 1949 by the American Jewish Committee.

"hearty," "mellow," "cheerful and good-humored" voice as, decade after decade, he presents his Brer Rabbit stories to the nation.

But Remus too is a white man's brainchild: he was created in the columns of the Atlanta *Constitution*, back in the early 1880's, by a neurotic young Southern journalist named Joel Chandler Harris (1848–1908).

When Remus grins, Harris is pulling the strings; when he "gives" his folk stories, he is the ventriloquist's dummy on Harris's knee.

The setting for these stories never varies: the little white boy, son of "Miss Sally" and "Mars John," the plantation owners, comes "hopping and skipping" into the old Negro's cabin down in back of the "big house" and the story telling session gets under way. Remus's face "breaks up into little eddies of smiles"; he takes his admirer on his knee, "strokes the child's hair thoughtfully and caressingly," calls him "honey." The little boy "nestles closer" to his "sable patron" and listens with "open-eyed wonder."

No "sanctions of fear and force" here, Harris insists—the relationship between narrator and auditor is one of unmitigated tenderness. Remus "gives," with a "kindly beam" and a "most infectious chuckle"; the little boy receives with mingled "awe," "admiration," and "delight." But, if one looks more closely, within the magnanimous caress is an incredibly malevolent blow.

Of the several Remus collections published by Harris, the first and most famous is *Uncle Remus: His Songs and His Sayings.* Brer Rabbit appears twenty-six times in this book, encounters the Fox twenty times, soundly trounces him nineteen times. The Fox, on the other hand, achieves only two very minor triumphs—one over the Rabbit, another over the Sparrow. On only two other occasions is the Rabbit victimized even slightly, both times by animals as puny as himself (the Tarrypin, the Buzzard); but when he is pitted against adversaries as strong as the Fox (the Wolf, the Bear, once the whole Animal Kingdom) he emerges the unruffled winner. The Rabbit finally kills off all three of his powerful enemies. The Fox is made a thorough fool of by all the weakest animals—the Buzzard, the Tarrypin, the Bull-Frog.

All told, there are twenty-eight victories of the Weak over the Strong; ultimately all the Strong die violent deaths at the hands of the Weak; and there are, at most, two very insignificant victories of the Strong over the Weak. . . . Admittedly, folk symbols are seldom systematic, clean-cut, or specific; they are cultural shadows thrown by the unconscious, and the unconscious is not governed by the sharp-edged neatness of the filing cabinet. But still, on the basis of the tally-sheet alone, is it too far-fetched to take Brer Rabbit as a symbol—about as sharp as Southern sanctions would allow—of the Negro slave's festering hatred of the white man?

It depends, of course, on whether these are animals who maul and murder each other, or human beings disguised as animals. Here Harris and Remus seem to differ. "In dem days," Remus often starts, "de creeturs wuz santer'n 'roun' same like fokes." But for Harris—so he insists—his anthropomorphism is only incidental. What the stories depict, he tells us, is only the "roaring comedy of animal life."

Is it? These are very un-Aesopian creatures who speak a vaudeville dialect, hold candy-pulls, run for the legislature, fight and scheme over gold mines, compete for women in elaborate rituals of courtship and self-aggrandizement, sing plantation ditties about "Jim Crow," read the news-papers after supper, and kill and maim each other—not in gusts of endocrine Pavlov passion but coldbloodedly, for prestige, plotting their crafty moves in advance and often using accomplices. . . . Harris sees no malice in all this, even when heads roll. Brer Rabbit, he explains, is moved not by "malice, but mischievousness." But Brer Rabbit "mischievously" scalds the Wolf to death, makes the innocent Possum die in a fire to cover his own crimes, tortures and probably murders the Bear by setting a swarm of bees on him—and, after causing the fatal beating of the Fox, carries his victim's head to Mrs. Fox and her children, hoping to trick them into eating it in their soup. . . .

One dramatic tension in these stories seems to be a gastronomic one: *Will the communal meal ever take place in the "Animal" Kingdom?*

The food-sharing issue is posed in the very first story. "I seed Brer B'ar yistiddy," the Fox tells the Rabbit as the story opens, "en he sorter rake me over de coals kaze you en me ain't make frens en live naborly." He then invites the Rabbit to supper—intending that his guest will be the main course in this "joint" feast. Brer Rabbit solemnly accepts the in-vitation, shows up, makes the Fox look ridiculous, and blithely scampers off: "En Brer Fox ain't kotch 'im yit, en w'at's mo', honey, he ain't gwine ter." The Rabbit can get along very well without the communal meal; but, it soon develops, Brer Fox and his associates can't live without it.

Without food-sharing, no community. Open warfare breaks out im-mediately after the Fox's hypocritical invitation; and the Rabbit is invari-ably the victor in the gory skirmishes. And after he kills and skins the Wolf, his other enemies are so cowed that now the communal meal finally seems about to take place: "de animals en de creeturs, dey kep' on gittin' mo' en mo' familious wid wunner nudder—bunchin' der perwishuns ter-gidder in de same shanty" and "takin' a snack" together too.

But Brer Rabbit isn't taken in. Knowing that the others are sharing their food with him out of fear, not genuine communality, he remains the complete cynic and continues to raid the Fox's goober patch and the Bear's persimmon orchard. Not until the closing episode does the Fox make a genuine food-sharing gesture—he crawls inside Bookay the Cow with Brer Rabbit and gratuitously shows him how to hack out all the beef he can carry. But the communal overture comes too late. In an act of the most supreme malevolence, the Rabbit betrays his benefactor to the farmer and stands by, "makin' like he mighty sorry," while the Fox is beaten to death. ... And now the meal which aborted in the beginning, because the Fox's friendliness was only a ruse, almost does take place—with the Fox as the main course. Having brutally destroyed his arch enemy, Brer Rabbit tries to make Mrs. Fox cook a soup with her husband's head, and almost succeeds.

Remus is not an anthropomorphist by accident. His theme is a *human* one—neighborliness—and the communal meal is a symbol for it. His moral? There are no good neighbors in the world, neither equality nor fraternity. But the moral has an underside: the Rabbit can never be trapped.

Another tension runs through the stories: *Who gets the women?* In sex, Brer Rabbit is at his most aggressive—and his most invincible. Throughout he is engaged in murderous competition with the Fox and the other animals for the favors of "Miss Meadows en de gals."

In their sexual competition the Rabbit never fails to humiliate the Fox viciously. "I'll show Miss Meadows en de gals dat I'm de boss er Brer Fox," he decides. And he does: through the most elaborate trickery he persuades the Fox to put on a saddle, then rides him past Miss Meadow's house, digging his spurs in vigorously. . . . And in sex, it would seem, there are no false distinctions between creatures—all differences in status are irrelevant. At Miss Meadows' the feuds of the work-a-day world must be suspended, "kaze Miss Meadows, she done put her foot down, she did, en say dat w'en dey come ter her place dey hatter hang up a flag er truce at de front gate en 'bide by it."

The truce is all to the Rabbit's advantage, because if the competitors start from scratch in the sexual battle the best man must win—and the best man is invariably Brer Rabbit. The women themselves want the best man to win. Miss Meadows decides to get some peace by holding a contest and letting the winner have his pick of the girls. The Rabbit mulls the problem over. He sings ironically,

> Make a bow ter de Buzzard en den ter de Crow
> Takes a limber-toe gemmun fer ter jump Jim Crow.

Then, through a tricky scheme, he proceeds to outshine all the stronger contestants.

Food-sharing, sex-sharing—the Remus stories read like a catalogue of Southern racial taboos, all standing on their heads. The South, wearing the blinders of stereotype, has always tried to see the Negro as a "roaringly comic" domestic animal. Understandably; for animals of the tame or domestic variety are not menacing—they are capable only of mischief, never of malice. But the Negro slave, through his anthropomorphic Rabbit stories, seems to be hinting that even the frailest and most humble of "animals" can let fly with the most bloodthirsty aggressions. And these aggressions take place in the two most sacrosanct areas of Southern racial etiquette: the gastronomic and the erotic.

The South, with its "sanctions of fear and force," forbids Negroes to eat at the same table with whites. But Brer Rabbit, through an act of murder, *forces* Brer Fox and all his associates to share their food with him. The South enjoins the Negro, under penalty of death, from coming near the white man's women—although the white man has free access to the Negro's women. But Brer Rabbit flauntingly demonstrates his sexual superiority over all the other animals and, as the undisputed victor in the sexual competition, gets his choice of *all* the women.

And yet, despite these food and sex taboos, for two solid centuries— for the Rabbit stories existed long before Harris put them on paper— Southerners chuckled at the way the Rabbit terrorized all the other animals into the communal meal, roared at the Rabbit's guise in winning the girls away from the Fox *by jumping Jim Crow*. And they were endlessly intrigued by the O. Henry spasm of the miraculous in the very last story, right after the Fox's death: "Some say dat . . . Brer Rabbit married ole Miss Fox. . . ."

An interesting denouement, considering the sexual fears which saturate the South's racial attitudes. Still more interesting that Southern whites should even have countenanced it, let alone revelled in it. . . .

Significantly, the goal of eating and sex, as depicted in Uncle Remus, is not instinct-gratification. The overriding drive is for *prestige*—the South is a prestige-haunted land. And it is in that potent intangible that the Rabbit is always paid off most handsomely for his exploits. Throughout, as he terrorizes the Strong, the "sassy" Rabbit remains bland, unperturbed, sure of his invincibility. When he humiliates the Fox by turning him into a saddle-horse, he mounts him "same's ef he wuz king er de patter-rollers." ("Patter-rollers," Harris cheerfully points out, were the white patrols that terrorized Negro slaves so they wouldn't wander off the plantations.)

Brer Rabbit, in short, has all the jaunty topdog airs and attitudes which a slave can only dream of having. And, like the slave, he has a supremely cynical view of the social world, since he sees it from below. The South is the most etiquette-ridden region of the country; and the Rabbit sees all forms of etiquette as hypocritical and absurd. Creatures meet, address each other with unctuous politeness, inquire after each other's families, pass the time of day with oily clichés—and all the while they are plotting to humiliate, rob, and assassinate each other. The Rabbit sees through it all; if he is serene it is only because he can plot more rapidly and with more deadly efficiency than any of the others.

The world, in Brer Rabbit's wary eyes, is a jungle. Life is a battle-unto-the-death for food, sex, power, prestige, a battle without rules. There is only one reality in this life: who is on top? But Brer Rabbit wastes no time lamenting the mad unneighborly scramble for the top position. Because it is by no means ordained that the Weak can never take over. In his topsy-turvy world, to all practical purposes, the Weak *have* taken over. In one episode, the Rabbit falls down a well in a bucket. He can get back up only by enticing the Fox to climb into the other bucket. The Fox is duped: he drops down and the Rabbit rises, singing as he passes his enemy:

> Good-by, Brer Fox, take keer yo' cloze
> Fer dis is de way de worril goes
> Some goes up en some goes down
> You'll git ter de bottom all safe en soun'.

This is the theme song of the stories. The question remains, who sings it? The Rabbit is a creation of Uncle Remus's people; is it, then, Uncle Remus singing? But Uncle Remus is a creation of Joel Chandler Harris. . . .

There is a significant difference in age—some hundreds of years—between Uncle Remus and Brer Rabbit. The Rabbit had been the hero of animal stories popular among Negroes from the early days of slavery; these were genuine folk tales told by Negroes to Negroes and handed down in oral form. Uncle Remus was added only when Harris, in packaging the stories—using the Negro grin for gift-wrapping—invented the Negro narrator to sustain the dialect.

Harris, then, fitted the hate-imbued folk materials into a framework, a white man's framework, of "love." He took over the animal characters and situations of the original stories and gave them a human setting: the loving and lovable Negro narrator, the adoring white auditor. Within this framework of love, the blow was heavily padded with caresses and the genuine folk was almost emasculated into the cute folksy.

Almost, but not quite. Harris all his life was torn between his furtive penchant for fiction and his profession of journalism. It was the would-be novelist in him who created Remus, the "giver" of interracial caresses; but the trained journalist in him, having too good an eye and ear, reported the energetic folk blow in the caress. Thus the curious tension in his versions between "human" form and "animal" content.

Before Harris, few Southerners had ever faced squarely the aggressive symbolism of Brer Rabbit, or the paradox of their delight in it. Of course: it was part of the Southerner's undissected myth—often shared by the Negroes—that his cherished childhood sessions in the slave quarters were bathed in two-way benevolence. But Harris, by writing the white South and its Negro tale-spinners into the stories, also wrote in its unfaced paradoxes. Thus his versions helped to rip open the racial myth —and, with it, the interracial grin.

What was the slippery rabbit-hero doing in these stories to begin with? Where did he come from? As soon as Harris wrote down the oral stories for mass consumption, these questions began to agitate many whites. The result was a whole literature devoted to proving the "un-American" genealogy of Brer Rabbit.

Why, one Southern writer asks, did the Negro pick the Rabbit for a hero? Could it be because the Rabbit was "symbolic of his own humble and helpless condition in comparison with his master the owner of the plantation"? Perhaps the Rabbit represents the Negro "in revolt at . . . his own subordinate and insignificant place in society"?

But no: if the Negro is capable of rebelling against society—American society—even symbolically, he is a menace. The Negro must be in revolt against *Nature*, against the "subordinate and insignificant place" assigned to him by biological fate, not America. The writer reassures himself: the Negro makes animals act "like a low order of human intelligence, such as the Negro himself [can] comprehend." The Negro naturally feels "more closely in touch with [the lower animals] than with the white man who [is] so superior to him in every respect." No threat in Brer Rabbit; his genealogy, having no *American* roots, is a technical matter for "the psychologist or the student of folklore."

However, uneasy questions were raised; and as they were raised they were directed at Harris. Readers sensed the symbolic taunts and threats in the rabbit and insisted on knowing whether they were directed against white America—or against "Nature." Harris took refuge from this barrage of questions in two mutually contradictory formulas: (1) he was merely the "compiler" of these stories, a non-intellectual, a lowly humorist, ignorant of "folkloristic" matters; and (2) Brer Rabbit was most certainly, as Southerners intuited, an undiluted African.

"All that I know—all that we Southerners know—about it," Harris protested, "is that every old plantation mammy in the South is full of these stories." But, a sentence later, Harris decided there *was* one other thing he knew: "One thing is certain—the Negro did not get them from the whites; *probably they are of remote African origin.*" And if they come from the Congo, they offer no symbolic blows to Americans; they are simply funny. So Harris warns the folklorists: "First let us have the folktales told as they were intended to be told, for the sake of amusement. . . ."

But if the folklorists *should* find in them something "of value to their pretensions"? Then "let it be picked out and preserved with as little cackling as possible."

The South wavered; it could not shake off the feeling that Brer Rabbit's overtones were more than just funny. And Harris, too, wavered. To a British folklorist editor he wrote, suddenly reversing himself, that the stories were "more important than humorous." And in the introduction to his book he explains that "however humorous it may be in effect, its intention is perfectly serious. . . . It seems to me that a volume written wholly in dialect must have its solemn, not to say melancholy features."

What was it that Harris sporadically found "important," "solemn," even "melancholy" here? It turns out to be the *Americanism* of Brer Rabbit: "it needs no scientific investigation," Harris continues in his introduction, "to show why he [the Negro] selects as his hero the weakest and most harmless of all animals. . . . It is not virtue that triumphs, but helplessness. . . . Indeed, the parallel between the case of the 'weakest' of all animals, who must, perforce, triumph through his shrewdness, and the humble condition of the slave raconteur, is not without its pathos."

A suggestive idea. But such a "parallel" could not have been worked out in the African jungle, before slavery; it implies that Brer Rabbit, after all, was born much closer to the Mississippi than to the Congo. . . . This crucial sentence does not occur in later editions. Instead we read: "It would be presumptious [*sic*] in me to offer an opinion as to the origins of these curious myth-stories; but, *if ethnologists should discover that they did not originate with the African, the proof to that effect should be accompanied with a good deal of persuasive eloquence.*"

In this pressing sentence we can see Harris's whole fragmented psyche mirrored. Like all the South, he was caught in a subjective tug-of-war: his intelligence groped for the venomous American slave crouching behind the Rabbit, but his beleaguered racial emotions, in self-defense, had to insist on the "Africanism" of Brer Rabbit—and of the Negro. Then Miss Sally and Mars John could relish his "quaint antics" without recognizing themselves as his targets.

Against the African origin of Brer Rabbit one may argue that he is an eloquent white folk-symbol too, closely related to the lamb as the epitome of Christian meekness (the Easter bunny). May not the Negro, in his conversion to Christianity, have learned the standard Christian animal symbols from the whites? Could not his constant tale-spinning about the Rabbit's malevolent triumphs somehow, in some devious way, suggest the ascent of Christ, the meekness that shall inherit the earth; suggest, even, that the meek may stop being meek and set about inheriting the earth without waiting on the Biblical timetable?

But, there *is* more definite evidence as to Brer Rabbit's non-African origins—skimpy, not conclusive, but highly suggestive. Folklore study indicates that if the Negro did have stories about a rabbit back in Africa, they were not these stories, and the rabbit was most decidely not this rabbit. Brer Rabbit's truer ancestor, research suggests, hails from elsewhere.

"Most of these Negro stories," reported a Johns Hopkins ethnologist —one of the "cackling" folklorists—". . . bear a striking resemblance to the large body of animal stories made on European soil, of which the most extensive is that known as the *Roman de Renard.* The episodes which form the substance of this French version circulated in the Middle Ages on the Flemish border. . . . The principal actors . . . are the fox, who plays the jokes, and the wolf, most frequently the victim of the fox."

In incident after incident, the Brer Rabbit situations parallel the Reynard the Fox situations: the same props appear, the same set-to's, the same ruses, the same supporting characters, often the same dialogue. But there is one big difference: "In *Uncle Remus* the parts are somewhat changed. Here the rabbit, who scarcely appears (under the name Couard) in the *Renard*, is the chief trickster. His usual butt is the fox. . . ."

In Christian symbolism, then, the rabbit is the essence of meekness and innocence. And in an important part of white folk culture he stands for the impotent, the cowardly, as against the cunning fox. Suddenly, with the beginning of slavery, the Negro begins to tell stories in which the rabbit, now the epitome of belligerence and guile, crops up as the *hero*, mercilessly badgering the fox.

Could the Negroes have got the Reynard fables from the whites? Not impossible. The stories originated among the Flemish peasants. During the 12th century they were written down in French, Latin, and German, in a variety of rhymed forms. The many written versions were then widely circulated throughout Western Europe. And more than a few of the first Negro slaves were brought to France, Spain, and Portugal; and some of their descendants were transplanted to America. Also, many early slaves were brought to plantations owned by Frenchmen—whether in the Louisiana Territory, the Acadian-French sections of North Carolina, or the West Indies.

And many white masters, of French and other backgrounds, told these delightful fox tales to their children. And, from the beginning of the slave trade, many Negroes—who may or may not have had pre-Christian rabbit fables of their own back in Africa—could have listened, smiling amiably, slowly absorbing the raw materials for the grinning folk "gift" that would one day be immortalized by Joel Chandler Harris, Walt Disney, Tin Pan Alley, and the comics. . . .

The Harris research technique, we learn, was first-hand and direct.

Seeing a group of Negroes, he approaches and asks if they know any Brer Rabbit stories. The Negroes seem not to understand. Offhandedly, and in rich dialect, Harris tells one himself—as often as not, the famous "Tar-Baby" story. The Negroes are transfixed; then, suddenly, they break out in peals of laughter, kick their heels together, slap their thighs. Before long they are swapping Rabbit yarns with the white man as though he were their lifelong "hail-feller." "Curiously enough," Harris notes, "I have found few Negroes who will acknowledge to a stranger that they know anything of these legends; and yet to relate one of the stories is the surest road to their confidence and esteem."

Why the sudden hilarity? What magic folk-key causes these wary, taciturn Negroes to open up? Harris claims to have won their "esteem"; but perhaps he only guaranteed them immunity. He thinks he disarmed the Negroes—he may only have demonstrated that he, the white bossman, was disarmed.

And how much did the Negroes tell him when they "opened up"? Just how far did they really open up? Harris observes that "there are different versions of all the stories—the shrewd narrators of the mythology of the old plantations adapting themselves with ready tact to the years, tastes, and expectations of their juvenile audiences." But there seem to be gaps in Harris's own versions. At tantalizingly crucial points Uncle Remus will break off abruptly—"Some tells one tale en some tells nudder"—leaving the story dangling like a radio cliff-hanger. Did these gaps appear when the stories were told to Harris? When the slave is obliged to play the clown-entertainer and "give" his folk tales to his masters, young or old, his keen sense of the fitting might well delete the impermissible and blur the dubious—and more out of self-preservation than tact.

Of course, the original oral stories would not express the slave's aggressions straightforwardly either. A Negro slave who yielded his mind fully to his race hatreds in an absolutely white-dominated situation must go mad; and the function of such folk symbols as Brer Rabbit is precisely to prevent inner explosions by siphoning off these hatreds before they can completely possess consciousness. Folk tales, like so much of folk culture, are part of an elaborate psychic drainage system—they make it possible for Uncle Tom to retain his facade of grinning Tomism and even, to some degree, to believe in it himself. But the slave's venom, while subterranean, must nonetheless have been *thrillingly* close to the surface and its symbolic disguises flimsier, its attacks less roundabout. Accordingly his protective instincts, sensing the danger in too shallow symbolism, would have necessarily wielded a meticulous, if unconscious, blue pencil in the stories told to white audiences.

Harris tried hard to convince himself that Uncle Remus was a full-fledged, dyed-in-the-denim Uncle Tom—he describes the "venerable sable patron" as an ex-slave "who has nothing but pleasant memories of the discipline of slavery." But Harris could not completely exorcise the menace in the Meek. How often Remus steps out of his clown-role to deliver unmistakable judgments on class, caste, and race! In those judgments the aggressions of this "white man's nigger" are astonishingly naked.

"Why the Negro Is Black" tells how the little boy makes the "curious" discovery that Remus's palms are white. The old man explains: "Dey wuz a time w'en all de w'ite folks 'us black—blacker dan me. . . . Niggers is niggers now, but de time wuz w'en we 'uz all niggers tergedder. . . ." How did some "niggers" get white? Simply by bathing in a pond which washed their pigmentation off and using up most of the waters, so that the latecomers could only dabble their hands and feet in it.

But the stragglers who were left with their dark skin tone are not trapped—they may be able to wriggle out of it. In "A Plantation Witch," Remus, explaining that there are witches everywhere in the world that "comes en conjus fokes," hints that these witches may be Negroes who have slipped out of their skins. And these witches conjure white folks from all sides, taking on the forms of owls, bats, dogs, cats—and rabbits.

And in "The Wonderful Tar-Baby Story"—advertised on the dust-jacket as the most famous of all the Remus stories—Remus reverts to the question of pigmentation. ("There are few negroes that will fail to respond" to this one, Harris advises one of his folklore "legmen.") The Fox fashions a "baby" out of tar and places it on the side of the road; the Rabbit comes along and addresses the figure. Not getting any answer, he threatens: "Ef you don't take off dat hat en tell me howdy, I'm gwineter bus' you wide open." (Here the Rabbit's bluster reads like a parody of the white man's demand for the proper bowing-and-scraping etiquette from the Negro; it is a reflection of the satiric mimicry of the whites which the slaves often indulged in among themselves.) He hits the Tar-Baby—his fist sticks in the gooey tar. He hits it with the other hand, then kicks it—all four extremities are stuck.

This is "giving" in a new sense; tar, blackness, by its very yielding, traps. Interesting symbol, in a land where the mere possession of a black skin requires you, under penalty of death, to yield, to *give,* everywhere. The mark of supreme impotence suddenly acquires the power to render impotent, merely by its flaccidity, its inertness; it is almost a Gandhi-like symbol. There is a puzzle here: it is the Rabbit who is trapped. But in a later story, "How Mr. Rabbit Was Too Sharp for Mr. Fox," it turns out that the Rabbit, through another cagey maneuver, gets the Fox to set him free from the tar-trap and thus avoids being eaten by his enemy. The Negro, in other words, is wily enough to escape from the engulfing pit of blackness, although his opponents, who set the trap, do their level best to keep him imprisoned in it. But it is not at all sure that anyone else who fell victim to this treacherous black yieldingness—the Fox, say—would be able to wriggle out so easily.

The story about "A Plantation Witch" frightens his young admirer so much that Remus has to take him by the hand and lead him home to the "big house." And for a long time the boy lies awake "expecting an unseemly visitation from some mysterious source." Many of the other stories, too, must have given him uneasy nights. For within the "gift" that Uncle Remus gives to Miss Sally's little boy is a nightmare, a nightmare in which whites are Negroes, the Weak torture and drown the Strong, mere blackness becomes black magic—and Negroes cavort with cosmic forces and the supernatural, zipping their skins off at will to prowl around the countryside terrorizing the whites, often in the guise of rabbits. . . .

Harris's career is one of the fabulous success stories of American literary history. Thanks to Uncle Remus, the obscure newspaperman was catapulted into the company of Mark Twain, Bret Harte, James Whitcomb Riley, and Petroleum V. Nasby; Andrew Carnegie and Theodore Roosevelt traveled to Atlanta to seek him out; he was quoted in Congress. And all the while he maintained—as in a letter to Twain—that "my book has no basis in literary merit to stand upon; I know it is the matter and not the manner that has attracted public attention . . . my relations towards Uncle Remus are similar to those that exist between an almanac-maker and the calendar. . . ."

But how was it that Harris could apply his saccharine manner to such matter, dress this malevolent material, these nightmares, in such sweetness and light? For one thing, of course, he was only recording the tottering racial myth of the post-bellum South, doing a paste-job on its fissioning falseface. As it happened, he was peculiarly suited for the job; for he was crammed full of pathological racial obsessions, over and above those that wrack the South and, to a lesser degree, all of white America.

Even Harris's worshipful biographer, his daughter-in-law, can't prevent his story from reading like a psychiatric recital of symptoms. The blush and the stammer were his whole way of life. From early childhood on, we are told, he was "painfully conscious of his social deficiencies" and his "lack of size"; he felt "handicapped by his tendency to stutter" and to "blush furiously," believed himself "much uglier than he really was"; in his own words, he had "an absolute horror of strangers."

During his induction into the typographical union, Harris stutters so badly that he has to be excused from the initiation ceremony; trapped in a room full of congenial strangers, he escapes by jumping out of the window. "What a coarse ungainly boor I am," he laments, "how poor, small and insignificant. . . ." He wonders if he is mad: "I am morbidly sensitive . . . it is an affliction—a disease . . . the slightest rebuff tortures me beyond expression. . . . It is worse than death itself. It is *horrible.*" Again, he speculates about his "abnormal quality of mind . . . that lacks only vehemence to become downright insanity. . . ." Harris's life, it appears, was one long ballet of embarrassment.

"I am nursing a novel in my brain," Harris announced archly more than once. All along he was consumed with the desire to turn out some "long work" of fiction, but, except for two inept and badly received efforts (published after his forty-eighth year), he never succeeded. Over and over he complained bitterly of his grinding life in the journalistic salt mines— but when the Century Company offered him a handsome income if he would devote all his time to creative work, he refused. This refusal, according to his daughter-in-law, "can be explained only by his abnormal lack of confidence in himself as a 'literary man.' "

The urge to create was strong in Harris, so strong that it gave him no peace; and he could not create. That is the central fact in his biography: his creative impulses were trapped behind a block of congealed guilts, granite-strong; the works he produced were not real gushings of the subjective but only those driblets that were able to seep around the edges of the block.

Harris's stammer—his literal choking on words—was like a charade of the novelist *manqué* in him; his blush was the fitful glow of his smothered self, a tic of the guilty blood. And that smothered self had a name: Uncle Remus.

Accused of plagiarizing folk materials, Harris replies indignantly: "I shall not hesitate to draw on the oral stories I know for incidents. . . . The greatest literary men, if you will remember, were very poor inventors." Harris all his life was a very poor inventor; his career was built on a merciless, systematic plagiarizing of the folk-Negro. Small wonder, then, that the "plantation darky" was such a provocative symbol for him. For, ironically, this lowly Negro was, when viewed through the blinders of stereotype, almost the walking image of Harris's ego-ideal—the un-selfconscious, "natural," free-flowing, richly giving creator that Harris could never become. Indeed, for Harris, as for many another white American, the Negro *seemed* in every respect to be a negative print of his own uneasy self: "happy-go-lucky," socializing, orally expressive, muscularly relaxed, never bored or passive, unashamedly exhibitionistic, free from self-pity even in his situation of concentrated pain, emotionally fluid. And every time a Remus opened his mouth, every time he flashed a grin, he wrote effortlessly another novel that was strangled a-borning in Harris.

"I despise and detest those false forms of society that compel people to suppress their thoughts," Harris wrote. But he was himself the most inhibited and abashed of men. What fascinates him in the Rabbit stories, he confesses, is "the humor that lies between *what is perfectly decorous in appearance* and *what is wildly extravagant in suggestion.*" But, a thorough slave to decorum, he was incapable of the "wildly extravagant," whether in his love-making ("My love for you," he informs his future wife, "is . . . far removed from that wild passion that develops itself in young men in their teens . . . it is not at all wild or unreasoning") or in his writing.

Harris, then, was *awed* by Uncle Remus. It was the awe of the sophisticate before the spontaneous, the straitjacketed before the nimble. But was the Negro what Harris thought him to be? It is certainly open to question, for another irony of the South is that the white man, under his pretense of racial omniscience, actually knows the Negro not at all—he knows only the falseface which he has forced on the Negro. It is the white man who manufactures the Negro grin. The stereotype reflects the looker, his thwartings and yearnings, not the person looked at; it is born out of intense subjective need.

Harris's racial awe was only an offshoot of the problem that tormented him all his life: the problem of identifying himself. He was caught in the American who-am-I dilemma, one horn of which is white, the other often black. And there is abundant proof that, at least in one compartment of his being, Harris defined himself by identifying with the Negro.

As a child, Harris started the game of "Gully Minstrels" with his white playmates; and later in life, whenever he felt "blue" and wanted to relax, he would jump up and exclaim, "Let's have some fun—let's play minstrels!" Often, in letters and newspaper articles, and even in personal relations, he would *jokingly* refer to himself as "Uncle Remus," and when he started a one-man magazine, he decided to name it *Uncle Remus's Magazine* instead of *The Optimist!* Frequently he would lapse into a rich Negro dialect, to the delight of his admirers, from Andrew Carnegie down to the local trolley conductor. And, like Uncle Remus, he even toys with the idea that whites are only blanched Negroes: "Study a nigger right close," he has one of his characters say, "and you'll ketch a glimpse of how white folks would look and do without their trimmin's."

Harris seems to have been a man in permanent rebellion against his own skin. No wonder: for he was driven to "give," and it was impossible for him to give without first zipping out of his own decorous skin and slipping into Uncle Remus's. To him the artist and the Negro were synonymous.

And Harris virulently *hated* the Negro too. "The colored people of Macon," he writes in his paper, "celebrated the birthday of Lincoln again on Wednesday. This is the third time since last October. . . ." And: "A negro pursued by an agile Macon policeman fell in a well the other day. He says he knocked the bottom out of the concern." Again: "There will have to be another amendment to the civil rights bill. A negro boy in Covington was attacked by a sow lately and narrowly escaped with his life. We will hear next that the sheep have banded together to mangle the downtrodden race."

The malice here is understandable. Can the frustrate—the "almanac-maker"—ever love unequivocally the incarnation of his own taboo self—the "calendar"? What stillborn novelist can be undilutedly tender towards the objectivization of his squelched alter-ego, whose oral stories he feels impelled to "draw on" all his life?

Most likely, at least in Harris, the love went deeper than the hate—the hate was, in some measure, a *defense* against the love. *"Some goes up en some goes down."* Who sings this theme song? A trio: the Rabbit, Remus, *and* Harris. Literally, it is only a rabbit and a fox who change places. Racially, the song symbolizes the ascent of the Negro "Weak" and the descent of the white "Strong."

But to Harris, on the deepest personal level, it must have meant: collapse of the "perfectly decorous" (inhibition, etiquette, embarrassment, the love that is never wild, the uncreative journalist-compiler, the blush and the stammer) and the triumph of the "wildly extravagant" (spontaneity, "naturalness," the unleashed subjective, creativity, "Miss Meadows en de gals," exhibitionism, the folk-novelist). The song must have been *deliciously* funny to him. . . .

The Remus stories are a monument to the South's ambivalence. Harris, the archetypical Southerner, sought the Negro's love, and pretended he had received it (Remus's grin). But he sought the Negro's hate too (Brer Rabbit), and revelled in it in an unconscious orgy of masochism —punishing himself, possibly, for not being the Negro, the stereotypical Negro, the unstinting giver.

Harris's inner split—and the South's, and white America's—is mirrored in the fantastic disparity between Remus's beaming face and Brer Rabbit's acts. And such aggressive acts increasingly emanate from the grin, along with the hamburgers, the shoeshines, the "happifyin'" pancakes.

Today Negro attack and counter-attack becomes more straightforward. The NAACP submits a brief to the United Nations, demanding a redress of grievances suffered by the Negro people at the hands of white America. The election newsreels showed Henry Wallace addressing audiences that were heavily sprinkled with Negroes, protected by husky, alert, *deadpan* bodyguards—Negroes. New York Negroes voted for Truman—but only after Truman went to Harlem. The Gandhi-like "Tar-Baby" begins to stir: Grant Reynolds and A. Phillips Randolph, announcing to a Senate committee that they will refuse to be drafted in the next war, revealed, at the time, that many Negroes were joining their civil-disobedience organization—the first movement of passive resistance this country had seen.

Increasingly Negroes themselves reject the mediating smile of Remus, the indirection of the Rabbit. The present-day animated cartoon hero, Bugs Bunny, is, like Brer Rabbit, the meek suddenly grown cunning—but without Brer Rabbit's facade of politeness. "To pull a Bugs Bunny," meaning to spectacularly outwit someone, is an expression not infrequently heard in Harlem.

There is today on every level a mass repudiation of "Uncle Tomism." Significantly the Negro comedian is disappearing. For bad or good, the *Dark Laughter* that Sherwood Anderson heard all around white New Orleans is going or gone.

The grin is faltering, especially since the war. That may be one of the reasons why, once more, the beaming Negro butler and Pullman porter are making their amiable way across our billboards, food labels, and magazine ads—and Uncle Remus, "fetchin' a grin from year to year," is in the big time again.

The Wizard of Oz:
Parable on Populism

Henry M. Littlefield

Covert social commentary is often present in children's books—not only in those adult books judged acceptable for children, such as Mark Twain's Huckleberry Finn, *but also in stories written specifically for young readers such as the Rover Boys series and the "Dick and Jane" school readers. Knowledge of this has led to crusades against subversive tendencies in school books; it has also enticed talented scholars like Henry Littlefield into the field of children's literature. Littlefield has written a classic study of a favorite American novel,* The Wizard of Oz, *by Lyman Frank Baum.*

The Wizard of Oz, published in 1900, satirizes the politics of the 1890s, particularly the Populist movement and the agrarian myth. Littlefield's analysis prompts questions concerning the American public's favorable reaction to the novel. Its popularity may provide insights into America in 1900; however, it is possible that no one perceived Baum's message and that the initial popularity of the story had nothing to do with his satire. To discover the reasons for the continuing popularity of The Wizard of Oz one must look to Judy Garland and the film versions of the novel, since few people today read the original story. It might prove interesting to review the films in order to determine whether Baum's social themes remain intact.

More information on Baum is provided by Martin Gardiner and Russel B. Nye in The Wizard of Oz and Who He Was. *Russel B. Nye has surveyed juvenile fiction in his textbook* The Unembarrassed Muse: The Popular Arts in America.

On the deserts of North Africa in 1941 two tough Australian brigades went to battle singing,

> Have you heard of the wonderful wizard,
> The wonderful Wizard of Oz,
> And he is a wonderful wizard,
> If ever a wizard there was.[1]

It was a song they had brought with them from Australia and would soon spread to England. Forever afterward it reminded Winston Churchill of those "buoyant days." Churchill's nostalgia is only one symptom of the world-wide delight found in an American fairy-tale about a little girl and her odyssey in the strange land of Oz. The song he reflects upon came from a classic 1939 Hollywood production of the story, which introduced millions of people not only to the land of Oz, but to a talented young lady named Judy Garland as well.

Ever since its publication in 1900 Lyman Frank Baum's *The Wonderful Wizard of Oz* has been immensely popular, providing the basis for a profitable musical comedy, three movies and a number of plays. It is an indigenous creation, curiously warm and touching, although no one really knows why. For despite wholehearted acceptance by generations of readers, Baum's tale has been accorded neither critical acclaim, nor extended critical examination. Interested scholars, such as Russel B. Nye and Martin Gardiner, look upon *The Wizard of Oz* as the first in a long and delightful series of Oz stories, and understandably base their appreciation of Baum's talent on the totality of his works.

The Wizard of Oz is an entity unto itself, however, and was not originally written with a sequel in mind. Baum informed his readers in 1904 that he had produced *The Marvelous Land of Oz* reluctantly and only in answer to well over a thousand letters demanding that he create another Oz tale. His original effort remains unique and to some degree separate from the books which follow. But its uniqueness does not rest alone on its peculiar and transcendent popularity.

Professor Nye finds a "strain of moralism" in the Oz books, as well as "a well-developed sense of satire," and Baum stories often include searching parodies on the contradictions in human nature. The second book in the series, *The Marvelous Land of Oz,* is a blatant satire on feminism and the suffragette movement. In it Baum attempted to duplicate the format used so successfully in *The Wizard,* yet no one has noted a

From *American Quarterly*, 16 (1), Spring 1964, 47–58. Reprinted by permission of the author and the *American Quarterly* of the University of Pennsylvania. Copyright 1964 by Trustees of the University of Pennsylvania. (Footnotes have been omitted.)

1. From "The Wizard of Oz," lyric: E. Y. Harburg; music: Harold Allen. Copyright 1938, renewed 1967. Rights throughout the world controlled by Leo Feist Inc. Used by permission.

similar play on contemporary movements in the latter work. Nevertheless, one does exist, and it reflects to an astonishing degree the world of political reality which surrounded Baum in 1900. In order to understand the relationship of *The Wizard* to turn-of-the-century America, it is necessary first to know something of Baum's background.

Born near Syracuse in 1856, Baum was brought up in a wealthy home and early became interested in the theater. He wrote some plays which enjoyed brief success and then, with his wife and two sons, journeyed to Aberdeen, South Dakota, in 1887. Aberdeen was a little prairie town and there Baum edited the local weekly until it failed in 1891.

For many years Western farmers had been in a state of loud, though unsuccessful, revolt. While Baum was living in South Dakota not only was the frontier a thing of the past, but the Romantic view of benign nature had disappeared as well. The stark reality of the dry, open plains and the acceptance of man's Darwinian subservience to his environment served to crush Romantic idealism.

Hamlin Garland's visit to Iowa and South Dakota coincided with Baum's arrival. Henry Nash Smith observes,

> Garland's success as a portrayer of hardship and suffering on Northwestern farms was due in part to the fact that his personal experience happened to parallel the shock which the entire West received in the later 1880's from the combined effects of low prices, . . . grasshoppers, drought, the terrible blizzards of the winter of 1886–1887, and the juggling of freight rates. . . .

As we shall see, Baum's prairie experience was no less deeply etched, although he did not employ naturalism to express it.

Baum's stay in South Dakota also covered the period of the formation of the Populist party, which Professor Nye likens to a fanatic "crusade." Western farmers had for a long time sought governmental aid in the form of economic panaceas, but to no avail. The Populist movement symbolized a desperate attempt to use the power of the ballot. In 1891 Baum moved to Chicago where he was surrounded by those dynamic elements of reform which made the city so notable during the 1890s.

In Chicago Baum certainly saw the results of the frightful depression which had closed down upon the nation in 1893. Moreover, he took part in the pivotal election of 1896, marching in "torch-light parades for William Jennings Bryan." Martin Gardiner notes besides, that he "consistently voted as a democrat . . . and his sympathies seem always to have been on the side of the laboring classes." No one who marched in even a few such parades could have been unaffected by Bryan's campaign. Putting all the farmers' hopes in a basket labeled "free coinage of silver," Bryan's platform rested mainly on the issue of adding silver to the nation's gold standard. Though he lost, he did at least bring the plight of the little man into national focus.

Between 1896 and 1900, while Baum worked and wrote in Chicago, the great depression faded away and the war with Spain thrust the United States into world prominence. Bryan maintained Midwestern control over the Democratic party, and often spoke out against American policies toward Cuba and the Philippines. By 1900 it was evident that Bryan would run again, although now imperialism and not silver seemed the issue of primary concern. In order to promote greater enthusiasm, however, Bryan felt compelled once more to sound the silver leitmotif in his campaign. Bryan's second futile attempt at the presidency culminated in November 1900. The previous winter Baum had attempted unsuccessfully to sell a rather original volume of children's fantasy, but that April, George M. Hill, a small Chicago publisher, finally agreed to print *The Wonderful Wizard of Oz.*

Baum's allegiance to the cause of Democratic Populism must be balanced against the fact that he was not a political activist. Martin Gardiner finds through all of his writings "a theme of tolerance, with many episodes that poke fun at narrow nationalism and ethnocentrism." Nevertheless, Professor Nye quotes Baum as having a desire to write stories that would "bear the stamp of our times and depict the progressive fairies of today."

The Wizard of Oz has neither the mature religious appeal of a *Pilgrim's Progress,* nor the philosophic depth of a *Candide.* Baum's most thoughtful devotees see in it only a warm, cleverly written fairy tale. Yet the original Oz book conceals an unsuspected depth, and it is the purpose of this study to demonstrate that Baum's immortal American fantasy encompasses more than heretofore believed. For Baum created a children's story with a symbolic allegory implicit within its story line and characterizations. The allegory always remains in a minor key, subordinated to the major theme and readily abandoned whenever it threatens to distort the appeal of the fantasy. But through it, in the form of a subtle parable, Baum delineated a Midwesterner's vibrant and ironic portrait of this country as it entered the twentieth century.

We are introduced to both Dorothy and Kansas at the same time:

> Dorothy lived in the midst of the great Kansas prairies, with Uncle Henry, who was a farmer, and Aunt Em, who was the farmer's wife. Their house was small, for the lumber to build it had to be carried by wagon many miles. There were four walls, a floor and a roof, which made one room; and this room contained a rusty-looking cooking stove, a cupboard for the dishes, a table, three or four chairs, and the beds.
>
> When Dorothy stood in the doorway and looked around, she could see nothing but the great gray prairie on every side. Not a tree nor a house broke

the broad sweep of flat country that reached to the edge of the sky in all directions. The sun had baked the plowed land into a gray mass, with little cracks running through it. Even the grass was not green, for the sun had burned the tops of the long blades until they were the same gray color to be seen everywhere. Once the house had been painted, but the sun blistered the paint and the rains washed it away, and now the house was as dull and gray as everything else.

When Aunt Em came there to live she was a young, pretty wife. The sun and wind had changed her, too. They had taken the sparkle from her eyes and left them a sober gray; they had taken the red from her cheeks and lips, and they were gray also. She was thin and gaunt, and never smiled now. When Dorothy, who was an orphan, first came to her, Aunt Em had been so startled by the child's laughter that she would scream and press her hand upon her heart whenever Dorothy's merry voice reached her ears; and she still looked at the little girl with wonder that she could find anything to laugh at.

Uncle Henry never laughed. He worked hard from morning till night and did not know what joy was. He was gray also, from his long beard to his rough boots, and he looked stern and solemn, and rarely spoke.

It was Toto that made Dorothy laugh, and saved her from growing as gray as her other surroundings. Toto was not gray; he was a little black dog, with long silky hair and small black eyes that twinkled merrily on either side of his funny, wee nose. Toto played all day long, and Dorothy played with him, and loved him dearly.[2]

Hector St. John de Crèvecoeur would not have recognized Uncle Henry's farm; it is straight out of Hamlin Garland. On it a deadly environment dominates everyone and everything except Dorothy and her pet. The setting is Old Testament and nature seems grayly impersonal and even angry. Yet it is a fearsome cyclone that lifts Dorothy and Toto in their house and deposits them "very gently—for a cyclone—in the midst of a country of marvelous beauty." We immediately sense the contrast between Oz and Kansas. Here there are "stately trees bearing rich and luscious fruits ... gorgeous flowers ... and birds with ... brilliant plumage" sing in the trees. In Oz "a small brook rushing and sparkling along" murmurs "in a voice very grateful to a little girl who had lived so long on the dry, gray prairies" (p. 20).

Trouble intrudes. Dorothy's house has come down on the wicked Witch of the East, killing her. Nature, by sheer accident, can provide benefits, for indirectly the cyclone has disposed of one of the two truly bad influences in the Land of Oz. Notice that evil ruled in both the East and the West; after Dorothy's coming it rules only in the West.

The wicked Witch of the East had kept the little Munchkin people "in bondage for many years, making them slave for her night and day" (pp.

2. L. Frank Baum, *The Wonderful Wizard of Oz*, pp. 11–13. All quotations cited in the text are from the inexpensive but accurate Dover paperback edition (New York, 1960).

22–23). Just what this slavery entailed is not immediately clear, but Baum later gives us a specific example. The Tin Woodman, whom Dorothy meets on her way to the Emerald City, had been put under a spell by the Witch of the East. Once an independent and hard working human being, the Woodman found that each time he swung his axe it chopped off a different part of his body. Knowing no other trade he "worked harder than ever," for luckily in Oz tinsmiths can repair such things. Soon the Woodman was all tin (p. 59). In this way Eastern witchcraft dehumanized a simple laborer so that the faster and better he worked the more quickly he became a kind of machine. Here is a Populist view of evil Eastern influences on honest labor which could hardly be more pointed.

There is one thing seriously wrong with being made of tin; when it rains rust sets in. Tin Woodman had been standing in the same position for a year without moving before Dorothy came along and oiled his joints. The Tin Woodman's situation has an obvious parallel in the condition of many Eastern workers after the depression of 1893. While Tin Woodman is standing still, rusted solid, he deludes himself into thinking he is no longer capable of that most human of sentiments, love. Hate does not fill the void, a constant lesson in the Oz books, and Tin Woodman feels that only a heart will make him sensitive again. So he accompanies Dorothy to see if the Wizard will give him one.

Oz itself is a magic oasis surrounded by impassable deserts, and the country is divided in a very orderly fashion. In the North and South the people are ruled by good witches, who are not quite as powerful as the wicked ones of the East and West. In the center of the land rises the magnificent Emerald City ruled by the Wizard of Oz, a successful humbug whom even the witches mistakenly feel "is more powerful than all the rest of us together" (p. 24). Despite these forces, the mark of goodness, placed on Dorothy's forehead by the Witch of the North, serves as protection for Dorothy throughout her travels. Goodness and innocence prevail even over the powers of evil and delusion in Oz. Perhaps it is this basic and beautiful optimism that makes Baum's tale so characteristically American—and Midwestern.

Dorothy is Baum's Miss Everyman. She is one of us, levelheaded and human, and she has a real problem. Young readers can understand her quandary as readily as can adults. She is good, not precious, and she thinks quite naturally about others. For all of the attractions of Oz Dorothy desires only to return to the gray plains and Aunt Em and Uncle Henry. She is directed toward the Emerald City by the good Witch of the North, since the Wizard will surely be able to solve the problem of the impassable deserts. Dorothy sets out on the Yellow Brick Road wearing the Witch of the East's magic Silver Shoes. Silver shoes walking on a golden road; henceforth Dorothy becomes the innocent agent of Baum's ironic view of the Silver issue. Remember, neither Dorothy, nor the good Witch of the North, nor the Munchkins understand the power of these shoes. The allegory is abundantly clear. On the next to last page of the book Baum has Glinda, Witch of the South, tell Dorothy, "Your Silver Shoes will carry you over the desert. . . . If you had known their power you could have gone back to your Aunt Em the very first day you came to this country." Glinda explains, "All you have to do is to knock the heels together three times and command the shoes to carry you wherever you wish to go" (p. 257). William Jennings Bryan never outlined the advantages of the silver standard any more effectively.

Not understanding the magic of the Silver Shoes, Dorothy walks the mundane—and dangerous—Yellow Brick Road. The first person she meets is a Scarecrow. After escaping from his wooden perch, the Scarecrow displays a terrible sense of inferiority and self doubt, for he has determined that he needs real brains to replace the common straw in his head. William Allen White wrote an article in 1896 entitled "What's the Matter With Kansas?" In it he accused Kansas farmers of ignorance, irrationality and general muddle-headedness. What's wrong with Kansas are the people, said Mr. White. Baum's character seems to have read White's angry characterization. But Baum never takes White seriously and so the Scarecrow soon emerges as innately a very shrewd and very capable individual.

The Scarecrow and the Tin Woodman accompany Dorothy along the Yellow Brick Road, one seeking brains, the other a heart. They meet next the Cowardly Lion. As King of Beasts he explains, "I learned that if I roared very loudly every living thing was frightened and got out of my way." Born a coward, he sobs, "Whenever there is danger my heart begins to beat fast." "Perhaps you have heart disease," suggests Tin Woodman, who always worries about hearts. But the Lion desires only courage and so he joins the party to ask help from the Wizard (pp. 65–72).

The Lion represents Bryan himself. In the election of 1896 Bryan lost the vote of Eastern labor, though he tried hard to gain their support. In Baum's story the Lion, on meeting the little group, "struck at the Tin Woodman with his sharp claws." But, to his surprise, "he could make no impression on the tin, although the Woodman fell over in the road and lay still." Baum here refers to the fact that in 1896 workers were often pressured into voting for McKinley and gold by their employers. Amazed, the Lion says, "he nearly blunted my claws," and he adds even more appropriately, "When they scratched against the tin it made a cold shiver run down my back" (pp. 67–68). The King of Beasts is not after all very cowardly, and Bryan, although a pacifist and an anti-imperialist in a time of national expansion, is not either. The magic Silver Shoes belong to

Dorothy, however. Silver's potent charm, which had come to mean so much to so many in the Midwest, could not be entrusted to a political symbol. Baum delivers Dorothy from the world of adventure and fantasy to the real world of heartbreak and desolation through the power of Silver. It represents a real force in a land of illusion, and neither the Cowardly Lion nor Bryan truly needs or understands its use.

All together now the small party moves toward the Emerald City. Coxey's Army of tramps and indigents, marching to ask President Cleveland for work in 1894, appears no more naively innocent than this group of four characters going to see a humbug Wizard, to request favors that only the little girl among them deserves.

Those who enter the Emerald City must wear green glasses. Dorothy later discovers that the greenness of dresses and ribbons disappears on leaving, and everything becomes a bland white. Perhaps the magic of any city is thus self imposed. But the Wizard dwells here and so the Emerald City represents the national Capitol. The Wizard, a little bumbling old man, hiding behind a facade of papier mâché and noise, might be any President from Grant to McKinley. He comes straight from the fair grounds in Omaha, Nebraska, and he symbolizes the American criterion for leadership—he is able to be everything to everybody.

As each of our heroes enters the throne room to ask a favor the Wizard assumes different shapes, representing different views toward national leadership. To Dorothy, he appears as an enormous head, "bigger than the head of the biggest giant." An apt image for a naive and innocent little citizen. To the Scarecrow he appears to be a lovely, gossamer fairy, a most appropriate form for an idealistic Kansas farmer. The Woodman sees a horrible beast, as would any exploited Eastern laborer after the trouble of the 1890s. But the Cowardly Lion, like W. J. Bryan, sees a "Ball of Fire, so fierce and glowing he could scarcely bear to gaze upon it." Baum then provides an additional analogy, for when the Lion "tried to go nearer he singed his whiskers and he crept back tremblingly to a spot nearer the door" (p. 134).

The Wizard has asked them all to kill the Witch of the West. The golden road does not go in that direction and so they must follow the sun, as have many pioneers in the past. The land they now pass through is "rougher and hillier, for there were no farms nor houses in the country of the West and the ground was untilled" (p. 140). The Witch of the West uses natural forces to achieve her ends; she is Baum's version of sentient and malign nature.

Finding Dorothy and her friends in the West, the Witch sends forty wolves against them, then forty vicious crows and finally a great swarm of black bees. But it is through the power of a magic golden cap that she summons the flying monkeys. They capture the little girl and dispose of her companions. Baum makes these Winged Monkeys into an Oz substitute for the plains Indians. Their leader says, "Once ... we were a free people, living happily in the great forest, flying from tree to tree, eating nuts and fruit, and doing just as we pleased without calling anybody master." "This," he explains, "was many years ago, long before Oz came out of the clouds to rule over this land" (p. 172). But like many Indian tribes Baum's monkeys are not inherently bad; their actions depend wholly upon the bidding of others. Under the control of an evil influence, they do evil. Under the control of goodness and innocence, as personified by Dorothy, the monkeys are helpful and kind, although unable to take her to Kansas. Says the Monkey King, "We belong to this country alone, and cannot leave it" (p. 213). The same could be said with equal truth of the first Americans.

Dorothy presents a special problem to the Witch. Seeing the mark on Dorothy's forehead and the Silver Shoes on her feet, the Witch begins "to tremble with fear, for she knew what a powerful charm belonged to them." Then "she happened to look into the child's eyes and saw how simple the soul behind them was, and that the little girl did not know of the wonderful power the Silver Shoes gave her" (p. 150). Here Baum again uses the Silver allegory to state the blunt homily that while goodness affords a people ultimate protection against evil, ignorance of their capabilities allows evil to impose itself upon them. The Witch assumes the proportions of a kind of western Mark Hanna or Banker Boss, who, through natural malevolence, manipulates the people and holds them prisoner by cynically taking advantage of their innate innocence.

Enslaved in the West, "Dorothy went to work meekly, with her mind made up to work as hard as she could; for she was glad the Wicked Witch had decided not to kill her" (p. 150). Many Western farmers have held these same grim thoughts in less mystical terms. If the Witch of the West is a diabolical force of Darwinian or Spencerian nature, then another contravening force may be counted upon to dispose of her. Dorothy destroys the evil Witch by angrily dousing her with a bucket of water. Water, that precious commodity which the drought-ridden farmers on the great plains needed so badly, and which if correctly used could create an agricultural paradise, or at least dissolve a wicked witch. Plain water brings an end to malign nature in the West.

When Dorothy and her companions return to the Emerald City they soon discover that the Wizard is really nothing more than "a little man, with a bald head and a wrinkled face." Can this be the ruler of the land?

Our friends looked at him in surprise and dismay.

> "I thought Oz was a great Head," said Dorothy.... "And I thought Oz was a terrible Beast," said the Tin Woodman. "And I thought Oz was a Ball of Fire," exclaimed the Lion. "No; you are all wrong," said the little man meekly. "I have been making believe."

Dorothy asks if he is truly a great Wizard. He confides, "Not a bit of it, my dear; I'm just a common man." Scarecrow adds, "You're more than that ... you're a humbug" (p. 184).

The Wizard's deception is of long standing in Oz and even the Witches were taken in. How was it accomplished? "It was a great mistake my ever letting you into the Throne Room," the Wizard complains. "Usually I will not see even my subjects, and so they believe I am something terrible" (p. 185). What a wonderful lesson for youngsters of the decade when Benjamin Harrison, Grover Cleveland and William McKinley were hiding in the White House. Formerly the Wizard was a mimic, a ventriloquist and a circus balloonist. The latter trade involved going "up in a balloon on circus day, so as to draw a crowd of people together and get them to pay to see the circus" (p. 186–87). Such skills are as admirably adapted to success in late-nineteenth-century politics as they are to the humbug wizardry of Baum's story. A pointed comment on Midwestern political ideals is the fact that our little Wizard comes from Omaha, Nebraska, a center of Populist agitation. "Why that isn't very far from Kansas," cries Dorothy. Nor, indeed, are any of the characters in the wonderful land of Oz.

The Wizard, of course, can provide the objects of self-delusion desired by Tin Woodman, Scarecrow and Lion. But Dorothy's hope of going home fades when the Wizard's balloon leaves too soon. Understand this: Dorothy wishes to leave a green and fabulous land, from which all evil has disappeared, to go back to the gray desolation of the Kansas prairies. Dorothy is an orphan, Aunt Em and Uncle Henry are her only family. Reality is never far from Dorothy's consciousness and in the most heartrending terms she explains her reasoning to the good Witch Glinda,

> Aunt Em will surely think something dreadful has happened to me, and that will make her put on mourning; and unless the crops are better this year than they were last I am sure Uncle Henry cannot afford it (p. 254).

The Silver Shoes furnish Dorothy with a magic means of travel. But when she arrives back in Kansas she finds, "The Silver Shoes had fallen off in her flight through the air, and were lost forever in the desert" (p. 259). Were the "her" to refer to America in 1900, Baum's statement could hardly be contradicted.

Current historiography tends to criticize the Populist movement for its "delusions, myths and foibles," Professor C. Vann Woodward observed

recently. Yet *The Wonderful Wizard of Oz* has provided unknowing generations with a gentle and friendly Midwestern critique of the Populist rationale on these very same grounds. Led by naive innocence and protected
by good will, the farmer, the laborer and the politician approach the
mystic holder of national power to ask for personal fulfillment. Their desires, as well as the Wizard's cleverness in answering them, are all self-
delusion. Each of these characters carries within him the solution to his
own problem, were he only to view himself objectively. The fearsome Wizard turns out to be nothing more than a common man, capable of shrewd
but mundane answers to these self-induced needs. Like any good politician
he gives the people what they want. Throughout the story Baum poses a
central thought; the American desire for symbols of fulfillment is illusory.
Real needs lie elsewhere.

Thus the Wizard cannot help Dorothy, for of all the characters only
she has a wish that is selfless, and only she has a direct connection to
honest, hopeless human beings. Dorothy supplies real fulfillment when
she returns to her aunt and uncle, using the Silver Shoes, and cures some
of their misery and heartache. In this way Baum tells us that the Silver
crusade at least brought back Dorothy's lovely spirit to the disconsolate
plains farmer. Her laughter, love and good will are no small addition to
that gray land, although the magic of Silver has been lost forever as a
result.

Noteworthy too is Baum's prophetic placement of leadership in Oz
after Dorothy's departure. The Scarecrow reigns over the Emerald City,
the Tin Woodman rules in the West and the Lion protects smaller beasts
in "a grand old forest." Thereby farm interests achieve national importance, industrialism moves West and Bryan commands only a forest full
of lesser politicians.

Baum's fantasy succeeds in bridging the gap between what children
want and what they should have. It is an admirable example of the way
in which an imaginative writer can teach goodness and morality without
producing the almost inevitable side effect of nausea. Today's children's
books are either saccharine and empty, or boring and pedantic. Baum's
first Oz tale—and those which succeed it—are immortal not so much
because the "heart-aches and nightmares are left out" as that "the won-
derment and joy" are retained (p. 1).

Baum declares, "The story of 'the Wonderful Wizard of Oz' was written solely to pleasure children of today" (p. 1). In 1963 there are very few
children who have never heard of the Scarecrow, the Tin Woodman or the
Cowardly Lion, and whether they know W. W. Denslow's original illustrations of Dorothy, or Judy Garland's whimsical characterization, is imma-
terial. *The Wizard* has become a genuine piece of American folklore

because, knowing his audience, Baum never allowed the consistency of the allegory to take precedence over the theme of youthful entertainment. Yet once discovered, the author's allegorical intent seems clear, and it gives depth and lasting interest even to children who only sense something else beneath the surface of the story. Consider the fun in picturing turn-of-the-century America, a difficult era at best, using these ready-made symbols provided by Baum. The relationships and analogies outlined above are admittedly theoretical, but they are far too consistent to be coincidental, and they furnish a teaching mechanism which is guaranteed to reach any level of student.

The Wizard of Oz says so much about so many things that it is hard not to imagine a satisfied and mischievous gleam in Lyman Frank Baum's eye as he had Dorothy say, "And oh, Aunt Em! I'm so glad to be at home again!"

America's Manufactured Villain—
The Baseball Umpire

David Q. Voigt

Within the emerging urban centers of the nineteenth century, entertainment became commercialized. Baseball quickly developed into a professional sport and "the national game." Its popularity may have been due to its pastoral setting or have sprung from its reflection of the nation's indecision over the ideals of individualism versus teamwork. Or, perhaps more to the point, the devotion baseball aroused might simply have been due to the fact that it was the only game in town.

Voigt's analysis of the evolution of the role of the umpire probes at the American personality. Certainly the creation of a villainous arbitrator indicates something about American attitudes toward authority in contrast to the respect shown for umpires in Cuba and Japan.

Hundreds of studies of baseball are available. Those interested in another study by Voigt should read American Baseball: From Gentleman's Sport to the Commissioner System. *One of the most fascinating works is Robert W. Peterson's account of the Negro leagues,* Only the Ball Was White. *For a glimpse at how baseball functions within one native American culture see J. R. Fox's "Pueblo Baseball: A New Use for Old Witchcraft" in this book.*

By their heroes you shall know a people, and the reverse seems equally true. "The villainy you teach me, I will execute and it shall go hard but I will better the instruction," said Shakespeare's *Merchant of Venice*. Thus, it would seem that if certain societal roles and behaviors are popularly despised, to know these would afford a glimpse into that fugitive will o' the wisp we call "national character." A deceptively simple proposal this, it promises the rewards of social insights for those willing to become villain-watchers. But, as ever, the complicating factor is that of trying to explain what one sees.

A case in point is the much villified American baseball umpire, who in the closing years of the nineteenth century became a target of popular abuse. A strange phenomenon in the annals of villainy, the umpire emerges as a manufactured villain, "a villain by necessity" in Shakespeare's words, thrown to ravenous spectators by shrewd owners who encouraged the fans' ritual abuse as a means of abetting the profits of baseball promotion.

For public consumption at major league parks, the umpire was packaged as a special kind of villain. That villains are different, with certain types serving special purposes, is well established in social theory. In a solid book entitled *Heroes, Villains, and Fools,* sociologist Orrin E. Klapp drove home the point that even in 19th century America there were varied villains, although not so varied a smorgasbord as we find today. In his lineup, Klapp lists five orders within the animal kingdom of American villains, and the one that best fits the umpire is that of "status abusers and arrogators." Within this order lies a genus which Klapp calls "oppressor types," and under this lies another subdivision called "moral persecutor," so labeled because this type has the habit of abusing power held over subordinates. It is this model that best explains the image of the umpire held by 19th century baseball fans. As an oppressor, or moral persecutor, the umpire was seen as a threat to the fortunes of the hometown team or to the splendid performance of a local hero. Since both had off days, disgruntled fans found it salving to blame the umpire. Thus, the umpire became the sacrificial lamb; the villainous blamesake upon whom fans could toss their collective frustrations. As a hate symbol, he still functions as a device for restoring the morale of disgruntled fans.

If Klapp's social psychological explanation serves to place the umpire in a credible villain mold, it is certain that pioneer organizers of American Baseball never intended the functionary to fall to such an estate. From the earliest amateur organizations of the 1840's to the opening of the first commercialized major league in 1871, all official rules of baseball

From *Journal of Popular Culture,* 4 (1), Summer 1970, 1–21. Reprinted by permission of the author and the editors. (Footnotes have been omitted.)

aimed at making the umpire the most esteemed member of a baseball club. Indeed, in that early "gentleman's era" of baseball, most clubs tried to restrict membership to "gentlemen." With such genteel company, it was thought to be an honor to be designated an umpire, since it implied that the honored one knew the rules well enough to make his own interpretations. Naturally, such license also meant that the game lacked a clear codification of rules, so it was not surprising that many protested the fuzziness of these "interpretations." However, in that era of organization umpires had powerful champions, such as the directors of the prestigious Knickerbocker Club of New York who invoked a set of graduated fines for cursing or otherwise offending umpires.

But the cherished idea of baseball as a rich-man's game did not last. By 1870 intense inter-city competition spurred commercialism as the most successful clubs hired husky proletarians to strengthen their teams. With admissions charged and players paid, the end came to the "gentlemen's era," and with it the umpire's status lowered.

For a brief time after the establishment in 1876 of the National League the umpire could still draw upon his former status of gentlemanly expert. Helping to keep the old myth alive was Henry Chadwick, a pioneer baseball organizer, rules-maker, and leading reporter of the game. More than anyone he was baseball's pope, and he gloried in his title of "father of the game," while using his pen to pontificate on the game's moral mission. Although realist enough to retreat from the lost cause of amateurism, he stoutly opted for retaining the amateur umpire. Arguing that to pay was to demean, he insisted that, "no higher compliment can be paid to a member of the fraternity, than to select him to act as umpire in a first class contest, as such choice implies. . .confidence in his knowledge of the rules. . . and in his ability to enforce them resolutely."

Up until 1876, which included the five years of the first commercial league known as the National Association, Chadwick's views carried weight. During that era, volunteer umpires officiated, guided only by a manual published by Chadwick. While the Association lasted, umpires varied in dress, dedication, and decision-making. To the consternation of fans and players different umpires took different positions, some going behind the batter, some behind the pitcher, while others stood in foul territory facing the batter. Even more confusing was the varied approach to calling balls and strikes, while the difficulty of calling an unseen play led Chadwick to suggest that an umpire ask some "gentleman" in the crowd for his objective opinion! Inconsistency in umpiring was a *leitmotiv* of the Association era, and is illustrated by this matter-of-fact comment about Umpire Theodore Bromeisler; while "experienced. . .prompt and impartial in his decisions," he called balls and strikes "with unusual strictness."

Even Chadwick admitted that these highly personalized decisions often erred, but he blamed players for provoking umpires to err by raucous protesting. A smart captain, advised Chadwick, would quiet his men to insure objectivity. And lest such rational advice fail, Chadwick urged club directors to eject insulting players or spectators.

Not surprisingly, there were times when umpire dignity collapsed in the face of angry assaults. In July 1873, during an Association game in Philadelphia, the umpire "had to be protected from the assaults of the gambling portion of the crowd." Sometimes umpires provoked players as did hot-tempered Bob Ferguson who accused a lethargic New York Mutual player of being in cahoots with gamblers. Angrily retorting, the player called Ferguson a liar, provoking Ferguson to hit the player with a bat. The incident provoked a mob scene and Ferguson got away with the help of a police escort. But usually players provoked umpires and during the Association era Chadwick often warned against the "vile habit" of disputing umpires.

With the organization of the National League in 1876 umpires faced a new era of adjustment. From the start the new league determined to systematize officiating, and began by retaining a professional staff paid at the rate of five dollars per game per man. Behind this move lurked the fear that umpires could be bribed and the new league wanted a clean public image to insure its success.

Another step toward professional umpiring came when the League ruled that umpires be chosen from an approved list. A groping move toward uniformity of experience, this led directly to the idea of a salaried staff. First tried in 1882 by the American Association, the plan aimed at silencing arguments over what team might choose the game umpire. Under the new plan, three umpires, each paid $140 a month, were assigned to cover all the seasonal games. And each umpire was ordered to wear blue cap and coat trimmed with gold cord and buttons. Notwithstanding a later attempt to outfit umpires in white, the early notion of umpires in blue persists in practice and folklore.

The new plan with its good pay lured many applicants. Scanning an early list a *Chicago Tribune* reporter noticed many "played out ball tossers," and sneered that such men would only hurt the game's image: "the average league umpire is a worthless loafer easily tempted and swayed. . .a very unsafe and eminently unworthy person in whose hands to place the arbitration of a game of ball played in the presence of great crowds of ladies and gentlemen."

At least some officials agreed, as evidenced by the bitter arguments over the appointees of the first staff of umpires. Eventually the four $1000 a year National League posts went to unknowns. Lacking experience, denied tenure, each soon fell before a harsh League rule calling for the immediate ouster of an umpire at the behest of four clubs. With clubs sniping at the staff only one survived; and of the banished trio, A. F. Odlin admitted that the job had lost its glamour:

> I was unaccustomed to appearing before the public, and as soon as the customary and inevitable howls of disapproval arose...I became more or less nervous and was thus unable to exercise accurate judgment....

Increasing an umpire's frustration were the rapidly changing rules and playing tactics of the 1880's. In that decade hardly a year passed without some change in the balls and strikes pattern. Moreover, pitchers contributed to the bewilderment, by introducing baffling curves and trick motions. Since existing rules did not define an illegal pitch, the problem of ruling on the legality of a pitch fell to the umpire. At the same time offensive style changes brought the bunt, the hit-and-run play, and tactics in base-stealing. On the basepaths, daring runners like Mike Kelly of Chicago maddened rival fans by cutting directly from first to third when the umpire's back was turned. A tough atmosphere for survival, umpires gained little by the pre-season seminars arranged by rules-makers who hoped to get uniform interpretations thereby.

By the mid-'eighties officials faced a mounting number of trouble cases involving umpires. Obviously the villification of umpires by players, owners, reporters and fans was getting out of hand. Underscoring the despised status of umpire were the mob scenes of 1884. After experiencing several, the Baltimore club of the Association installed barbed wire to forestall more. And in Philadelphia, League umpire Gunning was mobbed for calling a game because of darkness; while earlier in the same town Billy McLean was mobbed. An ex-boxer, Umpire McLean bore the taunts of loud mouthed fans until, goaded beyond endurance, he threw a bat which struck a fan. Within minutes McLean was besieged and only the timely arrival of a police escort saved him. The following year McLean faced a repeat of the experience in Cincinnati, with police again arriving in time to save him.

During the 'eighties umpires found angry players more menacing, and often umpires were beaten up on the field. In 1884, League umpire John Gaffney suffered a cut eye in a fight with John Ward. This incident prompted officials to impose fines of up to $200 with suspension for similar affronts. But club owners seldom enforced the penalty.

Hopes of improving the image of the besieged profession prompted Umpire Joseph Ellick to write an article analyzing his troubled life. In Ellick's opinion, it was the "kicking player...anxious to save face in front of a home crowd," who provoked fans into desiring "to kill you and wish you an unpleasant time in the next world." And events supported the thesis. Certainly players of the 'eighties were skilled hecklers and were encouraged by owners who often paid their fines. In 1886 Umpire Ben Young wearily testified that Charles Comiskey of the Browns was a "most aggravating player," whose trick of conversing with an aggrieved player within earshot of an umpire took the form of a barrage of "indirect" abuse.

Clearly any workable plan for insuring the dignity of umpires would require the full cooperation of major league officials, owners, and reporters. Yet at no time in the 'eighties or 'nineties was this achieved. Indeed, owners found umpire-baiting to be quite profitable. Although official League policy aimed at strengthening the role of umpire by increased pay and by granting his right to eject boorish players or fans, enforcement depended on the owners. And in the parks it was evident that owners had a vested interest in acquiescing in the degradation of umpires.

Certainly Chris Von der Ahe, the fat, boisterous "boss president" of the St. Louis Browns, saw no reason to curb umpire-baiters. Rather, he encouraged the practice by paying fines. In this way St. Louis became an umpire's torture chamber while Von der Ahe found that his permissiveness paid off at the turnstile. Nor was his the only experiment. In Boston a reporter supported the policy, stating that umpires "are too fully equipped with the foibles of our common flesh to assume the business. . .of repressing the hasty passions of others. What's the use of coining a player's unpremeditated damn into dollars and cents when you can do nothing with. . .the threats and acts of a mob?" Concluding, he urged umpires to accept abuse as a natural part of the spectacle. Once set, this permissive pattern was hard to change and harder to adjust to. A pragmatic solution of a sort came from President "Nick" Young of the National League who advised an umpire in 1887 to placate local fans by giving "the closest and most doubtful decisions to the home club."

In approving the public right to bait umpires, Albert G. Spalding, the Chicago owner and sporting goods king, argued that by harassing umpires fans were exercising their democratic right of opposing tyrants! And in 1897 when umpires protested the ambiguity of new rules, they were reminded that as employees, they "were not to question their superiors." And in his ghosted memoirs, John J. McGraw claimed that fans of the 'nineties preferred a rowdy, umpire-baiting style. In agreement was McGraw's Baltimore manager, Ned Hanlon, who advised umpires to accept abuse as part of their role:

> Ball players are not school children, nor are umpires schoolmasters. It is impossible to prevent expressions of impatience or actions indicating dissent with the umpire's decision when a player, in the heat of the game thinks he has been unjustly treated. . . . Patrons like to see a little scrappiness in the game, and would be very dissatisfied, I believe, to see the players slinking

away like whipped schoolboys to their benches, afraid to turn their heads for fear of a heavy fine from some swelled umpire.

Given a free rein, fans and players made the most of it. During the 'nineties fights and mobbings mounted and the turnover among umpires soared so high that scarcely a season went by without multiple firings or resignations. By now the practice of "kicking" at umpire decisions was widespread and it contributed mightily to the umpire's villification. Noting this scene in 1890 a *Brooklyn Eagle* writer sarcastically implied that a good player had to be a good kicker:

> How does the busy baseball player
> Improve each shining minute?
> He plagues the umpires all the day
> Because there's glory in it.

Other writers of the 'nineties welcomed the umpire-scapegoat as a prop for their stories. Seizing the villain with gusto, they poured reams of half-humorous, half-serious abuse. Thus, ace reporters like Tim Murnane of the *Boston Globe* headlined local defeats with phrases like "UMPIRE'S GAME." A *Clipper* writer introduced the umpire as the fan's "mortal enemy," whom "it is the proud privilege of every man seated. . .to hiss at and 'bullyrag' and abuse when he does not especially favor the local club." One who umpires, commented *Sporting News,* "must have a deformed head." And the sarcastic *Washington Post* writer, Joe Campbell, made a specialty of running lurid headlines like this:

> UMPIRE KELLY FLEES
> Women Spectators Smite Him With Their
> Parasols, Police Escort Him to the Cars

By such prose as this Campbell probably goaded fans: "Umpire McFarland, the yellowest piece of bric-a-brack that ever disgraced Nick Young's staff of indicator handlers, was responsible for the noisy brawl. . . after which McFarland, chattering from fear, fled through the gate behind the backstop, and was overtaken by Reilly and McJames, which pair of Senators bestowed a volley of billingsgate on the head of the mush-hearted umpire."

In this age other entertainers found salable themes in the national habit of umpire-baiting. In 1888 it was reported that John Philip Sousa had scored the orchestral part of a comic opera with a theme built around the evil designs of a villainous umpire. Written by a Washington newsman, the plot pitted clean-cut Eli Yale, a Giant pitcher, against villainous Umpire Moberly who lusted after the heroine Angela, at the same time scheming to cheat Yale's team out of the pennant. Embellishing this tired plot were songs with titles like, "He Stands in the Box With

the Ball in His Hands"; "The Umpire and the Dude"; and, "An Umpire I,
Who Ne'er Say Die."

Knocking umpires also inspired poets, few of whom matched this
doggerel effort in the *Washington Critic* of 1886:

> Mother, may I slug the umpire,
> May I slug him right away,
> So he cannot be here, mother,
> When the clubs begin to play?
>
> Let me clasp his throat, dear mother,
> In a dear, delightful grip,
> With one hand, and with the other
> Bat him several in the lip.
>
> Let me climb his frame, dear mother,
> While the happy people shout;
> I'll not kill him, dearest mother,
> I will only knock him out.
>
> Let me mop the ground up, mother,
> With his person, dearest, do;
> If the ground can stand it, mother,
> I don't see why you can't too. . . .

Umpires generally stood helpless as the everyday prose of writers
cemented their image as villainous oppressors. If they fought back, as
did Umpire Dunnigan in 1886, assaulting a writer for spelling out his
"glaring errors," they lost their jobs. Sometimes they lost the fight too, as
in the case of Umpire Jennings who in 1884 tried to lick a Washington
writer for the same reason. Arriving at the plant, Jennings ran afoul of
the paper's formidable sports editor who beat Jennings with a pastepot
and threw him out.

Even without pastepots writers had the upper hand. A headline in the
Louisville Commercial cried, "Robbed at Mob City—An Umpire's Daylight
Crime!" And in 1888, a *Sporting News* writer claimed that Umpire Herman
Doscher "has always been a home umpire and every manager. . .knows
it. . .he plays for the crowd, and as a grand stand umpire he is a pro-
nounced success." Indeed, so frequent were such sallies that the official
Reach Guide of 1890 begged writers to stop baiting umpires; at least
stop using umpires as examples of robbers!

Somehow, someway, enough umpires survived the hostile environment, adapting so as not to go the way of the bison or the passenger
pigeon. A handful of adaptive arbiters developed ingenious ways of serving the troubled habitat. In this era John Gaffney surpassed most in storing up merit and tenure, thereby gaining the uneasy crown of "King of
the Umpires." Almost without experience in joining the League in 1884, his

reception alerted him to the dangers of the role. Called to work in a crucial game, he nervously suited up in a remote corner of the player dressing room when an outspoken player blurted, "What do you think Nick Young has gone and done? He's sent down to the rural districts of Worcester County and got a hayseed to come here and umpire. . . . He'll be lucky if he gets out with his life."

To defy this grim forecast, Gaffney became a tireless, imaginative and efficient worker. Although suspended once for drinking, and constantly heckled, he accepted his villainous status, comforting himself with the doubtful assurance that only the "riff-raff" gave trouble. As an innovator he raised the status of the profession; even his beating helped by moving officials to enact heavy fines and suspensions for future acts of the kind. Meanwhile his decisions on practical problems of ballgames, such as how to call a ball that goes foul after passing out of the park, became official rulings. In this case, Gaffney's decision was that once out of the park, a batted ball is out of his jurisdiction!

By 1888 sports journals called attention to the Gaffney system of umpiring. They liked his tactic of umping behind the catcher until a runner reached first, after which Gaffney went behind the pitcher for a better view of the action on the bases. For awhile others were advised to imitate it, and although finally discarded, it remained a practical solution to the problems of a single umpire.

True, some of his ideas were ludicrous. He once told a writer that the "kicking problem" could be solved by making players pay money to the offended umpire. Gaffney reasoned that no sane player would ever want to enrich an umpire! Perhaps one reason why the suggestion died was that club directors of the 'nineties habitually reserved money from player fines to finance their annual banquet!

Asked for the secret of his success, that found him earning $2500 in 1888, Gaffney explained that he knew the rules, that he followed the ball "with dispatch," that he remained calm amongst players, and that he studied different styles of baserunning. He seldom fined and he boasted that in seven years of League work he fined a total of only $300.

As King Gaffney's rival, doughty Bob Ferguson at least held a patent of nobility. Famous as a player and manager, as an umpire he was aloof, stubborn—the archetype of the dictator-umpire. His philosophy was tough-minded, nearly the polar opposite of Gaffney's:

> Umpiring always came as easy to me as sleeping on a feather bed, and it would come to the rest of 'em if they would stand up and give it out that what they say must go. Never change a decision, never stop to talk to a man. Make 'em play ball and keep their mouths shut, and . . . people will be on your side and you'll be called the king of umpires.

Perhaps the Ferguson type deepened the villainous image of umpires; if so, it profited Ferguson who demanded $1500 in 1886, which was $500 more than the scale. Asked why, he blustered that he didn't care what others got; he was worth more.

Ranged between the Gaffney-Ferguson extremes were intermediary types like the intellectual Ben Young whose promising career ended in death in a railroad accident which happened while he was traveling to an assignment. A battler for a respected professional image, Young in 1887 proposed a ten point plan which urged that umpires work in both major leagues, that they each get a year's tenure, that owners be forced to protect them from insult and assault. For their part, Young pledged umpires would set high ethical standards, avoiding saloons and the company of players. And such strictures as these dominate the ethical code of umpires of today. Meanwhile in much the same manner Bob Emslie tried to re-educate sportswriters: "If we could only have base ball reporters whose partisanship was mild enough to treat us all alike the game would be greatly benefited in the end."

But in the closing years of the last century all such voices seemed hopelessly utopian. In that era abuses mounted as umpires were cursed, bombarded with beer bottles, and beaten. Perhaps 1897 was the nadir for the profession, since so many that year were harried out. By August, indeed, League president Young was losing sleep over lack of officiating:

> I thought I had secured Dan Campbell ... but he begs to be excused from working in the league until the business gets semi-respectable. I would have been in a pretty fix but for the courage of Tom Lynch and Bob Emslie. Lynch is a sick man and he needs ... rest. ...

> Bob Emslie received a sharp blow over his left lung, and coughed up a large clot of blood. He was advised to rest for a week or two, and was just about to start ... when Sheridan resigned, Hurst was arrested and Dan Campbell jumped the track. Immediately Lynch and Emslie came to my aid, and I believe I will be able to pull through ... if Joe Kelly of the Interstate League ... shows up satisfactorily.

In 1903 came the national agreement that ended the American League war and established the modern dual major league system. But for umpires there was no immediate peace. In the National league mob scenes occurred in 1904 as owners and writers continued to use umpires as scapegoats for cooling the ire of fans. Even in the more enlightened American league, under President Ban Johnson's avowed policy of defending the dignity of umpires, there was a *cause celebre* in 1901. It came when Manager McGraw of the Baltimore club protested Johnson's suspension of pitcher Joe McGinnity for spitting in an umpire's face. Denouncing

Johnson as a "Czar," McGraw triggered a running feud which ended with his defection to the National league.

As before, baseball's early modern era of 1903–1920 had umpires in a state of siege. On one flank fans fired verbal missiles, including curses, boos, and waves of maniacal laughter, the latter coming when umpires were struck by foul tips. So familiar by now was the rite of booing umpires that it found musical expression in a popular song entitled, "Let's Get the Umpire's Goat." Most menacing, however, was the lethal pop bottle; a new artifact, harbinger of America's belching cola age. One launched by a clerk in the St. Louis office of the German consulate in 1907 fractured the skull of Umpire Bill Evans. While the young umpire lay between life and death, President Johnson issued stern orders compelling owners to patrol the stands or face fines. In retrospect, the Evans beating was a turning point; henceforth, it was upward for umpires, but only within the villain pantheon! Not for them a heroic status.

Meanwhile on the other flank carping newsmen kept up their storied jibes. An extreme example of such flak found a writer using a fan's fatal heart seizure, which occurred at a game, as inspiration for this headline: "Umpire Klem Kills Innocent Fan." But as ever the center continued to be the worst front, for there umpires faced players. As usual umpires came off second best in the war of swearing, kicking, spiking and spitting. As a defense, cold comfort came from league advice urging umpires to walk away, and later file reports—trusting the league to right the wrongs with fines. Gradually the procedure paid off, so that a 1904 study showed that 85% of umpire trouble cases involved mere verbal abuse. However, umpires paid a price for their tattle-tale defense inasmuch as they were sneered at as "men of the cloth."

Not that umpires needed to validate their manhood. Stationed behind the plate he daily shared twice a catcher's share of bruises and blows, since a catcher spent half of each inning in a shaded dugout while the umpire toiled on without rest. Until 1911 single umpires were assigned each big league game, and because one could not be everywhere, players got away with tricks like doctoring balls, fouling runners, and prancing impudently around bases without touching bags. An impossible work environment, it ended in 1911 with the re-establishment of the dual umpire system, first tried, then abandoned, in the 'eighties.

Lacking power and tenure, the loneliness of the working umpire was deepened by the knowledge that at anytime the votes of five owners could end his career. Forced to live lives high above suspicion, most umpires learned to shun the company of owners, players, managers, or fans. A dreary monastic existence this, at least for some it was gentled by marital togetherness. The new king of umpires, Bill Klem, freely acknowledged his debt to his wife, while "Silk" O'Loughlin's last moments on earth testified to the depth of his relationship. Dying of flu during the ravaging 1919 epidemic, O'Loughlin's last request was for another embrace from the wife who lay beside him, stricken with the same disease.

In their harried lives during this early modern era umpires travelled without certain knowledge of their itinerary. Not until the 'teens did they get travel allowances and always they paid the cost of uniforms and protective equipment; even today the uniform allowance is inadequate. Yet, the biggest expense was their forfeited dignity. To fans nothing was sacred, certainly not an umpire's name. When an earnest neophyte named Colliflower joined the American staff he was cruelly mocked. To stop it, he changed his surname to James; a bad choice, inasmuch as fans took to calling him "Jesse"! Under such conditions survival called for moral athletes; something writer Grantland Rice understood when he urged that President Theodore Roosevelt try umping awhile: "it will curb your rash, headlong stren-u-os-it-tee."

Although Umpire Tim Hurst once rationalized that "you can't beat the hours," the fact was that umpires' pay lagged behind rising player salaries. In 1910 the top umpire salary was $3000, and that year the National league paid only $25,000 (a sum which included $8000 in travel expense) for its total officiating expense. A cheap price, it changed little, so that in 1920 under a dual umpire system, total costs came to only $41,000. Of course, star umpires like Klem picked up extra money for working World Series games, but in 1917 Series assignments still brought in only $650 extra. Emboldened by his fame, Klem in 1918 demanded and got $1000, but President Johnson stubbornly held the other three at the old $650 rate.

How ironic then, that these despised villains should have to carry the integrity of American baseball on their shoulders! A fact only vaguely appreciated by owners, it took a scandal like the Black Sox affair of 1919–1920 to drive it home. Daily exposed to irrational emotions of anger and villification, it was remarkable that the thin blue line held morally firm. Fascinated by this paradox, writer Hugh Fullerton wondered about the psychological propensity of umpires to err. As Fullerton thought, some gratified their love needs by playing the role of "homers," meaning that they threw close decisions to the home team. Others, however, were "bullheads," powered by self-righteousness into defying crowds. As an example, Fullerton cited Umpire Hank O'Day who boldly called Fred Merkle out in a riotous 1908 decision that helped Chicago wrest the pennant from McGraw's Giants.

Disliking either stance, Fullerton warned league leaders to mount a close watch since the best umpires had off days in objectivity. But Fullerton was too far ahead of official thinking, and the latter worthies continued to choose models like Bill Klem, who seemed to know the rules. Stubbornly self-assured, ex-bartender Klem awed players with his knowledge and cowed them with fines. As others aped his style, Klem accepted plaudits with pride and arrogance. Not until the twilight of his life did he admit to making mistakes; then he explained that his much quoted "I never called one wrong," really meant, "in my heart I never did." A proud martinet, so self-righteous was he that his claimed purity gave a new twist to the umpire villain image. As a septuagenarian Dean of National league umpires in the 1940's, he wrote a Grundyian code of umping etiquette that included the warning that no umpire should point his *gluteus maximus* at fans when dusting off home plate!

While Klem traversed an Olympic road to official dignity, others took humbler paths to the same goal. For his long service and quiet dignity Bob Emslie in 1919 capped a 25 year career by accepting the first umpire's pension. Meanwhile in the American league, President Johnson's policy of hiring stars like O'Loughlin, Hurst, Evans, Jack Sheridan and Tom Connolly paid off in respect, making this "big five" famous for leadership and efficient control. Of the quintet only Hurst was fired. Too brusk for such controlled professionalism, Hurst was ousted for spitting in the face of Eddie Collins of the Athletics, and for daring to give as his reason, "I don't like college boys."

Except for Hurst, Johnson's star system worked to elevate the status of umpires. Most outstanding was Connolly, an expert on rules, who retired in the 1940's and won a niche in baseball's Hall of Fame. Also important to the cause was Bill Evans, who retired in the 1920's, but left a remarkable pamphlet entitled, "The Billy Evans Course on Umpiring." A professional primer for rookie umps, Evan's 51 points told how to avoid arguments by practicing diplomacy, by concentrating on the ball and by avoiding eye contact with the dugouts or the fans. Also he urged greater tolerance for star players, urging young umpires to take their time before calling a play.

Such advice contributed mightily to the professional approach which in the years since the 1920's saw the establishment of training schools for umpires. Today such schools regularly turn out graduates; men professionalized to the hilt and backed by the combined power of officials and owners united at last in the common cause of maintaining order in a game now vastly enhanced by the prying eyes of television cameras. Lured by steadily rising salaries, umpires of the present era are comforted by the application of the rule of safety in numbers. Now four men work each major league game, rotating at the various observation points, while six are assigned to cover World Series and All Star Games!

True, their rights to organize and to bargain collectively, rights which the spreading "union ethic" brought to players after World War II, are denied to umpires. Recently American league president Joe Cronin fired two umpires for their organizing activities, but concessions already granted National league umps and threats of Congressional investigations promise an imminent breakthrough for umpires in this matter.

In an America growing increasingly legalistic, umpires no longer need fear mobbings. If not the laws which protect civil rights and personal liberty, then the spacious, well-policed ballparks have made such scenes as the fan pummeling the late Umpire George Magerkurth in 1940 so rare as to be part of a legendary age. Indeed, so safe is the climate today that a comely young matron, part of the "now" generation aspiring for female equality, is demanding a chance at a major league umping career. A holder of a *cum laude* degree from an umpire school, she has said that her only real problem is that of finding an adequate chest protector!

Today's baseball scene makes it appear that fans are finding it difficult to play the century long game of umpire-baiting. But lest it be supposed that the umpire has escaped his villainous status, the verbal abuse continues. It takes the form of ritualized booing every time the team of umpires is announced, and mocking jeers still debate each close decision, while cheers ring out when one is struck by a foul tip or otherwise discomfited. Such rites are painful enough, but when national celebrities support the ritual, it hurts more. Thus, when General Douglas MacArthur spoke out that Americans must always cling to familiar freedoms, like the right to boo umpires, Umpire Larry Goetz laid aside the general and began looking for a new hero.

The "Tin Lizzie's" Golden Anniversary

F. Eugene Melder

A farmer, so the story goes, stripped the tin roof off his barn and sent it to the Ford factory. Soon he received a letter informing him that although his car was badly damaged they could have it repaired in a week! Hundreds of jokes, sayings, and stories surrounded the most beloved mechanical device in the history of America, the "Tin Lizzie." In just fifty years the automobile has changed from a curiosity into the necessity Henry Ford thought it would be; F. Eugene Melder explains the role the "Lizzie" played in that development.

The automobile has not only transformed every aspect of America's material existence, it has become, in B. A. Botkin's opinion, not just an icon but a "supericon." Its importance to the American psyche is illuminated by the casual acceptance of 55,000 deaths each year which result from what are curiously labeled "accidents."

Ken W. Purdy's Wonderful World of the Automobile *is entertaining. Two penetrating articles, collected in* Icons of Popular Culture, *edited by Marshall Fishwick and Ray B. Browne, are Botkin's "Icon on Wheels: Supericon of Popular Culture," and Harry Hammond's "The Image in American Life: Volkswagen."*

Centennial, golden, silver and other anniversary observances, like human birthdays and national holidays, are occasions of celebration in American society as in many others. They symbolize achievement and growth. They serve as unifying and centripetal forces in a community threatened with civil conflict by the discordant and centrifugal pressures of disparate interests. They are reminders of past events which shape current culture.

Two centenaries celebrated in 1959 were the Oregon Centennial of Statehood and the observance in Titusville, Pennsylvania, of the hundredth anniversary of "Colonel" Drake's "bringing in" the world's first oil well. However, a "Golden Anniversary" of significant import which has received almost no public attention is the advent of the Model T Ford.

Perhaps the most recent attention of significance the Model T Ford has received in the American press is a protest of derision. An early Model T was included in the United States exhibit in the Brussels World Exposition of 1958. The doors of the fair had barely opened when the car became the object of a complaint which was carried ultimately to the White House. It prompted the President to dispatch a special representative to Brussels and left the President "very irritated" about the quality of the American contribution to the Brussels fair.

It may seem to many Americans who are not well along into middle age, as it seemed to the complainant, that the Model T is an anachronism in an international exhibit. However, to Americans who are in their golden years, the "tin Lizzie" may well seem to be an appropriate symbol of the American way of life in an Age of Plenty. Few would argue that American life is not largely centered around the automobile. From conception to the grave, the automobile is an ever present and powerful force. What better symbol of modern American life?

Before the advent of the Model T in 1908, the automobile was little more than an expensive plaything of the rich. An observer of the period, Stuyvesant Fish, later declared, "Nobody dreamed that automobiles would come into general use." In 1907, car registrations for the entire United States were 140,300, and only 157,000 cars had been produced and sold by the hundreds of producers of the American car industry. Nineteen years later, 1926, the last full year of Model T production, the automobile had attained its present role in American life as an ubiquitous necessity. A majority of the 22,044,600 cars registered were Model T Fords.

The introduction of the Model T was a marked contrast to the birth of a new name in cars recently. The Model T was developed in a small room partitioned off in one corner of the early Ford Motor Company plant

From American Quarterly, 12 (4), Winter 1960, 466–481. Reprinted by permission of the author's estate and the American Quarterly of the University of Pennsylvania. Copyright 1960 by Trustees of the University of Pennsylvania. (Footnotes have been omitted.)

on Piquette Street, in Detroit. Most of the design was worked out by a Hungarian immigrant, Joe Galamb, under the watchful eye of Henry Ford, over a period of about two years. Its development cost was but a few thousand dollars. In contrast, the Edsel, a recent addition to the roster of American cars, cost the Ford Motor Company a quarter of a billion dollars over a period of seven years before it was shown to the public in September, 1957.

The Model T had little advance publicity and no market research to forecast its appeal or demand. It had only the inspired hunch of Henry Ford that a cheap, small, lightweight, standardized and reliable car would find a wide market, and, more important, that profits would be satisfactory if a policy of price reductions were combined with the economies of mass production.

The publicity budget of the Edsel for the first five months was $12,000,000, of which $1,000,000 was spent before the date of public showing. After intensive market research, the Edsel was planned with a "market personality" as "the smart car for the younger executive or professional family on its way up." The Model T was first announced to the world in an obscure trade periodical, "The Horseless Age," in one sentence: "Yet other surprises—yes, a light touring car—that will be the delight of prospective buyers, the despair of competitors." That was the complete statement of the Ford Motor Company—as yet the Model T was unnamed. A typical advertiser's boast, it proved to be a great understatement.

Upon reaching the market, the Model T was successively advertised as "the family car at an honest price," "the farmer's car," "the doctor's car," "the merchant's car" and finally, in sweeping terms, as the *Universal* car, which it remained. Introduced with no fanfare, the Model T developed the most remarkable and widely heralded "personality" in the entire history of the automobile in the nearly twenty years of its production.

Perhaps the best-known summary of the Model T's personality is that provided in a classic epitaph by Lee Strout and E. B. White in 1936. Fact, legend and experience were woven together when they wrote: "The Fords were obviously conceived in madness: any car which was capable of going from forward into reverse without any perceptible mechanical hiatus was bound to be a mighty challenging thing to the human imagination." Again in 1953, White wrote, ". . . Model T was not a fussy car. It sprang cheerfully toward any stretch of wasteland whether there was a noticeable road under foot or not. It had clearance, it had guts, and it enjoyed wonderful health."

Not only did the Model T acquire a public reception and personality that exceeded that of any other car in history, each individual of the species is reputed to have displayed peculiarities of its own. As Allan Nevins wrote: "No two cars were quite alike. Mastery of any one involved highly personal qualities of courage, skill, intuition, and luck. As of Cleopatra, it could be said that time could not wither nor custom stale the infinite variety of the flivver; with all its superior dependability and simplicity, it combined an arch and mercurial eccentricity. It was more like a human being (of feminine gender) than any other car ever known to man."

In 1953, John Steinbeck remembered his first Model T, not as a female but as a neuter gender personality. He recalled:

"I guess Model T's would run forever, if you would let them. I was well gone in adolescence before I came by one at a price I could afford to pay— fifty dollars. It was almost as old as I was, and it had been around a helluva lot more than I had and was probably smarter to begin with. . . . I think I loved that car more than any car I ever had. It understood me. It had an intelligence not exactly malicious, but it did love a practical joke. It knew, for instance, exactly how long it could keep me spinning the crank and cursing it before I would start kicking its radiator in. It ran perfectly when I was in blue jeans, but let me put on my best suit and a white shirt, and maybe a girl beside me, and that car invariably broke down in the greasiest possible manner.

"I never gave it a name. I called it 'It.'

"The Model T was not a car as we know them now—it was a person— crochety and mean, frolicsome and full of jokes—just when you were ready to kill yourself, it would run five miles with no gasoline whatever."

If one theme runs through all of these sketches, it is that of a public image with durability and simplicity marked by a strain of humor mixed with temperamental idiosyncrasy. For millions of rural Americans, it occupied a place of affection synonymous with the horse or mule which it replaced. For urban and rural Americans alike, it was an invitation to the open road, to broader horizons, to escape from the drudgery and fatigue of the kitchen or the farm.

Meanwhile, the Model T ushered in the inexpensive automobile and placed individual motor transportation within reach of masses of Americans. The near-universal ownership of the motor car opened new horizons and whetted consumer appetites for a host of changes which add up to a social and cultural revolution in America more rapid than any large society had ever experienced before.

A vast body of humor and folklore grew up around the Model T which largely remains to be systematically investigated and analyzed in terms of its relations to American folk literature and value systems. For approximately a decade after 1913, dozens of editions of "Ford Joke Books" collected and spread the stories, mostly humorous, about the foibles of the car, of Henry Ford, its maker, its users, its uses and almost every imaginable feature of the machine. In one multi-volume interpretation of recent American social history, there was a chapter on the Ford joke. An endless series of stories, limericks, puns, conundrums and verse attested to Model

T's reputed characteristics and personality. Its noisiness, diminutiveness, tinniness ("Tin Lizzie"), cheapness, rough-riding qualities, toughness, economy of operation and many other traits were themes of the stories. It contributed new words to the dictionary, among them "flivver" and "jitney."

Legends grew up about the Model T, which are still with us. For instance, a writer in 1958 drew upon this body of legend when he likened the eighteenth-century harpsichord to the Model T Ford, "made for people with lots of time on their hands." "Every time the Model T owner took his car out, there was a contest to see who'd succeed, the car or the driver. Every driver brought a tool kit with screwdrivers, pliers, heavens knows what." This is sheer legend, on a par with the 1916 story of the Ford car which broke down in front of a junk shop. The driver entered the shop, quickly picked over a pile of miscellany and paid twenty cents for a bedspring, a remnant of garden hose and various odds and ends. The junk dealer observed that on the driver's return to his car, he lifted the hood, tinkered briefly with the motor while attaching his newly acquired junk, closed the hood, cranked the motor, mounted the driver's seat and rattled away down the road. The junk-shop man, after a few moments of apparent mental concentration, looked up at the sign above his shop door, stepped to the rear of his store, returned with brush and paint, painted out "Junk of all Kinds," and replaced it with "Ford Parts and Accessories."

The Model T ushered in a revolution in American rural social life for it was the Model T which made the automobile a common article of consumption for the American rural family. The farm family began to experience the freedom of a startling increase in mobility. The crossroads store and the country church received death blows in the decades in which the Model T was the dominant farm vehicle. Increasingly, the farm folk could get to town for their shopping and worship. The whole family could be whisked to an evening movie in the nearest town, or to larger centers than the nearest village for a Saturday afternoon of shopping or to worship in a more colorful church than the rural edifice. The relative isolation of rural society in the open-country neighborhood was on its way to replacement and rural sociologists soon noted its breakdown.

The Polk records of motor vehicle registrations in the United States snow that for 1924, 1925 and 1926, more than fifty per cent of all registrations were Model T cars and Model TT Ford trucks. The more prevalently agricultural the state and the lower the per capita income, the greater the percentage of Model T's to all other cars. In 1926, for example, Mississippi, with the lowest per capita income in the nation, showed three Model T registrations to every other car registered.

One reason the Model T was so popular with farmers was its low first cost—but a more important basis of its popularity was its flexibility. It was nicely adapted to appeal to the strong streak of practical ingenuity of the American or Canadian farmer, and the farmers took to Model T as to no other vehicle in history. Here was a car that, with a bit of imagination and energy, could be used to do a hundred tasks.

Among the many uses of the Ford on the farm were transport of all sorts, and as a power plant to turn such machines as cream separators, wood saws, feed mills, ensilage cutter and cider presses. Many a Ford car could and did find use to tow a wagon, pull a stump, drag a log or lead livestock. By 1915, truck conversion kits and tractor attachments by the thousands actually converted Model T's to usher in the day of the small truck and the farm tractor which came in the form of the Model TT trucks and the full-fledged Fordson tractor in 1917.

Wheeler Coy, a rural bard, summarized the farmer's son's sentiments in verse in 1916.

Things are changing over our way,
Better than they were by far,
No more longing; no more sighing;
Father's gone and bought a car.
Now as daylight comes serenely,
In the calm and dewy morn,
Father wakes me with the summons:
"Take the Ford and plow the corn."

Time was, when I spent an hour,
Watering, feeding, brushing mules,
Chasing up and down the pasture,
For the on'ry pesky fools;
But we've sold our mules and horses,
All those beasts have had their day,
Father merely smokes and mentions,
"Take the Ford and rake the hay."

In the eve I once walked weary,
Over where the cattle browse,
Now I hear my father calling:
"Take the Ford and get the cows."
Quick I start and quick I'm back there,
Hardly started, so it seems,
After milking, father tells me:
"Take the Ford and churn the cream."

So it changes ever better
Farmer's lives are full of play,
Father says we have it easy,
Different from the olden way,
But the best thing, Father told me
Best thing happened in my life,
Father said so nice and quiet:
"Take the Ford and find a wife."

That great American educational institution, "the little red school-house" immortalized in American folklore, suffered a sharp decline as the number of consolidated rural schools rose by 275 per cent, from 1915 to 1927. School consolidation has continued since but never again at the rate of growth in the heyday of the Model T—when the Model TT truck chassis, equipped with a bus body, was the outstanding vehicle in use for transport of children to the rapidly growing number of consolidated rural schools.

The influence of the Model T on town and city life was hardly less than on the farm. In the first decade of its production, the little car was the near universal vehicle of the village R.F.D. mail carrier, the doctor and the traveling salesman or "drummer." Fire and police departments soon used them in large numbers. During 1911, Police and Fire Departments of New York City put fleets of Model T roadsters in service as district head-quarters cars. Los Angeles replaced twenty downtown patrolmen with four officer-driven Model T roadsters per shift, in 1916.

The use of Model T's as taxis in many cities ushered in motorized taxicabs across the nation from the very advent of the little car. In 1914, the Model T foreshadowed the failure of the electric trolley car when hundreds of privately operated "jitneys" began service in Los Angeles. The movement mushroomed, and by 1915, it had spread to every corner of the country. The trolley car was doomed as the motor bus was soon developed to provide the more flexible and rapid service so forcibly demonstrated by the jitney.

Mass production of Model T's got underway with the world's first moving assembly lines in 1913, and touring cars sold for $490 the following season. At this point the motorized vacation tour rapidly became a commonplace for urban families. "Tourist camps" became standard equipment of thousands of town and city parks across the nation. The widespread ownership of the popular little car by manual laborers as well as white collar workers, contributed much to bringing to the townsman the pleasures of the country. The significance of touring and tourist tent camps as forerunners of the later tourist cabins and the modern day motel requires little documentation.

Another role of Model T, almost unsung, was to reinforce capitalism by giving to millions of workers a stake in the system in the form of motor car ownership or the expectation of such ownership. Plentiful evidence of the shortcomings of American capitalism to the workingman was accumulating in the years from 1890 to 1915. Virtual civil war marked the relation of labor and capital in the mining camps of the Rocky Mountains. The "Bull pens" of the Coeur d'Alene and Colorado mining camps into which striking miners were herded bore a striking resemblance to the concentration camps of Hitler Germany a generation or so later. The battles of

Homestead, Pennsylvania, and Pullman, Illinois and the Ludlow, Colorado, "massacre" were widely interpreted as notice that workers could not expect to better their lot under capitalism. There were indications, too, that labor increasingly accepted the socialist-communist-syndicalist rallying cry that worker wage-slaves "had nothing to lose but their chains." After 1905, the Industrial Workers of the World were creating havoc in the empires of the "lumber barons" of the west. To add to their challenge to capitalism, the I.W.W. made sallies into the textile centers of Lawrence, Massachusetts, and Paterson, New Jersey. Incidents of warlike activities as widely spaced as Spokane and Everett, Washington and McKee's Rocks, Pennsylvania, followed I.W.W. organizing activities. After years of struggle and strife, in 1915 needle trades workers of both men's and women's clothing were brought in to labor organizations committed to the destruction of capitalism. John Wayland's weekly newspaper, the socialist *Appeal to Reason,* achieved the widest circulation of the American press, with weekly sales of from four to six million per edition in the years from 1910 to 1915 or so. To make matters worse, workers' real full-time weekly earnings remained at the same level in 1914 as they had been in 1891, more than twenty years earlier. In 1920 amidst the troubled days of postwar discontent, Eugene V. Debs, as Socialist party candidate for President, polled an all-time record vote for his party of nearly a million ballots.

It was upon this scene that the Model T dramatically demonstrated to the workingman the possibility that he could acquire the status symbol of the middle and upper classes. Henry Ford's policies of continuous price reductions after 1909, and mass assembly line production coupled with the $5 daily wage after 1914, made him a workingman's hero. In consequence, the tide of worker opinion quietly and inconspicuously turned away from anti-capitalist ideologies as the "pie in the sky, bye and bye," taunt of the radicals promised to become a reality in the form of a cheap automobile in the "here and now." This shift in worker opinion was almost completely missed by the social scientists of the time, but not so by men in the labor movement itself. Probably the most accurate and authoritative opinion on the matter which survives is that of an old-line union man of Muncie, Indiana, made in the early twenties: "The Ford car has done an awful lot of harm to the unions here and everywhere else. . . . As long as men have enough money to buy a second-hand Ford and tires and gasoline, they'll be out on the road and paying no attention to union meetings."

Did American workers justify the complaints of the Muncie union leader by buying Fords? Apparently millions did, although no statistics by owner status were ever compiled. However, a quick look at facts is suggestive.

As the years of its production increased, rising money wages and

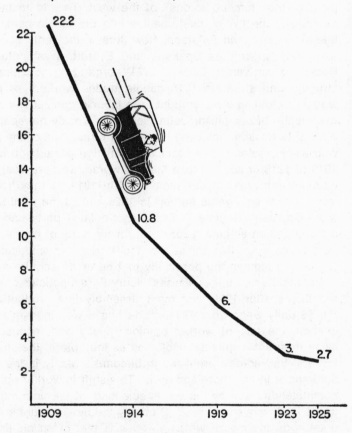

Henry Ford's policy of price reduction made it increasingly easy to own the little car. (See following chart.) In 1909, the first full year of Model T

Ratio of Prices of Model T Touring Cars to Wages of Factory, Coal Mining and Transport Workers, U.S.A., 1909–1925

Number of months' wages equivalent to Model T factory prices

22.2

22
20
18
16
14
12
10.8
10
8
6.
6
4
3. 2.7
2

1909   1914   1919   1923 1925

production, the factory price of a Model T touring car was $950 and the earnings of American workers in manufacturing, mining and transport were $516 a year. The average worker's total money income for 22 months would be insufficient to buy a Model T Ford. By 1919, the average worker's income had risen to $1,167 and the Ford touring car had declined to $575, so that six months' earnings would buy Mr. Average Worker a Ford. A small but growing number of workers could own new Fords, and second-hand cars could be bought by many more. Now came the big change. By 1923, the basic Ford touring car's factory price was $295 and the average annual earnings had risen to $1,256. An average workingman could buy a new Ford with three months' earnings, and by 1925, he could do even better—he could have a $290 touring car with two months' and three weeks' wages.

The relation of the automobile to religion and morals is no less significant. The impact of rapid transportation in reducing the importance of the rural houses of worship is clear and obvious. Thousands of rural worshippers found it easy to transfer their formal religious activities to more attractive and larger congregations and did. But as often as not, the younger generation found the call of the open road too attractive and discontinued their formal church attendance completely except for weddings and funerals. The reports of sermons of the time are full of ministerial protestations against the loss of support of the younger people to the rival enticements of the automobile.

Perhaps the cheap automobile had as great an impact on the religious thinking of the younger generation in those early years of its general use as it had on their church attendance. A recent recollection by an adolescent of the period serves to illustrate what Veblen termed "the impact of the machine process upon traditional religion." In this instance, however, the "machine process" in the form of the Model T Ford had its impact on the traditional religious beliefs of a user-consumer rather than on the fidelity of Veblen's factory worker to supernatural values. Our reporter recalls:

"Our little Epworth League flock of five high school boys and girls was returning for a religious retreat shepherded by our minister. The road home led up Pine Canyon from the Columbia River to Waterville [Washington]. It was a long steep grade of four miles or so. The day was hot. We were not yet halfway up when the minister's Model T balked. The radiator boiled and the motor failed. Our good minister suggested that we call for God's help so all six of us knelt in the road on the shady side of the car and prayed. The radiator soon ceased to boil, and we got under way again. Our prayers were answered but momentarily. Stops became frequent, and prayers increased in length. Three or four prayers later, the Model T topped the hill, and we were profoundly impressed with our convincing demonstration of the power of prayer.

"Imagine the shock to my newly demonstrated convictions at what we learned from the owner of the service station in Waterville where we stopped to replace the radiator water which had boiled away and for gas. On hearing of our difficulties on the Pine Canyon Grade, he commented that all Model T's behaved similarly on that hill. The customary and necessary way to get a Model T up that hill or any other which overheated the motor, he declared, was to stop at the instant the radiator boiled and wait to let the heated motor cool off as the Ford thermo-syphon cooling system operated too slowly on hills to keep the motor at a safe operating temperature. When I learned that our prayers had merely provided the time for the thermo-syphon to overcome the motor heat, I was crushed. My faith in prayer suffered a mortal blow."

This account suggests the possible influence of such everyday experiences with the Model T upon beliefs of the relationships of the spiritual and material orders.

The changes in morals, especially in sex behavior of unmarried young people in the years when the Model T was in greatest use, caused great concern on the part of the clergy and uneasy parents. They were quick to recognize the use of the Model T and other cars to carry young people quickly to secluded "lovers' lanes" or to the anonymity of distance in hotels or tourist cabins many miles from home. As Frederick Lewis Allen said, "One of the cornerstones of American morality had been the difficulty of finding a suitable place for misconduct; now the cornerstone was crumbling." He characterized the automobile as a veritable "living room" on wheels. The Lynds commented in 1928, "Buggy riding in 1890 allowed only a narrow range of mobility. . . . In an auto, however, a party may go to a city halfway across the state in an afternoon or evening." In their review of the records of the juvenile court of "Middletown," the Lynds reported that over half the girls charged with "sex crimes" in 1924 had committed the offense in an automobile. Although the Model T probably played a role no different than other makes as a participant in the changing behavior of the sexes, by sheer weight of numbers, the Model T must have been most important in the change of behavior from 1915 to 1925.

In 1927, when the Model T assembly lines ground to a final halt, more than fifteen million of the little cars had been produced in twenty calendar years. Never since has production of any single model of a motor car gone to a number even one-half as great. By 1927, the nation's population might all have been transported simultaneously, five to a car, and the car industry had grown up. No other country, except Canada, had reached an equivalent car-population ratio even by the year 1959.

The Model T had been so successful in making the motor car an article of common consumption that the country was well on its way toward its present-day organization of social life. By 1927, paved roads had been increased over one million times in the nineteen years since the Model T was born. The social forces were now all present—awaiting organization—to bring about the pattern of social life based on the automobile which we know in 1960. America had entered the "Age of Plenty," as *Business Week* observed in 1956, and "Model T" marked "a great divide in modern times. It can be used to date the transition from the Age of Production to the Age of Distribution."

The automobile industry of this country has matured. It operates mainly on the basis of the replacement market demand. In the recession year of 1958, leaders of the industry were earnestly seeking market stimulants or harbingers of consumer demand changes. General Motors, Ford and Chrysler companies were reported to be grooming small cars for presentation to the market in 1959. One unnamed auto company official was quoted as declaring, with an air of disgust, when asked if his firm would offer a small, modestly priced car of 100 inches wheelbase or thereabouts: "I can't say that. It's just not a sure thing yet. If we build one, it won't be in response to public demand—it'll just be a case of panic."

Meanwhile, as other nations of the world gear their economies to consumer demands in a world which shows promise of better standards of living for the common man, many candidates for the American role of the Model T in their respective countries have appeared. Among them are the Volkswagens and Lloyds of Germany, the Austin A-30's, Morris Minors and Ford Anglias and Populars of Britain, the Renault Dauphines and the Citroen 2-cylinder 2 CV's of France, the Saabs of Sweden, the Moskvitz's of Russia, the Vespa and Lambretta Scooters and the Fiat 600's of Italy, the Datsuns of Japan and the Holdens of Australia. In this decade, tourist camp grounds are becoming as common in Western Europe as they were in America forty years ago and "camping" has become a word common to all languages on this side of the Iron Curtain. If general war can be avoided by the powers for another decade, we may well see other counterparts of America's transportation revolution which was so largely based on the Model T, in these and other nations of the world. But it is doubtful if any one car model will ever again be as socially influential and dominant in the market as was the Model T. As a cultural classic and symbol of the Age of Plenty for the common man, it has a unique place in history.

Perhaps the planners of the United States exhibit at the 1958 Brussels Fair were thinking of the role of the Model T in making America and our social life what it is today when they chose to place an early model of the car in the exhibit. They may have been seeking to display symbols of the forces which made America's economic life the most bountiful in the world's history, rather than to exhibit, as sales bait, the chrome bedecked juggernauts of our current commercial offerings in a year when the American motor car industry was suffering the most severe slump in sales since the early years of the great depression of the thirties, and American imports of small foreign counterparts of the Model T are running at an all-time high after a rate of increase that had come close to doubling each year since 1953. The Model T had a revolutionary influence on America's social and economic life in ushering in an Age of Plenty and just possibly it may have carried that connotation to the millions of people who viewed it in the American Brussels exhibit.

The Model T exists now principally as memory. More than two hundred thousand Model T's were reported still running in June, 1953. For certain, a few thousand are still in existence—mainly in the hands of the dilettantes, collectors, car dealers and service stations who preserve the cars as conversation or human interest pieces. Occasionally, one is seen still carrying on in the day's work. Last year, at the Oxford-Cambridge boat race, there was a perfectly maintained Model T doing duty in hauling produce on the streets in West London. Last week in a New England supermarket parking lot, an elderly couple drove up in a well-groomed 1918 Model T. It is an unusual Sunday if there are no Model T cars offered for sale in the classified "Automobiles for Sale" columns of *The New York Times*. Even today, a limited variety of Model T parts may be purchased through the catalogues of Sears, Roebuck and Montgomery Ward mail order houses.

A strong case might be made for the proposition that the central material culture pattern of America at the end of the sixth decade of the twentieth century is the automobile complex. The present generation of Americans live in an environment of supermarkets, shopping centers, motels, service stations, used-car lots, wrecking yards and a series of "drive-ins"—movies, banks, restaurants, car washeries and so on. The American moves on rubber tires, over passageways characterized by traffic lights, complex road signs, highway numbers, toll booths, overpasses, underpasses, traffic separators, four, six, and eight lane separated turnpikes, trailer camps and parking meters. In terms of national consumption expenditures, the nation's motor transport accounts for more spending than does its food or its educational, health and library expenses combined, or its housing inclusive of depreciation and new construction outlays.

If American life of 1959 seems to be materially organized more around the motor car than around any other artifact, it is a safe generalization that the longest step in bringing about this material organization was that taken when the automobile first ceased to be a bauble of the rich and came within the reach of the common man. That step began just a half century ago with the advent of the Model T.

Wild Bird Hickok
And His Friends

James Thurber

From the earliest explorations, the European imagination has distorted the reality of American life. Tales of monstrous animals and cities of gold were believed, just as later the people of Paris convinced themselves that Ben Franklin was a half-savage, backwoods philosopher. In the twentieth century, European addiction to American popular culture was and still is responsible for many misconceptions—that all American girls are shapely blondes, that "good guys" prefer horses to women, that gangsters abound in America, and that all Americans are wealthy.

Until recently, Europeans have tended to borrow American popular culture rather than create their own. Mickey Mouse, the private eye, and the cowboy have found receptive audiences in Europe. The results have at times been sidesplitting, as James Thurber illustrates in the following article. Thurber, one of the eminent humorists of the twentieth century, scattered provocative insights into American culture throughout his writing; for another example see his "Food Fun for the Menfolk" also in this book. The Thurber Carnival is another fine collection of his work. The Italian use of American culture is clarified by Leslie Fiedler's "Italian Pilgrimage: The Discovery of America" in his book An End to Innocence.

In one of the many interesting essays that make up his book called "Abin-ger Harvest," Mr. E. M. Forster, discussing what he sees when he is re-luctantly dragged to the movies in London, has set down a sentence that fascinates me. It is: "American women shoot the hippopotamus with eye-brows made of platinum." I have given that remarkable sentence a great deal of study, but I still do not know whether Mr. Forster means that Amer-ican women have platinum eyebrows or that the hippopotamus has plati-num eyebrows or that American women shoot platinum eyebrows into the hippopotamus. At any rate, it faintly stirred in my mind a dim train of elu-sive memories which were brightened up suddenly and brought into sharp focus for me when, one night, I went to see "The Plainsman," a hard-riding, fast-shooting movie dealing with warfare in the Far West back in the bloody seventies. I knew then what Mr. Forster's curious and tantaliz-ing sentence reminded me of. It was like nothing in the world so much as certain sentences which appeared in a group of French paperback dime (or, rather, twenty-five-centime) novels that I collected a dozen years ago in France. "The Plainsman" brought up these old pulp thrillers in all clarity for me because, like that movie, they dealt mainly with the stupendous activities of Buffalo Bill and Wild Bill Hickok; but in them were a unique fantasy, a special inventiveness, and an imaginative abandon beside which the movie treatment of the two heroes pales, as the saying goes, into nothing. In moving from one apartment to another some years ago, I somehow lost my priceless collection of *contes héroïques du Far-Ouest,* but happily I find that a great many of the deathless adventures of the French Buffalo Bill and Wild Bill Hickok remain in my memory. I hope that I shall recall them, for anodyne, when with eyes too dim to read, I pluck finally at the counterpane.

In the first place, it should perhaps be said that in the eighteen-nineties the American dime-novel hero who appears to have been most popular with the French youth—and adult—given to such literature was Nick Carter. You will find somewhere in one of John L. Stoddard's pub-lished lectures—there used to be a set in almost every Ohio bookcase—an anecdote about how an American tourist, set upon by *apaches* in a dark *rue* in Paris in the nineties, caused them to scatter in terror merely by shouting, *"Je suis Nick Carter!"* But at the turn of the century, or shortly thereafter, Buffalo Bill became the favorite. Whether he still is or not, I don't know—perhaps Al Capone or John Dillinger has taken his place. Twelve years ago, however, he was going great guns—or perhaps I should say great dynamite, for one of the things I most clearly remember

From James Thurber, *Let Your Mind Alone* (New York: Harper & Bros.), pp. 185–190. Originally printed in *The New Yorker.* Copyright © 1937 by James Thurber. Copyright © 1965 by Helen W. Thurber and Rosemary Thurber Sauers. Reprinted by permission of Mrs. James Thurber.

about the Buffalo Bill of the French authors was that he always carried
with him sticks of dynamite which, when he was in a particularly tough
spot—that is, surrounded by more than two thousand Indians—he hurled
into their midst, destroying them by the hundred. Many of the most inspired paperbacks that I picked up in my quest were used ones I found
in those little stalls along the Seine. It was there, for instance, that I came
across one of my favorites, "Les Aventures du Wild Bill dans le Far-Ouest."

Wild Bill Hickok was, in this wonderful and beautiful tale, an even
more prodigious manipulator of the six-gun than he seems to have been
in real life, which, as you must know, is saying a great deal. He frequently
mowed down a hundred or two hundred Indians in a few minutes with
his redoubtable pistol. The French author of this masterpiece for some
mysterious but delightful reason referred to Hickok sometimes as Wild
Bill and sometimes as Wild Bird. *"Bonjour, Wild Bill!"* his friend Buffalo
Bill often said to him when they met, only to shout a moment later,
"Regardez, Wild Bird! Les Peaux-Rouges!" The two heroes spent a great
deal of their time, as in "The Plainsman," helping each other out of
dreadful situations. Once, for example, while hunting Seminoles in Florida,
Buffalo Bill fell into a tiger trap that had been set for him by the Indians—
he stepped onto what turned out to be sticks covered with grass, and
plunged to the bottom of a deep pit. At this point our author wrote,
" 'Mercy me!' s'écria Buffalo Bill." The great scout was rescued, of course,
by none other than Wild Bill, or Bird, who, emerging from the forest to
see his old comrade in distress, could only exclaim *"My word!"*

It was, I believe, in another volume that one of the most interesting
characters in all French fiction of the Far West appeared, a certain Major
Preston, alias Preeton, alias Preslon (the paperbacks rarely spelled anyone's name twice in succession the same way). This hero, we were told
when he was introduced, "had distinguished himself in the Civil War by
capturing Pittsburgh," a feat which makes Lee's invasion of Pennsylvania
seem mere child's play. Major Preeton (I always preferred that alias)
had come out West to fight the Indians with cannon, since he believed it
absurd that nobody had thought to blow them off the face of the earth
with cannon before. How he made out with his artillery against the forest
skulkers I have forgotten, but I have an indelible memory of a certain close
escape that Buffalo Bill had in this same book. It seems that, through an
oversight, he had set out on a scouting trip without his dynamite—he also
carried, by the way, cheroots and a flashlight—and hence, when he
stumbled upon a huge band of redskins, he had to ride as fast as he could
for the nearest fort. He made it just in time. "Buffalo Bill," ran the story,
"clattered across the drawbridge and into the fort just ahead of the
Indians, who, unable to stop in time, plunged into the moat and were

drowned." It may have been in this same tale that Buffalo Bill was once so hard pressed that he had to send for Wild Bird to help him out. Usually, when one was in trouble, the other showed up by a kind of instinct, but this time Wild Bird was nowhere to be found. It was a long time, in fact, before his whereabouts were discovered. You will never guess where he was. He was "taking the baths at Atlantic City under orders of his physician." But he came riding across the country in one day to Buffalo Bill's side, and all was well. Major Preeton, it sticks in my mind, got bored with the service in the Western hotels and went "back to Philadelphia" (Philadelphia appears to have been the capital city of the United States at this time). The Indians in all these tales—and this is probably what gave Major Preeton his great idea—were seldom seen as individuals or in pairs or small groups, but prowled about in well-ordered columns of squads. I recall, however, one drawing (the paperbacks were copiously illustrated) which showed two *Peaux-Rouges* leaping upon and capturing a scout who had wandered too far from his drawbridge one night. The picture represented one of the Indians as smilingly taunting his captive, and the caption read, *"Vous vous promenez très tard ce soir, mon vieux!"* This remained my favorite line until I saw one night in Paris an old W. S. Hart movie called "Le Roi du Far-Ouest," in which Hart, insulted by a drunken ruffian, turned upon him and said, in his grim, laconic way, *"Et puis, après?"*

I first became interested in the French tales of the Far West when, one winter in Nice, a French youngster of fifteen, who, it turned out, devoted all his spending money to them, asked me if I had ever seen a "wishtonwish." This meant nothing to me, and I asked him where he had heard about the wishtonwish. He showed me a Far West paperback he was reading. There was a passage in it which recounted an adventure of Buffalo Bill and Wild Bill during the course of which Buffalo Bill signalled to Wild Bird "in the voice of the wishtonwish." Said the author in a parenthesis which at that time gave me as much trouble as Mr. Forster's sentence about the platinum eyebrows does now, "The wishtonwish was seldom heard west of Philadelphia." It was some time—indeed, it was not until I got back to America—that I traced the wishtonwish to its lair, and in so doing discovered the influence of James Fenimore Cooper on all these French writers of Far West tales. Cooper, in his novels, frequently mentioned the wishtonwish, which was a Caddoan Indian name for the prairie dog. Cooper erroneously applied it to the whippoorwill. An animal called the "ouapiti" also figured occasionally in the French stories, and this turned out to be the wapiti, or American elk, also mentioned in Cooper's tales. The French writer's parenthetical note on the habitat of the wishtonwish only added to the delightful confusion and inaccuracy which threaded these wondrous stories.

There were, in my lost and lamented collection, a hundred other fine things, which I have forgotten, but there is one that will forever remain with me. It occurred in a book in which, as I remember it, Billy the Kid, alias Billy the Boy, was the central figure. At any rate, two strangers had turned up in a small Western town and their actions had aroused the suspicions of a group of respectable citizens, who forthwith called on the sheriff to complain about the newcomers. The sheriff listened gravely for a while, got up and buckled on his gun belt, and said, *"Alors, je vais demander ses cartes d'identité!"* There are few things, in any literature, that have ever given me a greater thrill than coming across that line.

The Serious Funnies: Adventure Comics During the Depression, 1929–1938

William H. Young, Jr.

Just who deserves credit for originating the first comic strip is disputed. In America, comics became widespread in the 1890s; 1897 marked the beginning of the first memorable strip, The Katzenjammer Kids. *Rudolph Dirks's two devil-may-care children, Mamma, the Captain, and the "Inspector" remain a unique creation in popular art. The kids assaulted the public order with a vigor that might land them in a reformatory today. "Society iss nix," they shouted, and they acted accordingly. By the time that Krazy Kat, Ignatz the mouse, and Offissa B. Pupp came on the scene in 1911 to play out their own version of law and order, the comic strip was an integral part of the newspaper business. Today many people could not face the day without* Peanuts *or* Dick Tracy *as an eye opener.*

In his comprehensive examination of the adventure comics of the thirties, William H. Young raises questions about the way in which social issues are dealt with in comic strips. For a learned study of an important strip, see Arthur Berger's Li'l Abner: A Study of American Satire. *Two rewarding introductions to comic books are Les Daniels and John Peck's* Comix: A History of Comic Books in America *and Jim Steranko's* A History of Comics. *Steranko is an artist for Marvel Comics.*

The comic strip as it is known today, with its series of rectangular panels, or frames, containing pen-and-ink drawings and dialogue in "balloons," is a relatively recent innovation. The strip concept (several linked panels arranged either horizontally or vertically) grew out of the cartoon. During the 1890's, the standard features of the comics emerged: 1) sequential narrative and pictures, 2) continuing characters who became identifiable for themselves, and 3) inclusion of dialogue within the picture itself.

With public acceptance, the comic strips mushroomed. The titles were constantly changing in the early years of the century, although virtually every strip was humorous—thus the names "comics" and "funnies." Until the early 1920's, such a thing as a strip without its gag or humorous situation existed as a rarity and had little following. Not until 1910 or so did the titles and the characters begin to achieve some permanence. Newspapers, artists, and syndicates continued to experiment with various shortlived series, and it was finally around 1925 that a semblance of stability was attained.

The purpose of this study is to see how the adventure comic strip reacted to the Depression during the years 1929–1938. For ease of discussion, three categories of comic strips have been devised for this investigation: 1) humorous strips, 2) serial strips, and 3) adventure strips. Not all adventure strips will be discussed; sheer numbers preclude treating them all; also many had extremely short runs and were then discontinued without leaving any discernible mark. Others were so patently patterned on successful strips that any mention of them would merely duplicate things said about the original model. Since the Depression was a time of disorder, and for many, a time of chaos, the diverting image of a stable, ordered world—or a disordered world being made stable—would be a reassuring one, if only for the length of time it took to read over a newspaper's comic page. This was the image presented to the reader by the adventure comics.

There exists always a certain time lag between actual events and a cultural depiction of them. The spirit of the "Roaring Twenties" gave way only reluctantly to the grimmer realities of the Thirties. Since cartoonists work anywhere from a few weeks to a year in advance of publication, this study, by commencing with 1929 (a period of relative stability), will be able to indicate whether or not the comics of the later 1920's differ sharply from those of the Depression, or if the two periods illustrate a continuum of cultural patterns.

Although the humorous comics were dominant at the outset of the Depression, another type of strip had by 1929 established a comfortable

From Journal of Popular Culture, 3 (3), Winter 1969, 404–427. Reprinted by permission of the author and the editors. (Footnotes have been omitted.)

niche for itself. This was the continued-story strip, or serial. With an almost unlimited choice of story approaches, in contrast to the humor comics, the serials could be funny or serious, or even a combination of the two. As the serials became more entrenched during the Twenties, more and more of them eliminated any pretense to humor, relying instead on straight story-telling.

At the time of the Depression, another form of comic evolved—and came into instant popularity. This was the straight adventure strip, working with a day-to-day serial plot, usually devoid of humor, and filled with physical action. In terms of techniques, the adventure comics grew out of the serial tradition, but their content was unique. Other adventure strips existed before the Thirties; Charles Kahles in 1906 was spoofing the movie serials with *Hairbreadth Harry* and filling his frames with action and suspense. In 1924 came *Wash Tubbs* by Roy Crane which also featured action—a strip destined to become a favorite of the 1930's after Crane made some changes in it. By 1938, the end of this study, the adventure strip would rank as the dominant form of comic strip, replacing the humorous funnies that had ruled the industry since its beginnings and also its erstwhile parent, the serial comic.

The adventure comic strip characteristic of the 1930's was something new, suddenly appearing, for all practical purposes, in 1929. Its story line and its visual format broke with the humorous and serial traditions. The adventure series had a bright, hard, sharp-edged style about them that caught the aesthetic movements of the Thirties. Pictorially, similar transitions in movie techniques, magazine illustration, and advertising art can be seen throughout the Depression years. In terms of plot, the work of writers like John O'Hara, Erle Stanley Gardner, James M. Cain, and Raymond Chandler finds echoes in the comic pages. The adventure strips were both innovative and eclectic: the changes they wrought on comic art were sweeping, yet they themselves borrowed more freely from other media than any previous comic form.

The first adventure series utilizing this new approach appeared in January of 1929, serving warning on the industry of what was to come. The strip was *Tarzan* (each episode carried a separate title, like *Tarzan the Ape-Man, Tarzan the Fearless,* etc. Here the entire series will be called simply *Tarzan*). It arrived with a backlog of popularity in other media. Edgar Rice Burroughs wrote *Tarzan of the Apes* in 1914, the first of a series totaling twenty-five volumes, all of which enjoyed huge sales. Hollywood quickly saw the potential in the *Tarzan* series, releasing its first movie version in 1918. Since that early effort, an endless succession of *Tarzan* films has been released, with over thirty-five separate features and serials produced at last count. Consequently it is not surprising that the comics finally recognized this commercially valuable property.

The difference between *Tarzan* and other comics occurs most obviously in layout and design. Virtually all strips up to 1929 used an essentially "flat" (i.e., two-dimensional) artistic style. Little attempt was made to give the illusion of depth; shading and cross-hatching were the exception rather than the rule. Also, landscape and extensive detail was relatively neglected. When detail was worked in, the effect was often one of busyness. It usually tended to distract attention instead of adding understanding of what was being portrayed. Those artists who did pursue a degree of realism in their drawings were wont to simplify the composition to such an extent that the final result was often the opposite of what they strove for: the realism was either lost or distorted. Finally, virtually all strips up to 1929 used what might be called a "proscenium presentation." The reader is in effect watching a stage play from a fixed vantage point. Seldom were such devices as an aerial view, a close-up, or a distance shot attempted. With the advent of *Tarzan,* the aesthetic standards of the comic strip came in for an abrupt change.

Credit for the changes *Tarzan* wrought on comic art cannot go to Edgar Rice Burroughs; by 1929 his success was such that he simply sold the rights to his stories to Metropolitan Newspaper Service, later United Features Syndicate. Eventually, of course, the demands of daily and Sunday publications eliminated even Burroughs (although the syndicate retained his name), and staff writers began to continue the saga of the ape-man. The credit must go to the artist hired to illustrate Tarzan's adventures: Harold Foster. Almost alone, he revolutionized the visual aspect of the comics. Foster came to the comics from advertising, a noteworthy point, with advertising's insistence on clarity coupled with detail and dramatic presentation. His approach to drawing was that of the academically trained artist, a sharp contrast to many of his fellow cartoonists who were self-taught. In addition to his formal training, Foster brought with him the advertiser's love of the unique: unique angles, unique lighting, unique composition. Whether or not Foster was unconsciously influenced by the movies is a moot point; that advertising and the films borrowed from one another is undeniable on the basis of the visual evidence. Although the series initially started rather timidly, within a short time it blossomed into something of a cinematic comic strip. No speech balloons obstructed the drawings; the narrative was included along the bottom portion of each panel. Just as the movie camera was finding increased freedom to move virtually anywhere, Foster never relied on the static proscenium approach to illustrate Tarzan's adventures.

Reader acceptance of this new style of comic strip was immediate. As far as the narrative content went, the stories appeared to be exercises in the purist escapism. Tarzan, son of an English nobleman, lives in the jungle, having renounced civilization. A man of amazing physical prowess, he is the law of the jungle. As such, he brings order to the chaotic tribal-animal life he commands, ruling fairly but firmly. What the *Tarzan* series was establishing, no doubt unknowingly on its part, was the criteria for a host of other yet-unborn adventure strips: 1) the physically strong and attractive male hero, 2) the helpless and acquiescent female heroine (the famous "Jane" in *Tarzan*), 3) the concept of justice administered by one man, answerable to no one. The new adventure strips, following in *Tarzan's* success, employed these standards rather closely, regardless if the hero were a nomadic adventurer, an aviator, a detective, or any of dozens of other occupations. Further, almost without exception the new series were placed in the hands of men with skill in realistic illustration (the word "cartoon," with its connotations of humor, really seems no longer applicable). Frequently this meant creative teams: one man for the drawing, one man for the story itself. This is a far cry from the old tradition of the cartoonist who writes and draws his own material. A professional sheen came to the comics, although there are those who maintain this came about at the expense of a certain lyricism the older strips possessed.

The impact of *Tarzan* must also be examined in terms of the Depression. Although the strip had its origins in early 1929, it did not really begin to attain its distinctive features until later in the year and on into 1930. Foster was frankly experimenting in the first months of the series, attempting to find a means of presentation that would express him and also the themes of the plot. Such a problem, of course, would be expected with any artist working with another man's story line. Only as he got more comfortable with the strip did he exercise more daring. The angles of perception become sharper, the use of perspective more camera-like (from distance to close-up and then to middle distance, etc.). But because he was also a trained artist, the resultant illustrations are always ordered and restful. Thus an action-filled jungle scene would not upset the viewer because of unfulfilled expectations (for example, a section of background detail that catches the eye and looks as though it is going to play a significant part in the illustration, but instead is simply extraneous in light of the total picture) or because of unbalanced composition. The apparent contradiction in terms of a "restful action" scene means that the various pictorial elements are in place—the subject of the illustration is relatively unimportant. This is not to suggest that all cartoonists previous to Harold Foster could not draw—on the contrary, many of their compositions rank as masterpieces in the field. But it does suggest that by the 1930's *more* artists were working at their drawing boards with more attention to the composition itself, and not just as a means of illustrating a story or a punch line. The somewhat slapdash construction of the early days of cartooning (and such an assertion must always take into account numerous exceptions—certainly Winsor McCay was practicing most of the "innovations" of the 1930's back in 1905) gradually was replaced by a new respect for more careful workmanship. The net effect of such an approach was a heightened order, an increased aura of stability for the visual side of the comic strips.

If the individual frames seem more ordered and stable, naturally there should be a carry-over to the story. The eye will impose on the mind the idea that the plot too is more ordered, that less chance for chaos exists. Adding to this is the very frame itself. Simply by enclosing a drawing within a defined boundary gives it a certain stability (not unlike framing a picture before hanging it on a wall). The drawing is thereby focused; it need not compete with the remaining page. Of course all cartoonists have used the frame approach; it should not be construed that this technique was born with the new adventure strips. Artists like Foster, however, did arrange their drawings *within* the frame with greater care, thus heightening the stability their compositions projected. Consequently, in Foster's *Tarzan* the idea of order is extremely strong. Tarzan himself brings stability to the wild jungle, and after bringing stability, he maintains it. Beasts, uncivilized natives, criminals from the outside world— all try to destroy Tarzan and thereby tear down the orderly system he has erected. His strength and jungle skills, however, always prove too much of a match for these would-be destroyers of law and order. Naturally, economic depressions play no part in Tarzan's jungle world. Foster has commented that he gave little thought to depicting economic conditions when doing *Tarzan.* But he goes on to say that he feels that he, and all cartoonists, "subconsciously . . . reflect their time and place. For instance, cartoonists from Florida or California seldom depict snow scenes." Of course, in *Tarzan* Foster was illustrating stories written by Edgar Rice Burroughs (or possibly staff writers; credits are not given) rather than his own material. But illustrationally, he clearly shows Tarzan's jungle world as superior to the "civilized" world beyond. The visual portrait of Tarzan is that of a man—significantly, white; the overtones of racial superiority are obvious, both in the stories and the drawings—who has carved out a system superior to the civilized urban jungle he has renounced. This visual judgment is reinforced in the stories themselves, where the villains represent a society more dangerous than the actual jungle. The reader can infer that the strip amounts to a renunciation of modern urban civilization. The mere thought of a man, no matter how fictional the man, capable of introducing a workable system into a chaotic world must have held an inward appeal to the Depression-weary reader who saw his own system falling into disorder around him.

Harold Foster found doing the daily and Sunday *Tarzan* too much of a burden, and he relegated the daily versions to Rex Maxon. Maxon, competent, but not of Foster's caliber, continued the photographic realism and balanced compositional approach. In 1936, Foster left *Tarzan* altogether that he might begin a strip drawn and written by himself, the justly famous *Prince Valiant*. His successor (for Sundays only; Maxon continued the daily chores) was Burne Hogarth. The appearance of this new artist marked for some critics ". . . the creation of a rare genius . . . one of the supreme moments of the comic strip." Hogarth continued Foster's level of excellence with tightly organized, well-ordered illustrations. He added to this, however, a decided flair for movement and action missing in Foster's more static techniques. Motion, or the implication of great movement, compels attention to a picture. Most of Hogarth's drawings demand that the eye follow their progression of events. Both Foster and Hogarth certainly imply artistically that harmony and order are essential components in a workable world. This concept is reinforced in both men's work by the absence of speech balloons. Since the drawings are highly realistic and the balloon is a symbolic device, they could concentrate completely on composition by dropping the balloon. All the new artists of the Thirties had to cope with the problem of placing the narrative element somewhere. Some apparently felt that running the narrative along the bottom of each frame was no more satisfactory than the older balloon, and therefore returned to tradition. But they tried making the balloon an integral *part* of the picture, and not merely the symbol of somebody talking. In the work of Milton Caniff, Roy Crane, and others, the careful placement of the balloons works to preserve order within the drawing, the balloon itself becoming an important component of the composition. Alex Raymond would later try speech scattered about the empty areas of the drawing but not enclosed within a balloon frame. The absence of the supple balloon line in Raymond's creations proves somewhat distracting; the speech of characters simply floats without any support, an effect bothersome to the eye. Only the sheer strength of Raymond's drawing overcomes this weakness.

In passing from *Tarzan* to other adventure strips of the period, aesthetic procedures similar to those just discussed become evident. In addition, the stories tend to go in one of two directions: 1) increased reality, a trend displayed by the many police-detective strips, or 2) greater escapism, particularly in the burgeoning science-fiction field. Interestingly, except for a short-lived failure or two, no one else tried the jungle milieu until Alex Raymond introduced *Jungle Jim* in 1934. Imitation may be the sincerest form of flattery, but apparently it was felt that *Tarzan* was so completely identified with a jungle setting that others would pale in comparison. *Jungle Jim,* in order to break out of the *Tarzan* mold, saw Jim as a man from the Western world who retains his civilized ways—even relishes them. He rules no savage empire, but simply has a continuing series of adventures within a jungle setting. His exploits, however, are frequently for the natives' benefit.

1936 saw *The Phantom* make its debut, drawn by Ray Moore and written by Phil Davis. More in the *Tarzan* line, the Phantom is a mysterious white man ("the ghost who walks," say the pygmies) who, like Tarzan, rules the jungle ("the Deep Woods"). He stalks about in a skintight purple costume—in contrast to Tarzan's loincloth—and presages in his way the fantastic heroes of the later Thirties and early Forties: Superman, Batman, Captain Marvel, *et al.* The Phantom also is mortal, but other than his jungle kingdom, bears little resemblance to Tarzan.

What these three strips did have in common, however, is the concept of one man imposing order on a chaotic land, and then making the newly found stability last. All show an avoidance of the present and instead return to more "natural" values, that is, a rejection of modern technological civilization in favor of a primitivism that accentuates individual worth. Such qualities as strength, understanding of nature, unbending honesty, and the like come to be seen as primary virtues. Although all engage in fantasy, their hearkening back to past values provides a symbolic response to the modern Depression. Whether or not their implied solution could work in a democratic setting is questionable. The adventure field, nonetheless, was a fertile one; a sampling of some of the representative strips within this new genre follows.

The early 1930's carried over much of the crime that had plagued the Twenties. The new decade was, in fact, the era of Al Capone, John Dillinger, "Legs" Diamond, Dutch Schultz, and many other notorious gangsters. Lawlessness was played up in newspaper headlines; Hollywood began to grind out innumerable films that purported to show that "crime does not pay," but actually celebrated the criminal, making him a veritable hero. Edward G. Robinson, James Cagney, and Humphrey Bogart began to be typecast as vicious killers, and the public loved them. Crime became a distracting antidote to the grim Depression; the escapades of criminals captured the public imagination. The stream of highly successful movies and stories dealing with crime did not go unnoticed by the syndicates. But comic-strip taboos forbade making gangsters into quasi-folk heroes. The solution was to celebrate the law enforcer, making him as colorful as the most flamboyant criminal. One of the first, and still the most successful, detective strips was *Dick Tracy.* Artist Chester Gould has stated his own reasons for inaugurating the strip: "Back in 1931 no cartoon had ever shown a detective character fighting it out face to face with crooks via the hot lead route." He further explained that he was fed up with "too much red tape" blocking the direct apprehension of criminals. Thus Tracy is direct—to the point of using criminal methods himself. Modern bureaucracy is seen to have become so sprawling that it can no longer perform its functions. Its impotence is contrasted to Tracy's virile brand of independence.

Although Dick Tracy is the nominal hero of the series, a continuing gallery of grotesques, usually with names and faces that somehow go together (Doc Hump, B. B. Eyes, Measles, Itchy, etc.) form part of each episode, giving Tracy and the police a steady diet of murders, robberies, assaults, and such to solve. These villains represent a threat to society, and society is seen in the strip as neat and stable, but hardly able to fend for itself. Gould implies that modern society has become weak; out of such reasoning could come the inference that an event like the Depression is the fault of such a social system. It is up to Tracy and the police to defeat these threats to order. The grotesque criminals that populate the series are products of modern civilization—and somehow it has failed. Tracy and his ruggedness are displayed for contrast, in this case, both to the criminal element and to the helpless world which needs Tracy's protection. Gould was at this point introducing a concept that novelists like Dashiell Hammett and Raymond Chandler were popularizing: the idea of the detective as a form of avenging angel. Tracy's face, especially the profile, has a hawk-like appearance to it. His nose really resembles a beak. Just as a bird of prey swoops mercilessly down on its victim, so does Tracy descend on criminals. The niceties of legal procedure are dropped; he is fighting crime and at times the ways of criminals are more effective in law enforcement. His motives supposedly make his methods right. As an avenger, he is beholden to no one; violence, often seemingly needless, dominates the strip as Tracy emerges as a mortal version of a wrathful Michael, gunning down those opposed to order.

The constant violence employed in *Dick Tracy* and its sister strips is akin to that used in some of the humorous funnies. It is controlled violence; the reader knows that the status quo will be regained at the end of a violent episode. People may be killed—mere policemen, lesser criminals, soldiers, and the like are killed with relative impunity in the more violent adventure strips. But important people survive, either to face the hero (who is mortal, but cannot be killed) at last if they represent evil, or to carry on to new adventures (this may happen to villains also, so they can continue to harass the hero). Regardless of how an episode concludes, the violence never becomes uncontrolled. The implication remains that the world of the adventure strip is an ordered world.

At first (the strip premiered in late 1931), *Dick Tracy* was drawn in a crudely realistic style. As it became established, Gould moved into a more stylized vein. It also began to appear in other media: adapted to film, there were four serials and several features. Also several compilations of Tracy's adventures appeared in book form. Unfortunately, no Hollywood actor could ever successfully duplicate Tracy's hawkish look. Yet as a comic strip, the series gives an aura of extreme realism. It also enlarges on the order motif so prominent in adventure strips of the Depression period. Whenever the police or law-abiding citizens are shown, care is taken to draw in detail using a sharp architectural purity of line, with everything extremely neat and uncluttered. But gangsters and their ilk get a more baroque treatment, with curves and general clutter coming to play a role in their presentation. The implications are clear: law *is* order, crime is disorder. The solution to a crime (more often than not coupled with the violent death of the gangster) is frequently accompanied with illustrations almost devoid of extraneous detail. The image that comes across to the reader of course is that order has been fully restored again.

Although the Depression itself does not appear in *Dick Tracy,* the strip's appeal to an audience suffering through such an upheaval would be understandable. The independent hero (Tracy has remarkably few restrictions on his police activities) who moves free of encumbering laws and restraints and thereby brings about order forcefully is a man who gets things done—the type of accomplishment doubtless wished for by many during the long years of the Depression. Unfortunately, the widespread admiration in the Thirties for dictators and extremists like Mussolini, Hitler, Huey Long, and Father Coughlin, all of whom promised a quick end to all problems, was frequently based on many of the same traits as those exhibited by Dick Tracy. Certainly *Dick Tracy* and its various imitators emphasized the need for a well-ordered society—only the means might be questionable. Democracy was a nice abstract concept in the adventure strips, but it usually moved too slowly for most of the new breed of heroes and was frequently put aside.

Another popular strip featuring the police and their activities was *Radio Patrol* by Eddie Sullivan and Charlie Schmidt. Again the villains are given much space, and again they are finally struck down at the very end of an episode. Like Gould, the authors were interested in the technical work of the police, and much time is consumed explaining and employing various gadgets. Even the title, with the use of "Radio," hints at the emphasis given the scientific side of law enforcement. But it is the individual officer who must apprehend the criminal—the gadgets can only help in detection. In this respect, the strip does not rely so strongly on the idea of a man who can step beyond the law he is supposedly upholding; the police are not so much avengers as they are simply men employing science to combat crime. The authors, however, do imply that crime threatens order—and thus must be defeated. The morality of right versus wrong is seldom touched on by the adventure strips; they offer what they feel is "recognizable villainy and skulduggery." They are in essence caricatured morality plays, and the many series apparently believed that their readers would accept all their villains as immoral. Thus they stressed what they believed was crime's threat to the community: the loss of order. With their roots in the Depression, these comic strips were responding to the loss of direction they saw in the country during the Thirties.

Artistically, *Radio Patrol* is a distracting strip. The artists go to extremes to be realistic and, apparently, "cinematic." Perspective is distorted and weird angles of vision are over-employed. Although the artists were undeniably talented, such an approach becomes wearisome; the story gets lost in the visual fireworks. Rather than by words, attitudes toward a subject in a cartoon are usually changed by the picture itself. *Radio Patrol's* over-reliance on the visually unique and its constant staginess at times work against the plot, and the concept of order is actually weakened.

Although most of the heroes (and the genuine *heroine* is almost non-existent; the comics are a man's world) of the adventure strips fought evil forces of one type or another, the great majority of them had no official connection with any law-enforcement agencies. They were instead the foot-loose wanderers who somehow keep encountering crime and feel compelled to challenge it. This type of hero could therefore meet many more types of law-breakers than could his police counterpart. Pirates, power-mad despots, even occasional gangsters from the realm of science fiction began to populate the serious strips. But characters like Ben Webster, Ned Brant, Bobby Thatcher, Tim Tyler, and Captain Easy were ready for them. Most of these heroes were adolescents, although Captain Easy emerges as a clearly defined adult. The use of boys in what are essentially men's roles can be partially attributed to the necessity of catering to the huge juvenile market, but another reason may be suggested also. The cartoonists, creating in the midst of a demoralizing depression, looked back fondly on the simpler days of their own youth (this would help to explain the many "nostalgic" panels then being done by people like J. R. Williams and Ed Dodd). Further, they tried to create in these adolescent characters the type of person they had once dreamed of being. All people daydream; here for once was the opportunity to picture those daydreams for others to see.

Gradually a set of "rules" developed for the behavior of these heroes. The conflicts they experience are seldom if ever internal ones, but rather external. The dangers may at first be ambiguous, and the hero must rely on himself to comprehend the situation. If he is truly a child (e.g., Bobby Thatcher), he will be called upon to act beyond the normal child's capabilities—and he will succeed. The adolescent and older heroes must face dangers which at first may temporarily defeat them. Often their motives will be misunderstood by others, and they will be forced to act in a hostile world. Because the problems are external, however, it only becomes a question of time before those problems are conquered and the heroes can move on, free of any entanglements. Such themes as these are remarkably similar to those employed in many Hollywood movies. The adventure comics project a world composed of the same characteristics as displayed in a grade "B" movie melodrama.

These adventure strips therefore show a simpler view of life, one that definitely eliminates such events as depressions, and provide for a vicarious re-enactment of fantasies. Further, it will be noted that, aside from the police and detective characters, few of these heroes have any apparent means of employment. Money, however, never arises as a problem; they eat well, dress well, and always have the mobility that normally only money can bring. In fact, money plays no role in *their* lives—only the villains are constantly lusting after money, which perhaps explains why they are villains. It would demonstrate that money by itself is not of great import. The strips instead suggest that the quality of life is what gives it meaning. Financial woes, psychological problems, trivialities—these demean living. Such a presentation in a time when many readers were unemployed or the victims of bank failures would be a reassuring one. And the strips' success indicates that many adults were ready for just this kind of presentation; the heroes' exploits hit a responsive chord in an audience that needed fresh dreams. Of course, adult heroes like Captain Easy live in essentially a boys' world, but they demonstrate that their boyish dreams of adventure need not be limited to boys.

As the Thirties progressed, more and more new strips began with men in the leads—and in many of the earlier comics the boys aged perceptibly. With maturity came increased opportunities to broaden the scope of the story; a love interest could be included, the hero could have access to more types of people, and with the oncoming war, he could eventually join one of the services. Also, the fashions of the time seemed more willing to accept the dashing adult hero. A parallel note to this trend can be found in 1930's dress: whereas the Twenties had emphasized a girlish-boyish look, the styles of the Thirties took on formality; skirts were lengthened, adult curves were rediscovered, hair styles were more dignified. Perhaps as the Depression became less severe, an escape to childlike

simplicity was no longer so appealing. In the changing comic world, probably the best of the whole genre, men or boys, was *Terry and the Pirates,*
by Milton Caniff.

"Terry" began with a juvenile male lead, sex appeal, action, and unusual danger—piracy along the China coast. Caniff built up a veritable
rogue's gallery of "sinister Orientals," with the deadly Dragon Lady as
Terry's most persistent foe. Terry is representative of most of the new
adventurers despite the locale of the strip. He is youthful; at the series'
inception he was extremely boyish, but Caniff allowed him to become a
teen-ager as the strip progressed, although the aging was virtually imper-
ceptible. (For added insurance, Terry has a handsome sidekick in the
adult Pat Ryan and comic relief in the character of Connie, a grotesque
Chinese.) Terry, like his other comic counterparts, is a rootless wanderer.
This latter characteristic probably found sympathy during the Depression.
Americans have traditionally been highly mobile geographically. By esti-
mates made in late 1932, some 25,000 families and some 200,000 young
men turned to a nomadic life, leaving home and friends behind, hitting
the road simply in search of a job or for something—anything. The mere
fact of movement suggested hope for change. It also perhaps served as
a substitute for class mobility during those troubled years. These were the
people John Steinbeck would later celebrate in *The Grapes of Wrath.* The
comic-strip wanderers reinforced the old idea of excitement on the road,
with the added promise of beautiful women, danger, riches, etc. Although
it is doubtful that many readers set out to become real-life Terries because
of the strip's influence, certainly the appeal must have existed in the bleak
Thirties. Caniff and his fellow artists were of course aiming at the imagination, but their escapism was based to a degree on the facts they saw about
them. As Caniff notes,

> The strip started on October, 1934, and the country was already on its
> way out of the muddle, but the people were so exhausted from the emotional
> drain that I used the simple picaresque device of attempting to take them out
> of their post-depression milieu and at least pretend for a Scheherazade mo-
> ment that they are somewhere else dreaming Walter Mitty dreams of their
> position (in the manner of Don Quixote). In the very nature of all this a certain
> order was implied.

The rootless hero is an old literary convention, but these strips were extremely contemporary. Their ingredients may have come from traditional
tales, but they offered a fictional alternative to the dreary Depression.

Caniff's *Terry and the Pirates* not only presented the nomadic hero—
it also pictured Asia, something which is unique in comic strips at the
time. The Oriental villain was a stand-by during the Thirties (Earl Derr
Biggers' *Charlie Chan,* later a comic strip, was about the only "good"

character of Asiatic extraction in any literary form at this time), but he usually had to go to the West to carry out his foul deeds. Gradually the tenor of "Terry" changed as Manchuria, then China, signaled the growing war threat in the Far East. Almost alone among American comic strips, *Terry and the Pirates* was ready for World War Two. International politics, normally a taboo subject, began to play a muted role in the background of the strip from the mid-1930's on, something most cartoonists studiously avoided until the actual outbreak of the war. As Caniff chronicled the growing fires of war, however, the sense of a response to the American Depression grew fainter and fainter. In fact, even the United States really passed from view until the nation's entry into the war. Caniff, in this way, perhaps made the most complete break from the Depression of any cartoonist—while the strip remained highly realistic and timely.

One side of life the late *Terry and the Pirates* focused on was aviation. But here Caniff was breaking no new ground; the flying strip was one of the first types of adventure series to appear in the wake of *Tarzan's* success. Among the leaders were *Barney Baxter in the Air* (by Frank Miller), *Smilin' Jack* (by Zack Mosley), and *Tailspin Tommy* (by Glenn Chaffin and Hal Forrest). One enterprising syndicate even capitalized on Eddie Rickenbacker's name by contracting him to write the continuity for *Ace Drummond* (drawn by Clayton Knight). Charles Lindbergh had captured the nation's imagination with his flight to Paris in 1927, and from then on, any distance or endurance flight made endless headlines. The movies frequently dramatized aerial exploits, but surprisingly the comic pages did not take advantage of aviation's popularity. True, Harold Teen flew a bit just before the Depression, but he flew for comedy, not drama. Mutt and Jeff, always ready to satirize any fads, took on the endurance flights that were so popular in early 1929. While Carl Spaatz flew "The Question Mark" to new records for staying aloft, Jeff hovered in "The Exclamation Point," certainly the most ungainly flying machine of all time. Finally several comic strips appeared that were to give a serious exposition of flight. *Tailspin Tommy* was among the first. The draftsmanship of it and its sister strips is meticulous; figures and landscape may leave something to be desired, but the airplanes are always letter-perfect. When Edgar Martin was including cutout dolls and chic outfits for the *Boots and Her Buddies* Sunday page, Chaffin and Forrest were adding detailed plans of popular planes of the day.

The aviation strips offered fast-moving plots that ranged, geographically, around the world. As much as possible, the heroes are seen in or near their airplanes, often for no other reason than to show some detail of the craft itself. In one way, these strips were the antithesis of the anti-mechanical bent that can be noted in some of the humorous comics. What they do is offer heroes who are self-reliant, free of dependence on a mechanized society. True, they have machines in the form of airplanes which are featured prominently in the various series, but these heroes are master of the machine rather than vice versa. In all of these strips, the achievement of the individual is the focus, not the accomplishments of their airplanes in which the heroes functioned only as pilots. But by celebrating the aircraft visually, the strips also look to the future, to an increasingly mechanized culture, in which the individual must learn to assert himself within the discipline imposed by mechanization. But an airplane offers no immediate threat to jobs and employment; it is often humanized (" 'she' got me through the storm," etc.) and not even looked on as a piece of machinery. In addition, in the flying strips the plane serves as a means to power, and power brings about order. The airplane therefore functions as more than a means of getting from one place to another speedily—it aids the hero in his quest to reestablish a harmonious situation. When the villains, who want to disrupt stability, also employ aircraft, their use of them is not so detailed and of brief duration. Only a perceptive reader would note this duality of function, and the stress on airplanes as powers for order remains dominant. While these symbolic overtones exist, it should be remembered that the planes—as planes alone—are also drawn with such loving detail simply to win that segment of the audience, usually boys, who found a fascination in aviation. Of course, the airplanes remained subordinate to their human pilots in the plots; their stress is pictorial. The story line as a rule follows that established by the various crime strips: a crime, exciting pursuit, eventual capture. Like all adventure strips, the material remains doggedly nontopical. The aircraft may be the latest models, but the stories divorce themselves from real time and events. Yet the persistent quest for order, the progressive outlook (in terms of scientific progress), and the financial nonconcern of the characters (where did they get all those airplanes?) were all muted responses to the times. Like their other adventure counterparts, one could be contemporary without being topical, and one could reply to the Depression without ever mentioning it.

Some cartoonists were not content with flying about the present world in search of adventure. Thus in 1930 Phil Nowlan and Dick Calkins introduced yet another new type of adventure strip: the science-fiction comic. Their particular contribution was *Buck Rogers, 2429 A. D.* (the year would eventually change to "the Twenty-fifth Century" to imply the passage of time). Still probably the most famous science-fiction strip, it quickly brought forth imitators. *Buck Rogers* was the first, however, and it laid down most of the ground rules the others would follow. Buck comes from the present, but, like a latter-day Rip Van Winkle, awakes to find himself in the future. He meets a beautiful girl, Wilma, and they share most of the adventures. Lurking in the background is a host of super-villains who appear at intervals to harass Buck and Wilma, threatening an apocalyptic end to just about everything if their demands are not met. Much of the strip's fascination lies in Buck's gradual introduction to twenty-fifth-century gadgetry. The innumerable machines, rockets, weapons, etc. (almost all of which seem extremely crude and dated today) that the strip displays constantly serve two purposes: they show one conception of the future and things to come, but they also show a world where science has eliminated such problems as depressions, unemployment, and poverty. The fondness for machines in the strip is especially strong during the early Thirties, the grimmest days of the Depression. It was during 1931–1932 that a movement began in the United States which claimed man was obsolescent, and many of his pursuits could be better accomplished by machines. The people behind these ideas were unemployed engineers, scientists, architects, and others in related fields. To them, the Depression was proof of the failure of the social system. Calling themselves Technocrats, they recommended control of the nation's economic life by trained technicians. The public developed a great enthusiasm for the movement, which came to be called Technocracy, and the fascination that *Buck Rogers* displays toward a mechanized future has its real counterpart in the concepts of the Technocrats. The strip, with its dependence on gadgets, goes somewhat against the "rugged individual" approach exemplified in the aviation series. Although both types of comics are progressive in terms of scientific outlook, in *Buck Rogers* the individual is less a master of his culture than he is simply a part of it.

The comic-strip future works well; any breakdowns come from without, not from the inner workings of the civilization itself. Eventually the Technocrats were discredited, and the public moved to the New Deal. In *Buck Rogers,* however, the idea of an ordered culture made possible by mechanical aids continued. This latter point of view is symbolically handled, with few overt references to mechanization, but the strip implies that contemporary problems will be unknown in the future. Not that the future world is a Utopia; on the contrary, the strip further implies that criminals have kept abreast of scientific advances, and crime is that much more dangerous to society. Additionally, the dangers from other planets and systems have multiplied, so that new threats pose new problems. The strip really offers only a variation in terms of time and locale from the other action comics—the adventures themselves remain essentially the same. For a Depression audience, *Buck Rogers* served to offer escapism pure and simple and also to reassure that audience that the Depression was not interminable. This latter approach is reinforced by the picture of a stream-

lined, smoothly running world in which all persons appear to fit designated roles—idleness is an unknown concept.

Although imitators of *Buck Rogers* sprang up, only one has had long-
term success: Alex Raymond's *Flash Gordon.* The two series were adapted
for the movies in the 1930's, both with Buster Crabbe in the lead—who
also occasionally portrayed Tarzan. Today, under different artists, the two
continue their science-fiction adventures. At the beginning, following the
successful trail blazed by *Buck Rogers,* Raymond had Flash (along with
the beautiful Dale and the brilliant Doctor Zarkov) move from the present
into a futuristic world where he must fight dangers similar to those faced
by Buck. But Raymond also borrowed a page from Harold Foster: whereas
Buck Rogers is, at best, crudely drawn, *Flash Gordon* demands attention
by its superlative illustrational style. Extremely cinematic, Raymond spent
far more time on his characters, allowing them to dominate the strip rather
than the gadgetry. The dichotomy of individualism versus machine technology that has been discussed in regard to the aviation strips and *Buck
Rogers* again appears. Raymond's decision to let Flash dominate the machines—and the strip—puts the series in close touch with virtually all the
adventure comics.

The basic story is really a morality tale, reduced to good versus evil,
with little shading. *Flash Gordon,* despite its futuristic environment, shows
a great affinity to *Tarzan, Dick Tracy,* and similar adventure comics. (Raymond, a prolific artist, in addition to *Flash Gordon* and the aforementioned
Jungle Jim, also did *Secret Agent X-9* in collaboration with Dashiell Hammett during the Thirties. This helps to explain the detective-like orientation
of *Flash Gordon.*) Its similarity to other popular strips probably explains
why it eventually grew to greater popularity than *Buck Rogers.* For the Depression audience, the theme of the self-reliant individual would be more
meaningful than one which shows the hero controlled by external forces
as did *Buck Rogers.* Although many readers' lives were being changed by
the Depression, the picture of the hero standing up to disorder carried
far more appeal. Thus Flash carries the story, implying that individuals
must command their destinies—not machines. The machines are present,
but the series relies on individual heroics.

The high point in *Flash Gordon,* however, is its art work. The strip
served as an ideal medium to express the 1930's sense of design. The
bulky, angular decor of *Buck Rogers* is replaced by the sleek, curvilinear
approach to composition. Modernity had reached the comic strips. The
streamlined, glistening architecture that would eventually dominate the
World's Fair of 1939 was presaged by the futuristic cities of Raymond's
strip. And implicit in his design is once again order—the villains (Ming the
Merciless was his most famous, a man who gradually came to symbolize
Japanese oppression in World War Two as Raymond slowly changed him

into the stereotyped "sinister Oriental"), just as in the other adventure strips, were out to destroy stability and thus accomplish their own ends. But what *Flash Gordon*'s basic plot lacked in originality was compensated for by the excellence of the illustrations.

One form of adventure never achieved any real success in the comics during the 1930's: the Western. Because of its great and enduring popularity in pulp magazines, books, and—in particular—the movies, the Western would seem a natural choice for comic-strip adaptation. Except for a few strips with modest circulations, however, no Western series reached the fame of the other adventure series. Several reasons can be advanced for this seemingly curious failure of acceptance. The leading cause of their low circulation lies with the distributors themselves: the syndicates and newspaper editors seem to shy away from the Western. Most comics, regardless of type, are oriented toward an urban audience, if for no other reason than that most comics readers are located in towns and cities. The humor strips normally portray urban situations, with little inclination to use rural characters other than the standby "bumpkin" or "hick." The serials, with their involved plots and numerous characters, usually take place in cities or small towns. When rural people appear, they frequently are shown to be unable or unwilling to cope with urban ways. The action adventures range all over the globe (and space) and through all areas of time (V. T. Hamlin's *Alley Oop* even went into the prehistoric past). But their rapid-fire dialogue, slick drawing, and sophisticated settings show a direct appeal toward an urban audience. As far as can be ascertained, virtually no geographical patterns existed for strip distribution. *Blondie, The Gumps,* and *Dick Tracy* went equally to rural, suburban, and metropolitan newspapers. The one exception to that generalization lies with the Western strip. A definite preference for this kind of comic exists in the various western states, where because of population distribution a large percentage of newspaper readers would come from rural environments and where a Western would naturally have greater popularity. One problem for the Western would therefore be distribution.

As a rule of thumb, a cartoonist is paid 50 per cent of the receipts taken in by his syndicate for distributing his comic strip. Normally an artist and his syndicate will strive to reach the larger city newspapers with huge circulations since the fee charged subscribing papers is commensurate with the readership. A paper serving a small community may therefore carry the same comic strip as its metropolitan counterpart but be charged only a fraction of the other's cost. Most cartoonists therefore strive to reach a broad, general audience. The syndicates' feeling apparently was—and still is—that an essentially urban audience would not like Westerns. What the syndicates apparently did not take into consideration was the amazing popular success of the movie Western and the Western novel. Both enjoyed continued popularity throughout the Depression. But the newspapers and the syndicates instead relied on the old formula of humor, serial stories, and adventure.

Another reason for the lack of successful Westerns is an aesthetic one. The view given of the West in stories and on film is an area of limitless space, with beautiful vistas at every turn. The small picture given in one comic-strip frame (about two inches by three inches at the most—the size varies with individual newspapers) hampers the feeling of great space. Man is usually seen to be rather small in contrast to the sprawling land in a Western movie; should a comic strip try the same idea, the figure would of course be little more than a speck. It is thus felt that the comic strip is a poor medium for reproducing the Western traditions. Yet the artistic quality of a strip like *The Cisco Kid* belies this point of view. But except for *Red Ryder, Little Joe, The Lone Ranger* and a few others, the Western has remained a neglected category in the comics. In fact, *The Lone Ranger* strip grew out of a 1933 radio serial by the same name. This is one of the few cases where the comics have borrowed directly from another medium; usually the reverse is true. Although the comic-strip version never achieved any great circulation, through the exposure of radio, movies, books, and comics *The Lone Ranger* emerged as a modern folk hero created by the mass media.

Even with the lack of Westerns, however, the adventure strips were a conspicuous success. It was in this genre that the worlds of violence and intrigue were explored. And it was also the field that opened comic art to illustrators with new ideas about drawing. Their highly realistic, at times cinematic, techniques gained acceptance for the equally realistic plots of the adventure strips. Most important of all, the adventure series made a definite response to the Depression and the chaotic Thirties. Although they may seem at first glance more escapist than any previous comic form, their very escapism involved a conscious reaction to the Depression era. Their slickly contrived action occurs so rapidly that the reader cannot think or object to what happens. Instead he sees in the adventure strips a symbolic visual and narrative search for order and stability. Any threats to these concepts are challenged by the heroes, and attempts are made to reestablish harmony. The Depression itself is never seen or referred to, but the implication is made that economic upheavals are never endless, and that the times must and will change for the better. As the decade drew to a close and the clouds of war looked more and more ominous, the adventure strips began to shed their escapist routine in order to line up against the Axis powers, the newest threat to order. Whereas the Depression was a taboo subject, the oncoming war allowed the comics an expression of reality.

The Gangster as Tragic Hero

Robert Warshow

Students of organized crime emphasize that it has a functional role in American society. Most criminals provide services for profit and thus from a sociological point of view are different in degree but not in kind from legitimate businessmen; the bookmaker and the insurance salesman are kinsmen. In contrast, the popular culture usually portrays the "gangster" as a creature who operates outside the law not merely for money but also because of dark psychological urges. His hatred for respectable people and his aggressive impulses are stressed—the cinema gangster invariably has a lust for murder. Robert Warshow's perceptive analysis of the stereotype of the gangster suggests that the stereotype (and its enduring popularity) may reveal more about urban America's attitude toward individualism and the myth of the self-made man than it does about the reality of criminality.

A valuable introduction to the gangster is "The Gangster Film" in Richard Griffith and Arthur Mayer's The Movies. *Daniel Bell discusses another point of view in his "Crime as an American Way of Life." Additional study of Warshow's approach to American culture should begin with his book* The Immediate Experience.

America, as a social and political organization, is committed to a cheerful view of life. It could not be otherwise. The sense of tragedy is a luxury of aristocratic societies, where the fate of the individual is not conceived of as having a direct and legitimate political importance, being determined by a fixed and supra-political—that is, non-controversial—moral order or fate. Modern equalitarian societies, however, whether democratic or authoritarian in their political forms, always base themselves on the claim that they are making life happier; the avowed function of the modern state, at least in its ultimate terms, is not only to regulate social relations, but also to determine the quality and the possibilities of human life in general. Happiness thus becomes the chief political issue—in a sense, the only political issue—and for that reason it can never be treated as an issue at all. If an American or a Russian is unhappy, it implies a certain reprobation of his society, and therefore, by a logic of which we can all recognize the necessity, it becomes an obligation of citizenship to be cheerful; if the authorities find it necessary, the citizen may even be compelled to make a public display of his cheerfulness on important occasions, just as he may be conscripted into the army in time of war.

Naturally, this civic responsibility rests most strongly upon the organs of mass culture. The individual citizen may still be permitted his private unhappiness so long as it does not take on political significance, the extent of this tolerance being determined by how large an area of private life the society can accommodate. But every production of mass culture is a public act and must conform with accepted notions of the public good. Nobody seriously questions the principle that it is the function of mass culture to maintain public morale, and certainly nobody in the mass audience objects to having his morale maintained. At a time when the normal condition of the citizen is a state of anxiety, euphoria spreads over our culture like the broad smile of an idiot. In terms of attitudes towards life, there is very little difference between a "happy" movie like *Good News,* which ignores death and suffering, and a "sad" movie like *A Tree Grows in Brooklyn,* which uses death and suffering as incidents in the service of a higher optimism.

But, whatever its effectiveness as a source of consolation and a means of pressure for maintaining "positive" social attitudes, this optimism is fundamentally satisfying to no one, not even to those who would be most disoriented without its support. Even within the area of mass culture, there always exists a current of opposition, seeking to express by whatever means are available to it that sense of desperation and inevitable

From *Partisan Review,* 15 (2), 1948, 240–244. Also included in Robert Warshow, *The Immediate Experience* (New York: Doubleday & Co., 1962). Reprinted by permission of the Robert Warshow estate. (Footnotes have been omitted.)

failure which optimism itself helps to create. Most often, this opposition is confined to rudimentary or semi-literate forms: in mob politics and journalism, for example, or in certain kinds of religious enthusiasm. When it does enter the field of art, it is likely to be disguised or attenuated: in an unspecific form of expression like jazz, in the basically harmless nihilism of the Marx Brothers, in the continually reasserted strain of hopelessness that often seems to be the real meaning of the soap opera. The gangster film is remarkable in that it fills the need for disguise (though not sufficiently to avoid arousing uneasiness) without requiring any serious distortion. From its beginnings, it has been a consistent and astonishingly complete presentation of the modern sense of tragedy.

In its initial character, the gangster film is simply one example of the movies' constant tendency to create fixed dramatic patterns that can be repeated indefinitely with a reasonable expectation of profit. One gangster film follows another as one musical or one Western follows another. But this rigidity is not necessarily opposed to the requirements of art. There have been very successful types of art in the past which developed such specific and detailed conventions as almost to make individual examples of the type interchangeable. This is true, for example, of Elizabethan revenge tragedy and Restoration comedy.

For such a type to be successful means that its conventions have imposed themselves upon the general consciousness and become the accepted vehicles of a particular set of attitudes and a particular aesthetic effect. One goes to any individual example of the type with very definite expectations, and originality is to be welcomed only in the degree that it intensifies the expected experience without fundamentally altering it. Moreover, the relationship between the conventions which go to make up such a type and the real experience of its audience or the real facts of whatever situation it pretends to describe is of only secondary importance and does not determine its aesthetic force. It is only in an ultimate sense that the type appeals to its audience's experience of reality; much more immediately, it appeals to previous experience of the type itself: it creates its own field of reference.

Thus the importance of the gangster film, and the nature and intensity of its emotional and aesthetic impact, cannot be measured in terms of the place of the gangster himself or the importance of the problem of crime in American life. Those European movie-goers who think there is a gangster on every corner in New York are certainly deceived, but defenders of the "positive" side of American culture are equally deceived if they think it relevant to point out that most Americans have never seen a gangster. What matters is that the experience of the gangster *as an experience of art* is universal to Americans. There is almost nothing we understand better or react to more readily or with quicker intelligence. The Western film, though it seems never to diminish in popularity, is for most of us no more than the folklore of the past, familiar and understandable only because it has been repeated so often. The gangster film comes much closer. In ways that we do not easily or willingly define, the gangster speaks for us, expressing that part of the American psyche which rejects the qualities and the demands of modern life, which rejects "Americanism" itself.

The gangster is the man of the city, with the city's language and knowledge, with its queer and dishonest skills and its terrible daring, carrying his life in his hands like a placard, like a club. For everyone else, there is at least the theoretical possibility of another world—in that happier American culture which the gangster denies, the city does not really exist; it is only a more crowded and more brightly lit country—but for the gangster there is only the city; he must inhabit it in order to personify it: not the real city, but that dangerous and sad city of the imagination which is so much more important, which is the modern world. And the gangster—though there are real gangsters—is also, and primarily, a creature of the imagination. The real city, one might say, produces only criminals; the imaginary city produces the gangster: he is what we want to be and what we are afraid we may become.

Thrown into the crowd without background or advantages, with only those ambiguous skills which the rest of us—the real people of the real city—can only pretend to have, the gangster is required to make his way, to make his life and impose it on others. Usually, when we come upon him, he has already made his choice or the choice has already been made for him, it doesn't matter which: we are not permitted to ask whether at some point he could have chosen to be something else than what he is.

The gangster's activity is actually a form of rational enterprise, involving fairly definite goals and various techniques for achieving them. But this rationality is usually no more than a vague background; we know, perhaps, that the gangster sells liquor or that he operates a numbers racket; often we are not given even that much information. So his activity becomes a kind of pure criminality: he hurts people. Certainly our response to the gangster film is most consistently and most universally a response to sadism; we gain the double satisfaction of participating vicariously in the gangster's sadism and then seeing it turned against the gangster himself.

But on another level the quality of irrational brutality and the quality of rational enterprise become one. Since we do not see the rational and routine aspects of the gangster's behavior, the practice of brutality—the quality of unmixed criminality—becomes the totality of his career. At the same time, we are always conscious that the whole meaning of this career is a drive for success: the typical gangster film presents a steady upward progress followed by a very precipitate fall. Thus brutality itself becomes at once the means to success and the content of success—a success that is defined in its most general terms, not as accomplishment or specific gain, but simply as the unlimited possibility of aggression. (In the same way, film presentations of businessmen tend to make it appear that they achieve their success by talking on the telephone and holding conferences and that success *is* talking on the telephone and holding conferences.)

From this point of view, the initial contact between the film and its audience is an agreed conception of human life: that man is a being with the possibilities of success or failure. This principle, too, belongs to the city; one must emerge from the crowd or else one is nothing. On that basis the necessity of the action is established, and it progresses by inalterable paths to the point where the gangster lies dead and the principle has been modified: there is really only one possibility—failure. The final meaning of the city is anonymity and death.

In the opening scene of *Scarface,* we are shown a successful man; we know he is successful because he has just given a party of opulent proportions and because he is called Big Louie. Through some monstrous lack of caution, he permits himself to be alone for a few moments. We understand from this immediately that he is about to be killed. No convention of the gangster film is more strongly established than this: it is dangerous to be alone. And yet the very conditions of success make it impossible not to be alone, for success is always the establishment of an *individual* preeminence that must be imposed on others, in whom it automatically arouses hatred; the successful man is an outlaw. The gangster's whole life is an effort to assert himself as an individual, to draw himself out of the crowd, and he always dies *because* he is an individual; the final bullet thrusts him back, makes him, after all, a failure. "Mother of God," says the dying Little Caesar, "is this the end of Rico?"—speaking of himself thus in the third person because what has been brought low is not the undifferentiated *man,* but the individual with a name, the gangster, the success; even to himself he is a creature of the imagination. (T. S. Eliot has pointed out that a number of Shakespeare's tragic heroes have this trick of looking at themselves dramatically; their true identity, the thing that is destroyed when they die, is something outside themselves—not a man, but a style of life, a kind of meaning.)

At bottom, the gangster is doomed because he is under the obligation to succeed, not because the means he employs are unlawful. In the deeper layers of the modern consciousness, *all* means are unlawful, every attempt to succeed is an act of aggression, leaving one alone and guilty and defenseless among enemies: one is *punished* for success. This is our intolerable dilemma: that failure is a kind of death and success is evil and dangerous, is—ultimately—impossible. The effect of the gangster film is to embody this dilemma in the person of the gangster and resolve it by his death. The dilemma is resolved because it is *his* death, not ours. We are safe; for the moment, we can acquiesce in our failure, we can choose to fail.

Food Fun for the Menfolk

James Thurber

Women take their problems to Ann Landers, boys learn how to be men from Paul Newman, and the jokes told in barrooms were written by professional humorists. Popular culture has substituted new modes of thought and behavior for many folkways. Thurber, in the following essay, ridicules this process while indirectly raising substantial questions about the domination of American life-style by the mass media. Coexistence between folk customs and popular culture may not be possible, Thurber suggests. Perhaps, the mere existence of a mass media transforms individuals from an "inner-directed" to an "other-directed" orientation. Gregory P. Stone's "Halloween and the Mass Child" in this book contains additional insights into this topic.
    Ethnic and racial minorities have not been immune to the homogenizing effect of popular culture, but the more isolated groups have preserved some of their traditional ways. A fascinating study of the mixture of pop and folk culture in a native American society is J. R. Fox's "Pueblo Baseball: A New Use for Old Witchcraft" also in this book. Lewis Atherton's Main Street on the Middle Border *is a useful account of the destruction of the middle-class midwestern folk culture.*

Five or six weeks ago, someone who signed himself simply A Friend sent
me a page torn from the Sunday magazine section of the *Herald Tribune*.
"I thought this might interest you," he wrote. Unfortunately, he failed to
mark the particular item he had in mind. On one side of the page was an
article called "New Thoughts about Awnings," which, naturally, didn't interest me at all. I turned the page over and came to this announcement:
"Why shouldn't you be among the prize winners in our reader-recipe contest for dishes made with plain or prepared gelatin?" The answer to that
was so simple as to be silly, so I went on to another column and a recipe
for "Plum Surprise." That couldn't have been what A Friend wanted me to
see, for the least of my interests in this world, the least of anybody's interests, is Plum Surprise. Gradually, by this process of elimination, I came
to an article called "Shower Parties, Up-to-Date!" (the exclamation point is
the author's). This was without doubt what A Friend wished to bring to my
attention. I read the article with mingled feelings of dismay and downright dread and then threw it away. But it haunted me for weeks. I realized
finally that "Shower Parties, Up-to-Date!" presented one of those menaces
which it is far better to face squarely than to try to ignore, so I dug it up
again and you and I are now going to face it together. If we all stand as
one, we can put a stop to the ominous innovation in shower parties which
the author of the article, Miss Elizabeth Harriman, so gaily suggests.

It is Miss Elizabeth Harriman's contention that *it is high time to invite
the bridegroom and his men friends to shower parties for the bride!* (The
italics and the exclamation point are mine.) "Nowadays," she says, flatly,
"the groom insists on being included in the party." Without descending to
invective, mud-slinging, or the lie direct, I can only say that you and I and
Miss Harriman have never met a groom and, what is more, are never going
to meet a groom who insists on being included in a shower party given
for his bride. A groom would as soon wear a veil and carry a bouquet of
lilies of the valley and baby's-breath as attend a shower party. Particularly
the kind of shower party which Miss Harriman, with fiendish glee, goes on
to invent right out of her own head. Let her start it off for you herself:
"After supper—which should be simple—comes the 'shower,' and here's
where we surprise the bride—and the groom—by not giving them a complete set of kitchen equipment. With a mischievous twinkle in our eye, we
deposit in front of the happy couple a bushel basket, saying 'The grocer
left this a little early for your new home, but you'd better open it now.'"
I will take up the story of what is supposed to happen next myself, with a
glint of cold horror in my eye.

From James Thurber, *Let Your Mind Alone* (New York: Harper & Bros.), pp. 199–206. Originally
printed in *The New Yorker*. Copyright © 1937 by James Thurber. Copyright © 1965 by Helen W.
Thurber and Rosemary Thurber Sauers. Reprinted by permission of Mrs. James Thurber.

It seems that the bushel basket is covered with a large piece of brown paper marked with the date of the forthcoming wedding. The very thought of a prospective bridegroom standing in a group of giggling women, with mischievous twinkles in their eyes, and looking at a bushel basket covered with brown paper bearing the date of his wedding is enough to convince anybody that Miss Harriman has got the wrong group of people together. But let us see what happens further (both according to Miss Harriman and according to me). In the basket, she says, are six brown-paper bags. The groom is made to pick up one of these, marked "What the Groom Gets." No groom in the United States would open a bag of that description—he is going through enough the way things are—but let us suppose that he does. Do you know what falls out of it, amid screams of laughter? A peach falls out of it. The bride now picks up a second brown-paper bag, labelled "What the Bride Gets." If you can't picture the look on the face of the groom at this point, I can. Well, out of this bag comes a box of salt marked "Genuine Old Salt." It seems that Miss Harriman has made the groom in this particular case "an ardent fisherman"—hence, Genuine Old Salt. Of course, that wouldn't work in the case of a groom who was not an ardent fisherman. All the guests would just stand there, with their mischievous twinkles turning to puzzled stares. If the groom is *not* an ardent fisherman, Miss Harriman suggests that the bride's bag contain "a gingerbread man cutter." You can hear the pleased roars of the groom and his men friends. "By George," they cry, "this is more fun than a barrel of monkeys!" Everybody is so interested that nobody wonders whether drinks are going to be served, or anything of that sort. There are four brown-paper bags yet to be opened, you see.

The bride now opens the first of these bags, marked simply "The Bride." From this emerge, amid the ecstatic squeals of the ladies, an old potato, a new potato, a borrowed rolling pin, and a blue plum. All the men stare blankly at this array and one of them begins to wonder where they keep the liquor in this house; but the girls explain about the contents of the bag. "Don't you see, Joe? It's 'something old and something new, something borrowed and something blue.' " "What's the potatoes for?" says Joe, gloomily (he is the man who was wondering where they keep the liquor). "I don't get it." "Well, Bert gets it," says the woman who has been explaining to Joe. Bert is a man whose guts Joe hates. "Let him have it," says Joe. This is one of his worst evenings, and there are still three brown-paper bags to be opened. The groom is now holding one of these, on which is printed "The Groom Is In the Kitchen Closet." There is a Bronx cheer from somewhere (probably from Harry Innis) and the groom grins redly; he wishes he were back in college. You and I know that the groom would simply put this bag back in the basket muttering something about it must be getting late, but Miss Harriman says he would open it. All right, he opens it. And pulls out a toy broom. At this point the groom's embarrassment and Joe's gloom are deeper than ever. "What's the idea?" Joe growls. "Stupid!" cries one of the ladies, gaily. "Don't you know 'Here comes the groom, stiff as a groom—stiff as a broom,' I mean?" "No," says Joe. He now moves directly on the pantry to see what there is in the way of drinks around the place. What he finds, in the icebox, is a Mason jar filled with cranberry juice. Joe instantly begins to look for his hat and overcoat, but the hostess captures him. There is more fun to come, she tells him—it is still *frightfully* early, only about eight-thirty.

The hostess leads Joe back to the bushel basket and pulls a fifth bag out of it, which she asks him to open; it is labelled "What the Guests Have." "What's the idea?" Joe grumbles, holding the bag as if it were a doily or a diaper. "Open it, silly!" squeal the excited girls, several of whom, however, are now squealing a little less excitedly than they have been. Joe finally opens the bag and pulls out a box of rice and a box of thyme marked "Good Thyme." "Thyme," mutters Joe, blankly, pronouncing the "h." He hands the boxes to the groom, who distractedly puts them back in the brown bag and puts the brown bag back in the bushel basket. One of the women hastily takes the bag out and opens it again, putting the rice and the thyme on a table. A slight chill falls over the party, on account of the groom's distraction and Joe's sullenness. There is a bad pause, not helped any by Harry Innis's wide yawn, but the hostess quickly hands the sixth and last brown bag to the bride, who extracts from it "a small jar of honey and a moon-shaped cooky-cutter." Joe takes the cooky-cutter from the bride; he is mildly interested for the first time. "What's this thing belong on?" he asks. Somebody takes it away from him. The groom glances at his wristwatch. It is not yet nine o'clock. "Isn't this fun, dear?" asks his bride. "Yeh," says the groom. "Yeh, sure. Swell." The bride realizes, with a quick intuition, that she is losing her hold on the groom. If she is a smart bride, she will be taken suddenly ill at this point and the groom will have to see her home (and Joe will have a chance to cry out with great concern, "Is there any whiskey in the house?"). But let us suppose that the bride is too dumb to realize why she is losing her hold on the groom. The party in this case goes right on. Miss Harriman has a lot more plans for it; she again has a mischievous twinkle in her eye.

The hostess—I shall just call her Miss Harriman—now hands each guest, including Joe, a piece of cardboard ruled off into twenty-five numbered squares (you can look up the article yourself). Each of the squares is large enough for a word to be written in it. Several of the men who have pencils swear they haven't, but Miss Harriman manages to dig up twenty-two pencils and two fountain pens from somewhere. Harry Innis puts his piece of cardboard on the arm of a davenport, stands up, and says, "Whatta you say we all run up to Tim's for a highball?" At this, Joe instantly puts on his overcoat, but one of the women makes him take it off, whispering harshly that he will break Miss Harriman's heart if he doesn't stay. "Aw," says Joe, and slumps into a chair. Mrs. Innis is quietly giving Harry a piece of her mind in a corner.

Miss Harriman now appears before everybody with an *enormous* piece of cardboard, also ruled off into twenty-five squares. Each square contains a dab of some kitchen staple or other: a dab of salt, a dab of pepper, a dab of sugar, a dab of flour, a dab of cayenne, a dab of sage, a dab of cinnamon, a dab of coffee, a dab of tea, a dab of dry mustard, a dab of grated cheese, a dab of baking powder, a dab of cocoa, and dabs of twelve other things. "The bride has her groceries all mixed up!" Miss Harriman sings out brightly. "You must all help her straighten them out! Everybody may look at the things on my cardboard and feel them, too, but nobody must dare taste! Then you write down in the corresponding squares on your own cardboard what you think the different things are!" Most of the men are now standing in a corner talking about the new Buick. One of them has folded his cardboard double and then folded that double and is absently tearing it into strips. Only Bert and two other men stick in the staples game; they identify the salt, sugar, pepper, coffee, and tea, and let it go at that. Ten of the twelve women present get all the answers right. The prize is a can of pepper and, not knowing whom to give it to, Miss Harriman just puts it on a table and claps her hands for attention. She announces that there is another food game to come. "Geezuss," says Joe.

Let Miss Harriman describe the next game in her own words. "In a large pan we gather together as many different vegetables and fruits as we can find—a bunch of carrots, a few beets, a turnip or two, potatoes white and sweet, parsley, lettuce, beans, oranges, grapefruit, pineapple, cherries, bananas—oh, anything. On a tray are placed string, toothpicks, paper towelling, waxed paper, pins, knives, scissors, melon-ball scoops, and any other kitchen implements. This game calls for partners, and as this is a food shower, we try to think of all the foods that seem to go together—Salt and Pepper; Liver and Bacon; Corned Beef and Cabbage; Cream and Sugar, etc. Half the ingredients are written on one color paper, the other on another color, and the guests match them for partners."

If, like Joe (who has drawn Liver and, for a partner, a Miss Bacon whom he has been avoiding all evening), you haven't got the idea yet, let me explain. The guests are supposed to manufacture the effigies of brides out of all these materials. Whoever makes the funniest or most original bride wins. (There are a lot of gags at this point, the men guffawing over in their corner. Bill Pierson tells the one about the social worker and the colored woman.) Of this bride-making game Miss Harriman writes: "Loud guffaws and wild dashes to the supply table will result." (She is right about the loud guffaws.) "Imaginations will run riot and hidden talents will come to the fore." But meanwhile, under cover of the loud guffaws and the wild dashes, Joe, Harry Innis, and the groom have slipped out of the house and gone on up to Tim's. When the bride discovers that the groom has disappeared she is distraught, for she thinks she has lost him for good, and I would not be surprised if she has.

An appropriate prize for this contest is, according to Miss Harriman, "a bridal bouquet of scallions and radishes with streamers of waxed paper, presented as someone plays 'Here Comes the Bride.'" You can imagine how Joe would have loved that if he had stayed. But he and Harry Innis and the groom are on their fifth highball up at Tim's. "And so our kitchen shower ends," writes Miss Harriman, happily, "with demands for another wedding as an excuse for more food fun." You have to admire the woman for whatever it is she has.

Who Knows What Evil Lurks

Jim Harmon

Public ownership of radio was never considered feasible by persons in a position to effect radio's development. From the first broadcasts, it was assumed that radio would be a private enterprise. Inevitably advertising followed—although Herbert Hoover predicted that the American people would not tolerate it—and with advertising came an obsession with the popularity of programs. Corporate consolidation through the "network system" began with the formation of NBC in 1926 and CBS in 1927. This started a movement toward standardized programming and nationwide advertising which produced the profits necessary for the hiring of "star" entertainers. The resulting "wasteland" of mediocre programming and irritating ads did not reach its nadir until television had replaced radio, but the decisions that led to it were made in the early days of radio.

Of the characters immortalized by radio, none is more celebrated than "The Shadow." The perfect radio hero, an invisible man, he stands in a long tradition of private citizens who uphold the law. The Shadow reflects the pervasive American notion that the police are either corrupt or bumbling "keystone kops" who are incapable of keeping order. For an account of a more frightening self-appointed guardian of the law see Christopher La Farge's "Mickey Spillane and His Bloody Hammer" in this book. Students interested in a comprehensive work should consult Erik Barnouw's three-volume The Image Empire: A History of Broadcasting in the United States.

"The Shadow, mysterious aide to the forces of law and order is, in reality, Lamont Cranston, wealthy young man about town who, years ago in the Orient, learned the hypnotic power to cloud men's minds so that they could not see him. Cranston's friend and companion, the lovely Margo Lane, alone knows to whom the voice of the invisible Shadow belongs. . . ."

There were electric thrills ahead when you heard that familiar opening, ominous and evocative as the theme of *Omphale's Spinning Wheel* that accompanied it. Mysterious friend to the law indeed was The Shadow. He was, and is, a classic figure of mystery itself. About him seems to hang the fog of Sherlock Holmes' London, and yet he is at home in the cheap dives frequented by the hard-boiled dicks of Dashiell Hammett and Raymond Chandler. And more than being a symbol of all this, The Shadow has become the chief fictional representative of all that was Radioland. After all, we knew even back then that here was the perfect hero for radio —the man you couldn't see.

This phantom avenger was never really created. Like Topsy, he just grew. Or more accurately, he was gathered out of those shadowy recesses of man's imagination. Long before the radio broadcasts and the magazine novels, The Shadow was a term used in many pieces of fiction to name a mysterious figure, sometimes hero, sometimes villain. In the nineteenth century, one writer speculated on "a certain shadow which may go into any place, by sunlight, moonlight, starlight, firelight, candlelight . . . and be supposed to be cognizant of everything." The Shadow would issue "warnings from time to time, that he is going to fall on such and such a subject, or to expose such and such a piece of humbug. . . . I want . . . to get up a general notion of 'What will the Shadow say about this, I wonder? What will the Shadow say about this? Is the Shadow here?' " The writer who speculated on using such a creature was Charles Dickens.

More recent predecessors of The Shadow in the early years of this century were the French villain Fantomos, who, like The Shadow, also lurked in dark recesses overhearing schemes and exchanging shots with adversaries garbed in black clothing and slouch hat, but with the distinction that, unlike The Shadow, he wore gloves; and Frank L. Packard's Jimmie Dale, alias The Gray Seal, who had a mask, signet ring, a civilian identity as a wealthy young man about town, a girl friend who sometimes used the pseudonym "Margot."

On radio The Shadow was the name given to a mysterious voice that introduced *Street and Smith's Detective Story Magazine Hour* by inquiring "Who knows what evil lurks in the hearts of men?" and then proceeded to answer the question by simply reading a story from the current issue of the crime magazine published by the sponsor.

From Jim Harmon, *The Great Radio Heroes* (New York: Doubleday), pp. 55–68. Copyright © 1967 by Jim Harmon, and reprinted by permission of Doubleday & Company, Inc., and the author.

The Shadow character became an instant hit and the whole show was devoted to his own exploits instead of merely introducing other stories. The program became a full-scale drama with actors, music, and sound effects. Street and Smith also issued a new magazine, *The Shadow Detective Magazine.*

In the first, Winter, 1931, the lead story was called "The Living Shadow." One of the early appearances of The Shadow on the radio was described in the text of this account from "the Secret Annals of The Shadow."

> There were those, of course, who claimed that they had heard his voice coming through the spaceless ether over the radio. But at the broadcasting studio, The Shadow's identity had been carefully guarded. He was said to have been allotted a special room, hung with curtains of heavy, black velvet, along a twisting corridor. There he faced the unseeing microphone, masked and robed.
>
> The underworld had gone so far as to make a determined effort to unravel The Shadow's identity, if it were truly The Shadow whose sinister voice the radio public knew, for there were doubters who maintained the voice was but that of an actor representing The Shadow. But all crookdom had reason to be interested—those without the law had to make sure.
>
> So watchers were posted at the entrance to the broadcasting chain's building. Many walked in and out. None could be labeled as The Shadow. In desperation, a clever crook, whose specialty was wire-tapping, applied for and secured a position as a radiotrician. Yet questioning of his fellow workers brought nothing but guesses to light. Around the studio The Shadow was almost as much a myth as on the outside. Only his voice was known.
>
> Every Thursday night the spy from crookdom would contrive to be in the twisting corridor watching the door of the room that was supposed to be The Shadow's. Yet no one ever entered that room!
>
> Could it be, then, that The Shadow broadcast by remote control? That his voice was conveyed to the studio by private wire? No one knew. He and his fear-striking laugh had been heard. That was all.

The original scripter for the radio series, Harry E. Charlot, died under puzzling circumstances, a mystery the solution of which is known perhaps only to The Shadow. After him a long line of free lancers contributed to the broadcasts: Jerry McGill, Max Erlich, even Alfred Bester, one of the great names in contemporary science fiction. Walter Gibson, a professional magician as well as a prolific writer who penned most of the nearly two hundred (178) *Shadow* magazine novels under the name of Maxwell Grant, unfortunately played no significant part in scripting *The Shadow* radio plays.

The writers for the magazine and the radio script fashioners borrowed freely from each other. Fans of the novels still complain that faithful sidekicks of The Shadow never appeared on the air, though this isn't quite true. In 1937 and 1938, among others, Commissioner Weston appeared along with his fellow police department member, Inspector Cardona, The Shadow's ally and nemesis. Radio fans, on the other hand, insist they never cared for the novels because in them, they say incorrectly, Margo Lane was not Lamont Cranston's friendly companion. While Margo was first born on the radio series, she certainly did appear in many of the magazine stories.

Aside from Margo, and cab driver Moe "Shrevie" Shrevnitz, who was an in-and-out comedy relief on radio, only Commissioner Weston was a familiar character in both media.

And who was it who knew what bitter fruit the weed of crime bears? James La Curto for one, also Frank Readick, who were among the very first actors to assume the role of the airwave's awesome avenger. Following in their shadowy footsteps was Robert Hardy Andrews, prolific radio writer who first scripted *Jack Armstrong* and *Just Plain Bill*. Then, in 1937, there was an actor who was only twenty-two when he stepped before the carbon mike to pronounce The Shadow's warning to crookdom. His name was Orson Welles.

The very young Orson Welles gave a lot of vigor to the then youthful career of The Shadow. His ominous rumble imparted a Shakespearian depth and urgency to every line of outrageous melodrama. Welles was convincing. On his other program, *The Mercury Theatre,* he convinced a good portion of the nation that we were literally being invaded by monsters from Mars when he adapted H. G. Wells' interplanetary novel, *War of the Worlds,* to sound like an on-the-spot newscast. That one broadcast earned him too much fame and notoriety to allow him to remain the anonymous star of *The Shadow,* so in the spring of 1939 Welles spoke for the last time to radio listeners of the evils that lurk in the minds and hearts of men.

Bill Johnstone, who had appeared in character roles on the show, succeeded Welles as Lamont Cranston. Although Johnstone's voice was vaguely similar to Welles', it was lighter and much, much more mature, barely this side of elderly.

By 1944, Johnstone had retired from the title role and the part was taken over by Bret Morrison, who had returned from army service to radio. He had been Mr. First Nighter before Pearl Harbor. But obviously military life had strengthened him for hardier stuff than attending a new play each week in radio's Little Theatre off Times Square. Actually, Morrison probably sounded more like a "wealthy young man about town" than any who played The Shadow—the right combination of sophistication and forcefulness.

Morrison's Margo was Gertrude Werner; Johnstone had played opposite Marjorie Anderson; and Orson Welles shared the kilocycles with a Margo Lane played by Agnes Moorehead.

The Brooklynite cab driver, Shrevie, was Alan Reed, who hasn't learned any better grammar as the voice of the home screen's "Fred Flintstone." Santos Ortega as Commissioner Weston completed the cast of regulars.

In cast and story, *The Shadow* was designed to convince you that The Shadow was real, he was earnest, and that he might be very near, lurking somewhere in the shadows, aware of your every guilty secret. For some listeners he was so convincing that during the war they wrote to the network broadcasting the exploits of The Shadow demanding to know why Lamont Cranston was not using his secret powers to fight the Nazis and Japanese. What the network replied to these correspondents is not known.

Anyone who ever tuned in on Sunday knew that Lamont Cranston had "the power to cloud men's minds so that they could not see him." In the most brightly lit room, The Shadow was invisible. He chuckled merrily as he drove the murder suspects he visited out of their minds. He was here, he was there, he was everywhere. Once in a while he would lift a mad scientist's flask of elixir into the air, or pull a gun out of nowhere and leave it hanging in the air to prove he was corporeal. But most of the time, he counted on his eerie voice to cause his victims to jump at every shadow.

It is strange that none of the people The Shadow ever visited on the airwaves ever suspected mechanical trickery. The Shadow, when invisible, sounded exactly as if he were speaking over a telephone. For some reason, no one ever snarled, "You can't fool me, buster. Somewhere you got one of them tin cans rigged up with a tight string!"

Moreover, Cranston was always telephoning people—crooks, suspects, Police Commissioner Weston. No one ever bleated, "Cranston, huh? So that's who you really are, Shadow! I'd recognize that voice anywhere!"

Of course, all this was more than a stupid mistake. We all realized, I think, that The Shadow was more than a voice. It was the *power* of The Shadow to cloud men's minds that made him able to go unrecognized when he didn't wish to be recognized.

In the show's early years, the decade before World War II, there was a time of experimentation, a search for the limitations and scope of The Shadow himself. The Master of Men's Minds was not limited to his power of hypnotic invisibility.

Those of the younger generation who think Shari Lewis invented ventriloquism would be surprised to learn that The Shadow was capable of projecting his voice up the entire slope of a volcanic mountain from its base. He did that in a 1937 radio episode called "White God" in order to cause a deranged scientist to blow himself and the mountain up in the mistaken belief that he would be taking his nemesis, The Shadow, along with him. The explosion didn't harm The Shadow, but it destroyed the volcano, which the scientist had turned into a gigantic magnet to pull planes and ships to their destruction. A madman in 1937, today he could probably get a good job with the government.

Many more purely psychic powers belonged to the youthful Shadow. The same year he caused the destruction of the "White God," he received a "Message from the Hills" delivered by sheer telepathy, the mind of an ancient native speaking directly to the mind of The Shadow to warn him of the forces of evil at work. The Shadow was able to answer the call for help both mentally and, at last, physically.

These were not all of the special powers of the Master of Darkness. When Margo was abducted by a lunatic who pined to be a vampire (another one of *those* weekends in the country!), The Shadow was able to silently "will" people he met to do his bidding and answer his questions. Finally, The Shadow located Margo just before the lunatic, a renegade medico, pumped the poor girl completely empty of blood. The "vampire" wasn't really thirsty, just greedy. He had gone a long way toward depopulating the countryside by siphoning the residents dry in order to sell their liquid contents to a blood bank.

After the thirties, the free-wheeling days of experimentation with The Shadow's powers were over. Someone decreed that Lamont Cranston was a detective and he would use his power as The Shadow exactly twice in each show. After the middle commercial, which urged you to rush right out and buy a ton of Blue Coal immediately, The Shadow would interview a reluctant witness to scare the bejabbers and the information out of him or her, and Cranston would become The Shadow for the second time in one show to capture the villain in the climax and, usually, rescue Margo Lane from his clutches.

Actually, it got so that The Shadow frightened people very little with his invisibility. It seemed everybody had been through that bit so many times that there were a few token lines about "Where's that voice coming from?" and "The Shadow has the power to cloud your mind . . ." and the interrogation would proceed in standard cops-and-robbers format.

Yet even into the forties and fifties an occasional broadcast of *The Shadow* had some element to help make it memorable—an interesting locale, a bit of business, a gimmick. The plays that were the most interesting were the ones concerned directly with The Shadow's power. While the furthest boundaries of his abilities were explored in the thirties, in the forties there was, on a rare occasion, a statement of his limitations.

The boundaries of hypnotic invisibility are known to science, since the feat can actually be performed by an expert. The subject, placed in a hypnotic trance and told "not to see" the hypnotist and his attire, will see a cigarette in the hand of the hypnotist eerily floating in the air. If the command is re-enforced by instructions not to detect any sign of the presence of the hypnotist, the subject will not even detect the smoking cigarette. Of course, any ordinary human hypnotist requires the right subject and careful preparation. Only the *superhuman* Shadow could cloud men's minds instantly. And even The Shadow was not infallible. Once he apparently neglected to instruct his subjects not to see *any* evidence of his presence, thus leaving himself open to being spotted in the home of a wealthy crook by the impressions of his feet in a deep-pile carpet. When guns came out, The Shadow's visible footsteps beat a hasty retreat, but, as I recall, he did catch up with the luxury-loving hood, no doubt in a place with hardwood floors.

Other much more complex methods were used to make The Shadow visible and expose his true identity. Aliens from space probed him with inspection rays and turned the data over to their calculators, which speedily beeped out a complete analysis when The Shadow hastily quit the scene. This happened back in 1939, when the audience must have really thought it was crazy Buck Rogers stuff.

Probably the highlight of all these "Shadow exposed" tales came in "The Shadow's Revenge," when Lamont Cranston stood mumbling furiously that he had the power to cloud men's minds while a pair of crooks were convulsed with laughter. "Hey, Cranston, you cracking up or something?" one amused gangster asked. It all seemed like a nightmare. And, unfortunately (as far as a good story was concerned) it was exactly that.

As a listener, after those first few years of pre-teen innocence, the greatest mystery about The Shadow to me was exactly what was meant by Margo being Lamont Cranston's "friend and companion." The question can be answered a bit more realistically than the innuendos about Lois Lane and Superman, or even the Lone Ranger and Tonto. There does seem to be some real, not purely imagined, evidence that the relationship between Margo and Lamont was very companionable. After all, Cranston and Margo did travel around the world together several times, generally unchaperoned, and many of the radio plays began with the wealthy young man about town and his "friend and companion" having breakfast together at Cranston's town house or apartment. While there was never mention of the possibility of marriage, there were often suggestions of romance, and Lamont and Margo referred to each other as "darling." All in all, it is apparent that Margo had a deep appreciation of the skills Lamont Cranston learned in the Orient.

The question, if one ever existed, seems completely settled in one of the 1965 paperbound revivals of The Shadow novels. In *The Shadow's Revenge,* under the traditional by-line of Maxwell Grant, the Master of Darkness pays a call to Margo Lane's boudoir.

> Margo Lane sat up in her bed. The slim body of the dark-haired woman was hidden by her light sheet. Awake, she smiled at the black-shrouded figure of her chief. The Shadow was not smiling, his great figure tall in the room, his glowing eyes piercing the dim bedroom light.
> "I must go now, Margo," The Shadow said. "I must find The Demon before it is too late. . . ."

So if Margo was The Shadow's "friend and companion," he was also her "chief" and she "smiled" at his entrance into her bedroom. Since The Shadow's prime motivation is power, he would exercise that power over the woman in his life. That part of the mystery of The Shadow seems solved.

Another "mystery" about Margo and Lamont that always interested me was why this companionable twosome never learned that no matter how bad the storm, no matter how perilous the road, they should never, never seek refuge in mysterious old mansions around which broke forks of lightning and winds of fury! They were sure to run into homicidal maniacs, gory corpses, and a legendary supernatural monster or two. It happened to them in "The Legend of Crown Shield Castle," "The House That Death Built," and "The Werewolf of Hamilton Mansion."

Hamilton Mansion wasn't the only place they ran into a lycanthrope menace. There was one in "Death Prowls at Night." There were zombies on "The Isle of the Living Dead," a relative of King Kong in "Night Marauders," and a crazy actor who thought he was the Frankenstein monster in "The Face."

Almost all of these creatures took after Margo Lane. It couldn't have been for her beauty alone. After all, so many of these fiends wanted to change her. One wanted to change her into a gorilla, and another madman tried to convince her to become a bitch—a she-wolf. She was menaced, tied up, tortured, threatened, and assaulted up to the point the censor would allow, and all because she traveled around the country with Lamont Cranston, who clearly wasn't going to make an honest woman of her. Such is the perversity of women!

The only other woman I can think of who has had to endure so much for a man is Lois Lane, perennial girl friend of Superman. With such a similarity in name and character, can there be any doubt that these two girls, so attracted to men who wear capes and mistreat them so, are sisters?

The perfect example of what Margo Lane had to go through appears in "The Ghost Walks Again," a script by Jerry Devine that was such a complete *Shadow* story that it was presented to writers as a sample of how to write the radio show.

When a ghost begins murdering the population of a small New England town, the town council gets together and comes to the only logical decision: call in Lamont Cranston. Needless to say, Cranston doesn't pay much heed to Margo (who is trailing him around again), and she is captured by the "ghost," who for kicks (there is no other reason) decides to put her to the torture.

EDWARD: In the days of the Puritans they had a very satisfactory method for dealing with meddlers . . . they branded them upon the forehead . . .

MARGO: No . . . no . . .

EDWARD: Soon, young lady, soon you shall feel the searing agony of that brand biting into your flesh!

MARGO: You're mad . . . you're mad!

EDWARD: (laughing) You won't feel the pain too long . . . no . . . you see, after you are branded I have another treat for you . . . the press . . . the torture press!

MARGO: You let me out of here!

EDWARD: The branding iron is glowing now . . . it is ready to use!

MARGO: You can't do this . . . please!

EDWARD: (laughing) Prepare yourself . . . prepare yourself, Miss Lane . . . I have the iron ready now . . .

MARGO: Keep it away from me . . . (screams) Keep it away!

SHADOW: Drop that iron, Mr. Darrow!

EDWARD: Who was that?

SHADOW: Release that girl . . .

EDWARD: No . . . no! Let go of my arm! Let me finish my work!
(Iron drops to floor)

SHADOW: There . . . your work is finished, Mr. Darrow!

EDWARD: Who are you?

SHADOW: (laughs) I am The Shadow!

EDWARD: The Shadow! I've heard of you . . .

SHADOW: Then you know too that I am here to put an end to your career of torture and murder, Mr. Darrow!

And so, once again, The Shadow does prove that he knows "what bitter fruit the weed of crime bears" and that "crime does not pay!"

The Shadow's exploits took place originally in the thirties, forties, and even into the fifties. The radio program lasted until 1954, nearly five years longer than *The Shadow Magazine*. And perhaps that was where Lamont Cranston should have stayed—in the shadows of the past. But many people didn't think so. They wanted radio drama back and, in particular, favorite shows like *The Shadow*. Of course, for the most part, the old recordings had been destroyed long ago because the program originators never considered the possibility that one day there would be a public demand to hear the old shows once again. But a few people still had radio recordings—private collectors, members of the cast, production crews of radio programs, and especially Charles Michaelson.

Charles Michaelson had been involved in the production of the original *Shadow* broadcasts and he had picked up syndication rights on this program and others when big-time radio began going out in the fifties. He salvaged literally thousands of transcription discs that might otherwise have been destroyed for all time. For nearly a decade all he had been able to do with the old recordings was store them. "When we started to clean out our vaults around Christmas of 1962, I couldn't bear to destroy those old radio recordings," Michaelson recalled. "Maybe it was the sentiment of the holiday season. I phoned ten large radio stations around the country and asked if they'd be interested in airing some of the old shows again. . . . I got six affirmative answers."

Charles Michaelson, a man alternately nostalgic and practical, had his problems to solve, many of them with unions. A committee of actors was set up to agree on the identity of voices heard on various episodes for residual payments. On some programs where the organist who played the theme and bridges couldn't be identified or located to sign an agreement, all the original music had to be edited out and stock transcription orchestrations inserted. In the end, Michaelson, the sentimental businessman, won over all obstacles. The Shadow returned!

WGN in Chicago was the first station to begin rebroadcasting *The Shadow.* Radio-TV columnists seized upon the programing idea and gustily informed Windy City citizens that "The Shadow is back on the air! Once again we'll hear of the evils that lurk in the hearts of men!"

Because of all the breezy banner waving that consequently drew audiences' attention back to radio drama, WGN's scheduling of the old *Shadow* shows received an overwhelming listener response as young and old alike, the neophytes and the nostalgics, all tuned in on Sunday afternoons in Chicago to brave the eerie adventures of the Master of Men's Minds. Students of the Pop Art culture at nearby Northwestern University even allegedly formed a Secret Shadow Society, complete with members garbed in black cloaks and slouch hats who huddled around an old Motorola floor-model radio, listening to *The Shadow.*

After this initial success, Michaelson added other stations to his list of customers and other titles to his catalogue of program offerings, including *Sherlock Holmes, Weird Circle,* and *The Green Hornet.*

The Shadow, though, became the most successful of the handful of old favorites the recordings of which had survived and were available for syndication, eventually reaching forty outlets. Though the market waxes and wanes, these old programs may be playing on some station somewhere as long as there is radio.

As one of the basic prototypes of what has come to be called Pop Art, The Shadow is unique and irreplaceable, a legend in his own time. A classic character who looms slouch hat and shoulders above all others of his kind, he is as inevitable as a guilty conscience, an unseen power that awakens within all of us our most deep-rooted fears of mortal retribution. There has never been a force quite like him.

None of the stories, or radio plays, or comic magazines, or motion pictures (and someday, no doubt, television programs), will ever be really good—not great art, not great literature. But The Shadow himself is great! For he is a creature of folklore, not created, but distilled.

Invisible as a radio beam, or cloaked in the blackness of night, The Shadow can achieve his full potential only in our imaginations. Whether by aid of a broadcast, or by the gift of memory, when The Shadow steals across the stage of our own consciousness, he *is* "the Master of Men's Minds."

INTRODUCTION: 1945–1970

$E=mc^2$. It has become a cliché to suggest that "the bomb" revolutionized the lives of Americans. "One must learn to breathe, eat, make love in its presence; it is a part of every living consciousness," declared Gene Feldman and Max Gartenberg. Jeff Nuttall in *Bomb Culture* offered a simple rule of thumb—no one who was past puberty in 1945 can conceive of living without a future, no one younger can imagine a future. If such a psychological upheaval did take place, it should be reflected by changes within the popular culture. What the period after World War II revealed was the growth of fear and hatred for technology and the industrialists who controlled it. The result was the creation of an anti-technological, non-commercial underground culture. However, that culture could not be sustained. "Money has reckoned the soul of America," cried Allen Ginsberg in 1958. By 1970 the underground, too, was dancing to a commercial tune.

Suppression can be blamed in some measure for the decline of the underground, but its failure issued for the most part from the propensity of its inhabitants to "sell out." In 1959 one could rent a beatnik; in 1969, a hippie. However "plastic" these particular individuals were, and despite the satiric intent, the willingness of underground people to rent themselves to people who used them to enliven their parties was indicative of deeper problems. The technological culture was alluring. Although it worked towards such horrors as an automated battlefield, it also gave rise to a variety of fascinating playthings, from wa-wa pedals to amphetamines.

Testifying to the flimsy nature of the noncommercial stance of the underground was the prominence of rock and drugs. Musicians who began by performing free in the park became hooked on multitrack tape recorders, sound engineers, and the quest for perfection within the studio. Large fees for personal appearances naturally followed, as did a tacit cooperation with promoters of exploitative festivals. Drugs, despite myths to the contrary, were always controlled by gangsters. From the perspective of 1970 the "free" world envisioned by Abbie Hoffman remains a pipe dream. Walt Kelly's famous line from "Pogo" can be applied to the underground: "We have met the enemy, and he is us." Or, as Captain America succinctly put it in *Easy Rider:* "We blew it."

In the mid-sixties, when the rage against technology was at its height, Marshall McLuhan magically appeared to uphold industrial progress. A savage critic of modern society throughout his early career, with the publication of *Understanding Media* he became the favorite philosopher of many American corporations. McLuhan argued that technological innovation, specifically change involving the media, was reordering society. Swiftly and inevitably a golden age of harmonious retribalization was being created through the electronic extensions of man's senses. Primitivistic resistance against this revolution was both idiotic and futile. McLuhan sidestepped questions pertaining to the control of this new world. Throughout his books he compared modern man with the sailor in Edgar Allan Poe's "Descent Into the Maelstrom." The sailor, caught in a whirlpool, must understand the action of the whirlpool if he is to have any possibility of saving himself. Presumably, after one grasps the nature of the electronic universe, he may then question its controllers.

McLuhan's emphasis upon the idea that "the media is the message" underscored the importance of popular culture, much of which is transmitted through the electronic media. His prestige also aided those students of culture who wished to eliminate arbitrary labels such as "high," "folk," "mass," and "kitsch." When a medium provides a "depth experience," these categories lose their meaning, McLuhan declared. Such divisions had always distorted the reality of American culture—the existence of Mark Twain, Winslow Homer, and Louis Armstrong proved as much—but it was not until the sixties that most critics were willing to accept the popular arts. Of course, the outcropping of brilliant popular artists since 1945 also served to demolish the snobbishness of critics. Jack Nicholson, Walt Kelly, Thelonious Monk, Andrew Wyeth, Kareem Abdul-Jabbar, Gus Arriola, and Bob Dylan (to name just a few) created art with no modifying adjectives.

Today many colleges offer courses in popular culture. Bowling Green State University has a Center for the Study of Popular Culture which publishes the *Journal of Popular Culture*. In the *Journal* the popular arts are frankly celebrated; in a recent issue Russel B. Nye asked: "I have never quite understood why, if a Ph.D. settles down with a Scotch and soda to read Ross MacDonald (who was recently favored with front-page *Times* and *Newsweek* reviews), it's sophistication, whereas a tool-and-die maker from Oldsmobile who watches *Mannix* on TV with a can of beer is automatically a slob. Whose values are the more genuine?" It is possible that the academic embrace will prove clammy. One can imagine bored students grinding out absurd term papers on homosexuality in "Little Queenie" and "The Ballad of a Teenage Queen" or memorizing the Wallet family tree from the comic strip *Gasoline Alley*. But that remains for the future. Today the study of popular culture is good (if not always clean) fun.

I Love Lucy; Charlie Brown (of Charles Schultz and The Coasters); mau-mauing; drafting (Elvis, Ali, and Junior Johnson); cancer and Acapulco gold; bopping at the high-school hop; soup cans; '51 Fords, '56 Chevys, and VW busses; homosexual fullbacks; sack dresses and midis; *Playboy;* Boston Braves, Milwaukee Braves, Atlanta Braves; mambo; Brenda Starr, Little Eva, and Suzy Creamcheese; *Peyton Place;* Silver Surfer; Marilyn Monroe and Robert Kennedy; flying saucers; point-shaving and quiz shows.... The jet propelled changes of the last twenty-five years are impossible to summarize. Such rapid cultural modification fragments the populace; "generations" only three to five years apart speak variant dialects and perform different rituals. "Where have you gone, Joe DiMaggio?" sang Simon and Garfunkel in *The Graduate,* and half the audience had only the fuzziest notion of what "the Yankee Clipper" symbolized. None of the following articles will answer Simon and Garfunkel's question, but they will provide an entering wedge into the complexity of modern American culture.

Remembrances of Bop in New York, 1945–1950

Gilbert Sorrentino

Before jazz spread beyond the boundaries of the Negro community, it was an authentic expression of black life. In the twenties and thirties jazz was grafted onto dance music to produce a pleasing product for the white middle class; the result was "swing." In the forties, some black musicians spurned swing to play jazz that expressed their own thinking, not the commercial necessities. Growing out of Harlem nightclubs, their music was labeled "rebop," "bebop," or simply "bop." It seemed eccentric and undanceable—"Chinese notes," in the words of one critic. Bop stirred a violent controversy among jazz players, but by the late forties it had won the day. Charlie Parker, Thelonious Monk, and Dizzy Gillespie became famous, and imitators proliferated.

Gilbert Sorrentino comments upon the social implications of bop; a more detailed study is Leonard Feather's Inside Be-Bop. *Marshall Stearns's* The Story of Jazz *is a perceptive survey.*

Jazz was an essential component of underground culture until rock supplanted it in the sixties. Some analysts have considered the importance of rock in the counter culture to be symbolic of the commercialism of the culture and of its anti-intellectualism. Others assert that this change only reflects the maturing of rock artists and the tendency of the more innovative of jazz musicians to withdraw into the black community.

This piece is not intended to be definitive, nor does it purport to be an historical treatment of New York jazz in the late 40s. It is simply my own personal recollections of what I heard, and what all my friends heard in New York jazz *at* that time. Anyone who was born in 1930 or so, who lived in New York at that time, and who listens, or listened, to jazz, will recall similar things. But there are many people who now listen to jazz who were either not interested in it then, or who were too young to be directly involved in listening. There are also many of us, who, although we were caught up in bop at that time, have forgotten, as I had until I started thinking about this piece, that we didn't think of jazz as an "art form" in *any* sense of that term when we listened. We were young, naïve, very romantic: above all, we wanted a music of our own, something removed from school dances, the Hit Parade, and "long-hair," which, when I was in my teens, was something I associated with the 1812 Overture, period. Or with Hollywood sound-tracks . . . Beethoven or Dimitri Tiomkin, they were the same to me. The whole thing was out of my realm and my experience. Before I "needed" music, this stuff was simply not in my air; after I "needed" it, I simply would not allow it into my air. I moved in a group which thought that music began and ended with be-bop: anyone who though differently was a square. To be called a square in those days was to be square in music only: which, in a strange sense, was much worse than being generally square. In a complex and certainly inarticulate way, we were right. Certainly, the chances are that a young man, who in 1945 didn't "dig Dizzy," would never in 1955 read Charles Olson. Bop, for me, was the entrance into the general world of culture, although at the time, I wouldn't have believed it. When I was 14, culture meant going to the opera and doing your homework every night.

In 1941, when the war broke out, I was 12 years old and lived in an all-white just-about lower middle-class neighborhood. A neighbor had given me a phonograph for Christmas the year before, and with the phonograph, about a dozen records. The neighbor's daughter, a girl of about sixteen, had chosen the records, one, because she worked in a record store, and two, because her parents had concluded, rightly, that she would know more about my "taste" than they would. I remember that among the records were Glenn Miller's *Little Brown Jug,* Harry James' *Flatbush Flanagan,* and Tommy Dorsey's *Marie.* I think that there was also the Andrews Sisters on *Here Comes The Navy,* a hokey "war" tune set to *Beer-Barrel Polka.* That was the first time I recall listening to swing. A year later I had about ten James records, but I think only one or two Miller and Dorsey. The same was true of my friends. I think the reason

From *Kulchur*, 3 (10), Summer 1963, 70–82. Reprinted by permission of Wender and Associates and Kulchur Press; copyright © by Kulchur Press, Inc.

for this was that we identified the Miller and Dorsey music with a group of people who were much older (that is, 3 or 4 years older—which was a lifetime), who went to high school, who enlisted, who were drafted, and who danced—at *real* dances. We wanted our *own* bands. Benny Goodman was completely out—he was more out of touch than the others. In 1943, when I entered high school, the situation was the same, although I think I had heard of Count Basie and Lionel Hampton. In about 1944 came the first great revelation—I heard Ellington. The tune was *Main Stem,* and I thought that I had never heard anything like it in my life—I hadn't. Instantly, the James band dissolved for me, and I spent all my time searching in the old 6th Avenue shops for 2nd-hand Duke records. I had an ally or two in this, and as we became more and more involved in Ellington, we found ourselves more and more removed from those who didn't know him. Then slowly, Basie came into our world. The concept of a big band that had a solo freedom was demonstrated, and I also heard Dicky Wells and Prez for the first time. There was still something, of course, turning me off these bands, and I think it was that they weren't *mine.* The music they played was great, but I had no identification at all with it, no "social" rapport with it, there wasn't even a chance to *see* the bands. In my neighborhood, none of the record stores carried any of their records.

Then came Herman, that fantastic herd, with *Caldonia* and *Apple Honey,* with its great bop writing for the brass section at the end. That's what got all of us, even those who didn't care about Duke, Dorsey, Miller, Basie, etc. It was the ragged, harsh, jumpy music of that great Herman band that excited us. We had found a band that was *really* ours, although what we had really found was be-bop. We didn't know at the time that bop writing, for the sections, was what made Herman's band so totally different from the rest. We had never even heard, as I recall, the word, be-bop. Bop had been played since about 1941, but there was a ban on records during the war, which was why we had all grown up on records that really belonged to people who were five or six years older: no records were released during the war at all, except those that had been pre-recorded. And all of us were, of course, too young to go to 52nd Street: my God, we didn't even know it was there!

Then, one day, when I was about 15 or 16, on my way to the movies, a friend of mine leaned out the window and called me to come in to his house. I went over and he told me that he wanted to play me a new record. "You've never heard anything like this in your life!" He put on this 78 Savoy, I think it was, and I sat there as if someone had hit me over the head: it was *Ko-Ko,* by Charles Parker and His Re-Bop Boys.

The Climate
In 1945, I and a great many other boys (and, perhaps, girls) were absolutely disoriented, and at a great remove from the "world" in general.
The "big guys" with whom we had at least occasionally played ball—or
been bullied by, had come back from the war, men—the tenuous contact
we had had with them was gone forever. The records that were played
at high school dances were the old pre-war swing records, new swing
records by people like Tex Beneke and Bobby Sherwood, or hopeless
tunes like *Dolly With A Hole In Her Stocking.* The big Negro bands were
considered too "wild," or, simply, were called "nigger bands"; their
music, "nigger music." The only "nigger music" tolerated was stuff by
Louis Jordan, etc. The old shufflin' along business. There was a general
feeling among older whites—and many younger ones—those who would
soon be damned by us "hipsters" as squares—that Negroes simply
picked up a horn, or a drum, and all this happy noise poured out. There
was no way to argue with these people, and the records that we pointed to
by Ellington and Basie were thought to be rather inept versions of what
those "great inventors" Goodman and Miller did. It never occurred to
these people to wonder if Ellington did it first, and none of us who defended these bands were at all aware of Benny Moten, Jay McShann, etc.,
and the other relatively regional bands that had been playing "swing"
when Glenn Miller was utterly unknown. In fact, there was a tendency to
"accept" the *known* Negro bands as being pretty good—"for niggers."
In a perverse way, this angered us, because we were at the point of
severing ourselves completely from this whole world: acceptance of the
big Negro bands didn't serve our purposes at all. Herman was a great
hero to us partially because of the strange fact that it was almost impossible to dance to him. The Lindy was *the* dance then and Herman's
music was either too fast, or the writing was too "musical" (in the sense
of being written for the *band,* and not the dancers) for the Lindy to be successful. We were overjoyed, because slowly a rift was occurring between
those of us who hungered for a music that meant something to us and
those who wanted the Hit Parade. There was also the element of snobbery
and the clique working. Those who "dug the Herd" were an elite—of their
own creation, to be sure, but an elite, nonetheless. Be-bop cut us off completely, to our immense satisfaction. It was even more vehemently decried
as "nigger music," but even to the tone-deaf it was apparent that it (the
music) didn't care what the hell was thought of it—jazz had broken itself
free of the middle-class world's *social* conception of what it should be. It
gave no quarter and asked none. It was, probably more than at any other
time in its history, including the present, absolutely non-popular: and its

adherents and devotees formed a cult, which perhaps more than any other force in the intellectual life of our time, brought together young people who were tired of the spurious. It was even more potent because it was impossible for those who hated it to parody it. You had to *know;* if you didn't know, you were on the other side, a square or a fig. The figs, to us, were even more hopeless than those who simply wanted to dance and tap their feet; they were people who listened only to "pure" jazz—which was Dixieland. They had their own *mystique* going for them, one which was held in contempt by us boppers. The reason that we loathed them more than the squares was because the squares didn't care at all, they were the ignorant ones—the figs purported to be "serious" about jazz—and yet wouldn't accept what be-bop was all about, an absolutely new method of playing.

 After I had heard *Ko-Ko* by Charley Parker, I bought early Gillespie 78s on the Musicraft label: *Salt Peanuts; That's Earl, Brother; Oop-Bop-She-Bam; Hot House; Groovin' High; Blue N' Boogie;* and many others. Dizzy was our king and our god. I recall having a jacket, Navy surplus, made of heavy canvas, on which I painstakingly copied a caricature of Dizzy—beret, horn-rimmed glasses, moustache and goatee, and a hand holding a trumpet. Above this drawing (which I put on the back of the jacket) I lettered the word BOP, and below it, DIZZY. Those who didn't know what the drawing was all about were out—those who knew, in. It was a tight little group and very few people who didn't care were admitted. The clothing worn was also unique, a uniform of "membership." It included one-button lounge suits, huge-shouldered jackets, pegged pants, "bop ties," (which were floppy bow ties that hung down to about the second shirt button) and horn-rimmed glasses. Symphony Sid was just about on the air at that time, or perhaps it was the next year, 1946, and he sold "bop glasses" for a dollar, mail order. One could either buy sunglasses or plain glasses. This phenomenon of wearing glasses was perhaps most "ideologically" indicative of the subtle undercurrents that were sweeping around us at the time. For a young man to wear glasses before bop was for him to open himself to the old "four-eyes" taunt. After bop, all the hipsters and boppers always wore them—but, of course, they had to be the heavy-framed type, black or tortoise-shell. What these glasses signified, it seems to me now, was a blind reaching out for rapport with not only the musicians who had "invented" them, but, more significantly, a rapport with a "world of the intellect" I would have normally scorned as "fruity." While the pre-bop musicians had removed themselves from nice society with their roughness, drinking, and lack of formal education, the bop musicians removed themselves even further by becoming identified with that most contemptible segment of American life, the *intelligentsia.* Yet at the same time, they lived hard, wild lives, identified themselves with the liquor (or, beginning with the boppers, the narcotics), the women, the night living, the vagrancy, the poverty, the insularity of the older musicians. Thus, they were twice-removed from the respectable, and so (hopefully) were we who adulated them. At this time, however, bop had no connection with street-fighting or overt criminality. That came later, perhaps starting about 1950 or 1951, when bop, *per se,* no longer existed. As usual, *Life* found out about bop at about the time it was entering its "cool" phase, and had a big spread on "how be-bop musicians live," and the rest of it, showing "typical" jam sessions, secret handshakes, and a lot of claptrap that was furnished so beautifully by Dizzy and Joe Carroll. Those who hated bop were led to hate it more, and we who were bop fans laughed ourselves silly over this lovely farce played at *Life's* expense. It was at about this time, too, that Lennie Tristano came on the scene with his trio, including Arnold Fishkin on bass and Billy Bauer on guitar. They made a 78 of *I Can't Get Started* and *Out On A Limb* on the other side, and Barry Ulanov, writing in Metronome, talked about a "fresh wind" blowing down the "stale corridors" of jazz. They were some stale corridors! Parker, Gillespie, Eager, Gordon, Monk, McGhee, Benny Green, JJ, Al Haig, Tadd Dameron, Kenny Clarke, Miles, Roach, the nonet, *et al.* Be-bop had become an art form—Metronome said so. That was in the days when Parker would get ratings of poor to fair—Bird was "old hat" by then. After Bird died, anything of his that was released, good, bad, or sloppy, evoked orgasms of enthusiasm in this same magazine, and cries of "the good old days."

In 1951 I went into the army. When I came out in 1953, bop was dead, people were talking about West-Coast jazz, musicians looked like Ivy Leaguers, people laughed at Lester Young's clothes, and who in hell is Fats Navarro? I remember calling Sid one night some time later and asking him to play *Ice Freezes Red.* He told me that they only played the "modern American sounds." Like Frank Sinatra.

The Clubs
In 1945, all of the jazz clubs that were considered "big-time," and which were not essentially after-hours joints were on 52nd Street, known then as simply "the Street." There were the Three Deuces, The Onyx, The Famous Door, and probably a dozen more, shoulder to shoulder, on both sides of the street. Every important jazz musician in the United States played in these clubs at one time or another during the five years I speak of. Those clubs that I went into, starting in late 1946, when I was still under 18, were totally unlike the jazz clubs that sprung up in emulation of the old Royal Roost, and which abound today. There was no admission, there *was* a minimum and, I believe, a cover at the tables, although there was nothing re-

sembling a "peanut gallery." One was allowed in on the basis of "looking old enough" and since most of the clubs were very dark, most of us got away with going in while we were still under age. The usual thing was to buy a beer and try to melt into the wall so that no one would notice that the beer was never drunk but remained in the glass, a prop. The great excitement of these clubs was that there was a fantastic amount of sitting-in. Musicians playing in one club would take their instruments during their break and walk across the street to sit in with the musicians playing there. Everyone was learning, everyone was excited, there were nightly "cutting" sessions and the audience responded warmly. A friend of mine told me that one night he saw Lionel Hampton, Red Norvo, Milt Jackson and Terry Gibbs all on the stand at one time playing vibes. This sort of thing was a common occurrence.

The clubs were incredibly small and intimate, the whiskey was terrible, the bars were always jammed, and there were very few women ever, either alone or escorted. While the audience was reserved, it was not the later audience that jazz fostered, that of the utterly bored sophisticate, listening with a frozen face, never applauding. Nor was it the "go! go!" audience that was born out of the JATP concerts at Town Hall and Carnegie Hall. The audience (it seemed to me then) was composed of young men in their late 20s, most of whom knew the musicians. They were habitués of these clubs, dressed in the Broadway manner, and wore sunglasses. I recall that the first time I ever saw anyone wearing sunglasses at night was in the Deuces. To me, that was the absolute zenith of hipsterism.

In about late '46 or early '47, the Chicken Roost, a small night club and restaurant that specialized in chicken-in-a-basket and Mickey Mouse Latin-American bands playing for dancing started a series of (I think) Tuesday night jazz concerts, or jam sessions featuring all the be-bop players in town at the time: Dizzy, Bird, Fats Navarro, Eager, and so on. These sessions were held under the auspices of Symphony Sid, whose all night DJ show was the only one in the country playing be-bop. It is almost impossible for me to think of these years, in any terms, without remembering Sid's show—the "all-night, all-frantic one." Around this time, the Chicken Roost changed its name to the Royal Roost and began a policy of regular nightly jazz, featuring boppers almost exclusively. The group which I remember most clearly was the incumbent group at the Roost, as the club came to be known. They were the regulars, men who lived in New York and who had a steady gig at the Roost for what seems to me to be at least a year. The group was made up of Tadd Dameron, leader and piano, Curley Russell, bass, Kenny Clarke, drums, Allen Eager, tenor, and Fats Navarro, trumpet. They played a clean, hard, swinging, driving bop, the best of which has never been surpassed. The star of the band was Fats, who was without a doubt the only trumpeter at that time who could approach Gillespie in range and power, in sheer ability to play the new music. He was a huge, genial man who seemed to blow effortlessly, and who sparked the rest of the group on original band tunes like *The Squirrel* and *Dameronia.* Eager played a beautiful tenor at that time, wholly derived from Prez, but with his own bop thinking supplementing Young's phrasing. It was a brilliant group. Either before or after this group, I can't remember, The Roost featured Tadd Dameron with Babs Gonzales, in a group called Babs' Three Bips and A Bop. Dameron was the Bop. Babs, while not the originator of scat bop singing, certainly brought it into prominence. They did "vocals" like *Oop-Bop-She Bam* and *Ool-Ya-Koo.*

The Roost charged 90 cents admission and we used to sit in the "peanut gallery." It was a new idea and relieved us all of the necessity of nursing beers secretly. On Sundays they instituted a policy of jam sessions from 4 to 8, during which time customers were allowed to sit at tables, without buying anything, for no more than the admission charge. These were excellent sessions, featuring sometimes two or three of the top men on each horn blowing in varying combinations. I saw groups with Miles Davis, Fats Navarro and Howard McGhee on trumpet, groups with Allen Eager, Brew Moore, and Dexter Gordon on tenor: there was one Sunday I recall on which they had three piano players and their groups playing continually: Monk with Sahib Shihab on alto and I think Blakey on drums, Tristano with Konitz, Fishkin and Bauer, and George Shearing (who was the first bopper to "sweeten it up" for the jukebox public with his *September In The Rain)* with Chuck Wayne and Denzil Best. The atmosphere was relaxed and informal, and there was a complete rapport between the musicians and the audience; I haven't seen such a thing recaptured since. At the same time, the "idea" of the bop played was much different from jazz today: I mean in the way the musicians went about it. There were always unspoken battles between men, and "fours" were an occasion for cutting. A great competition went on all the time. This fostered a lot of bad playing, but at the same time it gave to the atmosphere in which the audience existed a wonderful feeling of being "in" on things: we cheered the player who triumphed, we laughed, we had a good time. That seems to me to be the great single factor of that era which differentiates it from now: we were all completely, or almost completely, uncritical. When we were on the way home we never talked of who sounded bad, who sounded lazy, who was blowing clichés. It was all great music to us, it was bop—it *had* to be good. No one ever worried over whether it was "hip" to clap or not to clap. The whole damn thing was *our* music. The musicians were absolutely aware of this feeling, which is why the Roost always seemed to be

the most relaxed club in town. We who listened didn't comprise an "audience." We were members of the same cult as the musicians. What it came
to, simply, is that neither we nor the musicians were aware that bop was
an "art" to be "appreciated." It was something to which we were committed by necessity and intuition.

To return to George Shearing for a moment. It was Shearing who
"popularized" bop with his early records—popularized it to a point at
which The Roost came to be crowded on Sundays, and even on weekday
nights. About this time, due, I suppose, to the fact that most of those who
listened to bop were under-age, and had a tough time getting into the
clubs—this was about 1947 or 1948, and I had turned 18—the men who
owned The Roost closed it, and opened a huge, barn-like club on the second floor of a building around, I think, 49th and Broadway, called Bop City.
They had two different bars in Bop City, one with liquor and beer, the other
serving malteds, sodas, ice cream, etc. This was a hopeless place. The
acoustics were terrible, the musicians lost all touch with the audience,
and I, and my friends, who now considered ourselves "old" boppers, were
disgusted with the younger crowd that jammed the place. This was snobbery to a certain degree, but we were also justified in at least a few ways.
Bop City drew people to be-bop who were drawn to it because it was the
"thing" to do. I remember seeing the Herd about this time (this was the
later Herd, with Getz, Zoot Sims, Serge Chaloff, etc.) opposite Oscar Pettiford. In the middle of one of their numbers, somebody behind me asked
which one was Oscar Pettiford. It was this kind of thing that bugged us.
Also, at this time, the really old "hipster-types," the men who frequented
the 52nd Street joints, disappeared almost completely. The clubs on the
Street had almost all closed or turned into strip joints, and the older hipsters wouldn't dream of entering Bop City, with its malteds and marijuana
smoke in the air. Bop City was really a social event set to music. The zoots
from all the high schools came in in gangs, and sat around looking hip.
We were all very bitter, because not only was the audience absolutely un-
interested in the music, the musicians began to change. They all started
in on the by-now classic Miles Davis attitude, a combination of fear, disgust, and contempt. Cutting almost disappeared, there were those horrible
records that Bird made with strings, and Bird even had a gig at that time
with strings. I'll never forget him in his hopelessly baggy brown suit, laven-
der shirt and orange tie, blowing clichés in front of an assemblage of rot-
ten violinists from 802—and worse, looking as if he was worried he'd do
something wrong: all this in front of an audience of kids in sunglasses.
And Bird was *trying* to please: before this era, Bird always pleased, as did
everybody, but as I mentioned before, it was not a conscious attempt to
get to the audience—we were there to listen, we were part of the whole

thing. Now, it was something ugly and vulgar. I don't know how the musicians who made it through did it. Dizzy was in his leopard-skin cardigan phase, and had a conga drummer called, I think, Chino Pozo, who filled the spot left by Chano Pozo's death: but it was all different. Chano Pozo was, without a doubt, the most incredible drummer who ever involved himself with be-bop. To hear him play in person was enough to make you sweat with fear and wonder. There was nothing funny at all about his *Manteca*. It was black, deep, fantastically wild, and Dizzy's big band rode on top of it, absolutely unlimited. After his death, the conga drum and all the Latin-American tunes became flag-wavers that sounded stale and were stale. The rise and fall of Dizzy's big band was probably directly due to the popularization of be-bop. He started out with *Things To Come,* still one of the greatest big-band tunes ever made, maybe *the* greatest, and ended with funny hats. Apropos of this, I remember seeing Dizzy about three or four years ago in a club in Brooklyn called Town Hill; he was playing a kind of modified rock n' roll, and telling jokes about Little Rock to an audience of Miami Beach types. A friend of mine, just before one of the sets, walked up to the stand and asked him to play *Groovin' High.* Diz looked down in amazement and said, "Man, you don't look that old."

Well, at any rate, to return to the clubs. The Clique opened at that time, and later became Birdland. I rarely went to The Clique, because it was emceed by Fred Robbins and I was afraid that we'd have to listen to Frankie Laine. There was a place near 8th Avenue (on 47th?) called The Hickory Log that hardly anyone knew about and that used quiet jazz groups (no cover, no admission, no minimum). I recall hearing Billy Taylor there, and a quartet headed by Terry Gibbs. That was about it as far as the clubs went, although the Deuces hung on somehow, mostly by featuring Erroll Garner. Also, a place called The Circus Box (?) that had Georgie Auld and a small group, and later Charlie Barnet with a *sextet.* I don't mean to imply that these were the only clubs in the city. There were many uptown clubs, but neither my friends nor I ever went to them. The reasons for this were complex, but essentially it was because we were afraid to go, as whites, to all-Negro clubs, in all-Negro neighborhoods. Nobody relished the idea of getting caught in a strange neighborhood by a non-white gang that didn't care whether one was "hip" or not. Underscoring this was the fear that we would be taken for square white kids who were "slumming" in Harlem. The fear of being thought square was almost as great as the fear of being jumped.

What had happened in the incredibly short space of 3 or 4 years was that jazz had come out into the open, it had become "popular," the newer jazzmen had started to exhibit a fantastic contempt for the audience, and rightly so. The club had become less a place to hear jazz than a place to impress your date. By 1950, a great feeling of tension had come to the surface in the clubs. For the first time (in be-bop), the jazz player was forced to become a performer. As everyone knows, the toll was fantastic, in death, dissolution, and disappearance: curiously enough, the jazzmen who suffered most were the whites. New York jazzmen like Al Haig, Dodo Marmorosa, Remo Palmieri, George Wallington, Davy Schildkraut, *et al.,* simply vanished. It was the beginning of a new era.

The Musicians
Although it is risky to do so, the difference in the jazz musicians of today and the old boppers can be pointed up, at least partially, in a comparison of the current Miles Davis with the Miles of the late 40s. Everyone knows the Miles Davis attitude now prevalent: the slumped posture, the hauteur, the contempt for the audience, the "inability" to show up on time for many of his sets—the more than occasional refusal to play anything at all while on the stand. It is not my purpose here to judge or to gloss these characteristics, simply to point out what the old Miles was like. I happened to remember the other day, thinking of this, that when Miles played in the Roost in the 40s, he was incredibly shy, and, since his strivings toward a trumpet style different from either Gillespie's or Fats Navarro's was far from perfected, he was simply tolerated by the audience. As I recall, the listeners used his solo time to go to the bathroom, buy a beer, talk to friends, etc. This was something that was, of course, rude and stupid, since what Miles was doing was very new, and very different from anyone else—he was in the process of transition from bop to "cool," and in this process was tortured by the inadequacies of his playing. He probably hit more clinkers than any other trumpeter of his time, and when he played with Bird it was ridiculous. I cannot think of any other instrumentalist of that time who sounded so bad. Everyone knows the old story of how Dizzy doubled on trumpet *and* piano on Miles' first record with Bird, *Ko-Ko,* although the label names Davis as the trumpeter. I saw this happen to Miles at least once as I remember, and I think it was at that time that I really began to like him. He simply could not follow Bird with the usual trumpet clichés, and since he obviously couldn't out-do Bird's solo, he just stood there and let the rhythm take over for his solo time. When he "founded" the nonet it was all different. He was completely self-possessed, had found his way, and the cool bop had been born.

In a sense, Miles' change was a change that all musicians went through. As I suggested earlier, as bop became more and more popular, as audiences became less and less hip, the musicians became more remote and aloof. When they began to wear Ivy League clothes, the end was at hand; it was a sign that they were willing to disguise themselves in order to be able to live in a world which began to idolize them. Williams, in *Paterson,* speaks of the artist's plight in his reference to the dwarf who lived by the falls of the Passaic, "saved by his protective coloring." The bop musician was a loud figure as long as those who listened to him were "friendly" and equally loud. As soon as the "outsiders" began to listen, he affected the coloring that they had. The only bopper who never changed was Bird, and he probably would have changed had he lived—of course; in the figure of Monk we have someone who has remained almost exactly the same as he was years ago—even his music has remained the same. He was, in the late 40s, the only musician I know of who was, as it were, "beyond the pale" in his playing, and he certainly still is. Prez was also unique, a throwback to the old days of the 30s and Kansas City, the absolute king of them all. I saw him about a year before he died, and he was wearing the same drape suits, pegged pants, and conked hair that he always wore, as long as I knew him. But by and large, the boppers changed, not really *with* the times, but in a sense *against* them. The changes in dress coincided with the attempts to make jazz "respectable." The intellectual undercurrents at this same time were toward a "deeper understanding" of jazz as art, and toward a fuller realization of the jazzman's "problems." Out of this marvellous "care" came the hopelessness of the West Coasters and Dave Brubeck who was "influenced by e.e. cummings" and, of course, Revlon. One tends toward either bitterness or laughter when one thinks of Billie Holiday's unmarked grave in Potter's Field as against Brubeck's concert fees. But the jazzman survived, and the Ivy League clothes seemed an inside joke. It reminds me of the tale of Nathanael West in the expatriate Paris of the 20s, wearing a Bond Street suit, a bowler, and carrying a tightly rolled umbrella among the bohemians, and revelling each time he was sneered at as "bourgeois."

Conclusion

Looking back on this paper, it seems to me now merely a collection of notes, and rather unsorted notes at that. To closely develop these "notes" however, would entail writing a book, and the book would of course simply be a personal recollection of days that have already been treated historically. There are many questions that the notes raise, the most intriguing one for me being why the white boppers either disappeared entirely, or disengaged themselves from the newer aspects of jazz—to say that they simply could not play the "new" music is absurd when one thinks of Getz, Eager, Konitz, Tristano, and Mulligan. The second question that stands as important to me is why the Negro musician turned (not wholly—one thinks of Coltrane, Rollins, Coleman, etc.) away from the utterly "musical" complexities of bop to the rather "old" style that was once called rhythm and blues, and which is now called "soul" music. To anyone with ears there is more "soul" in almost any two bars of a blues by Bird or Prez than in the entire life output of someone like Cannonball Adderley or Ray Bryant. Then there is a third question, one of perhaps more complexity—and that is why the "hipster" (although he no longer exists in terms of what the 40s considered a hipster) of today feels that "soul" is "hipper" than "cool"— when five years ago he would have scorned "soul" as "race music." The social implications of these questions are obvious: where *is* the Negro musician? where *is* the white musician? what has happened to the audience (white and Negro alike) which once scorned all "race music" as square and something *for* the squares. As far as I can determine there is nothing musically superior in "soul" as against, let's say, Chet Baker. Both brands of "jazz" are weak and dull, yet we now have the phenomenon before us of the "hipster," complete in Ivy League suit and accoutrements, snapping his fingers to *Señor Blues,* or similar junk.

One suggestion that I have concerning these questions is that today's jazz is the most advanced tendril of old bop, but since it has become more difficult to do anything fresh and/or solid in jazz, the practitioners are few: the rest play what is "accepted" by the "hipsters." It's probably time for Illinois Jacquet to make a comeback as the founder of "soul."

Postscript

I want to make clear, finally, that I am not lamenting the passing of "pure" bop in the sense that nothing can be as good. But I am lamenting the passing of a time when both the jazz player and the jazz listener were free from the embroidery which "professional" hipsterism forced upon them.

As They Used to Say in the 1950's . . .

Howard Junker

When the 1950s ended, many Americans accepted the prevailing characterization of the decade as a time of gray-flanneled organization men, "happy people with happy problems," in the words of satirist Herbert Gold. It seemed appropriate in 1960 to summarize the fifties as the "age of Eisenhower." Youth, or "teenagers" as they were called, were an integral part of this portrait. Labeled the "Silent Generation" by Time, *they were depicted as apolitical, conformist, apathetic, and concerned only with automobiles, sex, and finding a secure niche in the world. Recently, historians aided by additional perspective have begun to revise these simplistic notions. They are working toward a more accurate understanding of the era, one that will most certainly involve a reevaluation of the youth culture. These revisions may culminate in Ike sharing his symbolic role with Elvis Presley or James Dean.*

One method of assessing the life of the young is through their slang, jokes, proverbs, insults, and code words. Howard Junker's delightful remembrance provides a starting point; Dan Wakefield's novel Going All the Way *is another useful source for the study of language usage in the fifties. James Dean's heroic stature is analyzed by Edgar Morin in this book in "The Case of James Dean."*

When the time comes, it may not be easy, despite the rebirth of Richard Nixon and Elvis Presley, to muster nostalgia for the Fifties. (Davy Crockett and Roy Cohn, Grace Kelly and the Playboy Bunny, *My Fair Lady* and adult Westerns, filter tips and instant coffee, Zen and the art of the Roller Derby, Ban the Bomb and togetherness, Harry Belafonte, Jack Kerouac, Dr. Kinsey, and The Golden Age of Television.)

But some of the words we used to use already have the power to charm, so great is the distance between then and now.

Jargonwise, the Fifties spoke a finalized version of advertisingese. Euphemists offered: the Police Action, peaceful coexistence, nuclear blackmail, freedom fighter, creeping Momism, desegregation, payola, cleavage, recession, pinko. Korea did little to enrich the language (brainwashing, gook). But from Russia came Sputnik, hence beatnik, jetnik. . . .

One kind of nostalgia for the Eisenhower Era looks back to an age of innocence. But this apparent innocence was protected at a cost. Irony, ambiguity, complexity were academic passwords that sophomores enacted as apathy. The common language was designed to not say what was meant: Would you like to have a cup of coffee/come up for a drink? (In the Sixties, *pace* Lenny Bruce: "Let's ball.") Sarcasm (Wanna lose ten ugly pounds? Cut off your head) and innuendo (I have here the names) were basic modes of conversation. Much literary imagination went toward developing acceptable variations on Mailer's (1948) fuggin, as in effing, frigging. Sick jokes finally mentioned other unmentionables, and with *Lady Chatterley's Lover* (1959) the unprintable became available in drugstores and at your local supermarket.

Beneath much of the (dirty) white buck, saccharine, other-directed innocence of the Fifties lurked a smug obliviousness. You could still say colored. (Ixnay, ofay.) Niggerlipping didn't seem such a terrible way to describe wetting the end of a cigarette. A riot was really funny. A soul kiss involved the tongue. The ghetto was where the Jews had escaped from. Race as in arms, rat and drag. A pill was like a dope. A bust was a pair of knockers, as in M.M., B.B. and Diana Dors. A joint was maybe a bar.

Getting stoned meant hitting the hard stuff (not horse, booze). A quick brew: quaff a foamy. Whales' tails, Thumper. Here's to the Cardinal once. Chug-a-lug. Getting blotto, stinko, loaded, smashed, plowed, bombed out of your ever-loving mind. Then: heaving, tossing, blowing your lunch (cookies). Upchuck, barf, puke. The problem of youth was getting served. Do you have proof (an I.D.)? Churchkey.

In short, in the Fifties, culture still enjoyed a literary base. Words (the novel) still mattered. Awareness was limited, not electronically total. And

From *Esquire*, 72 (2), August 1969, 70–71, 141. Reprinted by permission of Esquire Magazine and the author; copyright © 1969 by Esquire, Inc.

regionalisms, celebrated during the Thirties when the middle class stayed home, were not yet erased by television, which went coast to coast in 1951, and commercial jets, which crossed the Atlantic in 1958. Have gun, will travel.

In the Fifties, it was dangerous to take anyone at face value. (Are you for real?) In conformist times, you worried about Image (status), doubly anxious because words functioned as costume: are you hip?

Now you're talking (speaking my language). Certain key terms, dig, became juvenile gestures: L7 equaled square (cube or octagon meant supersquare). The three-ring sign indicated cool; screwy was the finger twirled at the temple, then flung at the nut.

Status was divvied up into geographical dualisms: in, out; with it, from squaresville. Hepcat. Beat/Jazz contributed: daddy-o, pad, bread, gig, slip me some skin. And all that, like, well, you know, man, incoherence. (Holden Caulfield, Marty, Brando and the Method, action painting, the silent generation, Nichols and May, taking the fifth.)

Don't hand me any of that jazz. Take five.

Alienation was the absurd egghead bit. (Did Adlai sell out?) Psychology was Krazy, man, like, I nearly flipped. The best minds. The orgone box. Or, as the get-well card said: I'm glad you're sick, but I'm sorry you're ill. You only got hung up when somebody flaked out on you. If you psyched a test, you had it made. What, me worry?

Yes, above all, anti-frantic. Stay cool. Hang loose. No sweat (negative perspiration). Under control. Made in the shade. Big deal.

Duhhhh!

The antithesis of cool was the slow burn, indicated by touching the index finger to the tongue, extending it toward the unfortunate victim and announcing "Psss" as if touching a hot stove. A variation: same gesture: Chalk one up for me! Tuftittie. The way the cookie crumbles. The Royal Screw, hence The Royal Shaft, hence The King's Elevator. Up the creek without a paddle.

Cruising for a bruising. Don't give me any grief. You want a knuckle sandwich. Get Bent. Your ass is grass. Blast off. Suck gas. Wise up. Don't bug me. Drop dead. DDT. Finally gonna shut you down. Dump all over you. How's that grab you? Forty lashes with a wet noodle.

Who cut the cheese? The true clue: he who smelt it dealt it. Silent but deadly.

Hardeeharhar.

Antlers In the Treetop or Who Goosed the Moose.

That went over like a pregnant pole vaulter with a broken stick.

What a fake out.

Almost everything was a drag (negative attitude), although some guys did get a charge (some kicks). Have a blast. Really hairy. Going ape. Bad, Mean, Wicked, Evil. Bitchin. I eat her up. She sends me. Gone, man, gone. Into the air, junior birdmen.

If you weren't grounded, you could take off. And hack, screw, mess around. Goof off.

Where did you go? (Take me to your leader.) I donno, waddya wanna do? Catch some rays. (Shades.) Play charades, spin-the-bottle, Frisbee, pogo stick, Hula-Hoop, bowling, knock-knock, why did the moron?

Precisely at age thirteen, you became a teen-ager. And there were pajama parties and sock hops with a thumbful of 45's. Only bird dogs cut in on a slow dance. Every party has a pooper, that's why we invited you. They tried to tell us we're too young. Grow up.

Certain college studs stuffed phone booths, smashed pianos and, from automobiles, displayed their naked asses to passersby, an act variously called dropping trou, mooning, handing out the b.a. gotcha. Slipping them some pressed ham involved pressing one's bare butt against the window. In the city, you could nerf a cab, i.e., bump it gently at a light. On the highway: chicken.

M*I*C*K*E*Y*M*O*U*S*E

The J.D.'s emerged. The hood. The Rock. (Don't knock the Rock.) Baddass. Tough as nails. Switchblade and zip gun for stomping, mixing it up, rumbles. (Squeezing a beer can.) Pegged pants and a greasy D.A.

Or: butch, crew cut, flat top. Charcoal-grey flannel, belt-in-the-back, paisley, Shetland, Madras, bermudas. Our fine-quality pink button-down. Tweedy and preppy.

The common ground: blue jeans, as in the one and only Levi's. (I'm wise to the rise in your Levi's.) As in shrink 'em in the bathtub. As in James Dean lives. As in engineer boots. Classy.

With a digression to honor circle pins, knee socks, saddle shoes, fruit boots, straight skirts, ponytails. On the one hand. On the other: beards, sandals and leotards—not yet called tights. Who wears short shorts? If you wore green on Thursday. . . .

As for sex, there was going steady (I.D. bracelet, ring-on-the-necklace, letter sweater or jacket). And breaking up. But mostly the eternal search for a little action, etc. Bedroom eyes. Hot lips.

The first thing a make-out artist asked: is she fast? (Nice or good.) Does she put out? Lay it on the line? Do the deed?

He, of course, was always horny. When really hard up, he would even overlook her b.o., cooties, flat chest. (Scuzzy, grungy.) Her zits.

It was suspected that sometimes she, too, was climbing up the wall. Hot to trot.

In that case, if he didn't get shot down (stood up), he might suggest catching a flick. The passion pit. Parking. Let's go watch the submarines race.

For openers, a snow job. Coming on like Gang Busters. Are you trying to feed me a line?

She might come across if he were a big wheel, a B.M.O.C. On the ball, divine, clean cut, casual, snazzy, a really good (great) guy, the living end. Cute. Neat. Smooth. Peachy keen. A hunk. Hey, bobo. She would certainly be turned off if he were grubby, a phony, a sex fiend, bad news, out to lunch, a banana, weenie, yo-yo, turkey, spastic, nebbish. Gross. A fink. With a bad case of the uglies. A dumb cluck. A loser, creep, simp. A nothing. Of course, if he were a straight arrow, there'd be no danger of his trying to go too far. (Goodnight kiss. Heavy petting.) Meanwhile, awaiting his chance to go all the way, a circular bulge etched itself into his wallet.

Back with the guys, he would be asked, especially if he had a rep as a hot ticket: Get much?

And at school next day, where the brains were grinds and usually brown-nosers, her friends noticed the hickey on her neck.

Which brings us to that ultimate, fabulous Fifties' experience: wheels.

Bombing around.

In a '49 Ford.

A '55 Chevy.

A Merc.

T-Bird.

Vette.

Coming and going in a Studey.

(Edsel.)

Stick shift, as in grind me a pound. Hang a left.

Fins and tails and two-tone and one year there was a three-tone.

Raked and flamed, decked and lowered, chopped and channeled.

Duals.

Glass pack.

Fuelie. Frenched lights. Coon tail.

I don't care if it rains or freezes, long as I've got my plastic Jesus.

A No. 4.56 rear end.

Driver ed.

I got to cut out. Peel out, lay rubber.

Take it easy.

Anyway I can get it.

See you later, alligator.

Mickey Spillane
and His Bloody Hammer

Christopher La Farge

Before the 1930s fictional detectives were usually portrayed as geniuses; Sherlock Holmes served as a model for aspiring writers. In the thirties some detective novelists began to create a new hero, a tough, enduring man who muddled through by hard work, courage, and patience. Dashiell Hammett and Raymond Chandler, the two most gifted creators of the tough private eye, have been hailed by critics, while Mickey Spillane, another successful practitioner of the genre, has experienced a negative reception. Reviewers of Spillane have ridiculed his inability to write, but the primary reason for the widespread antipathy he has aroused among critics is the message his books convey.

Hammett's and Chandler's detectives saw the world from a vaguely leftist perspective. Despite their cynicism, they wished to help the "little guy" and gained satisfaction from exposing the dissolute "upper crust." In contrast, Spillane's Mike Hammer, in the opinion of Christopher La Farge, embodies the attitudes labeled McCarthyism. La Farge perceived that Hammer's violation of the law in his pursuit of evil is part of American tradition; the outrage La Farge expressed must be understood as part of the outcry against Joseph McCarthy in the early fifties.

Mickey Spillane continues to publish novels containing the same themes, but his popularity has declined. This may denote a retrogression of McCarthyism or it may only disclose that Spillane's sexual scenes are sedate in comparison to those existing elsewhere in the popular media. For a more benign rendering of the vigilante spirit see Jim Harmon's "Who Knows What Evil Lurks" in this book. A recent study of Spillane is John G. Cawelti's "The Spillane Phenomenon." Thoughtful essays on the detective story are collected in Tough Guy Writers of the Thirties, *edited by David Madden.*

Many million people in the United States have bought, and presumably read, the books on the adventures of Mickey Spillane's creation, Mike Hammer, the Vigilante-Killer. I know that there have been at least six of these published since 1947; and that the one called *I, the Jury* had sold by August, 1953, 1,600,000 copies. As of June, 1954, 24,000,000 copies of Spillane's books had been published. One of these books, called *Kiss Me, Deadly,* even had the unusual record for a so-called murder mystery (Spillane's books have much murder and little mystery), of finding itself on the best-seller lists of the *New York Herald Tribune* and *The New York Times.*

This is a phenomenon that merits examination, although part of that examination has been made before. What is phenomenal about it is that a series of books can be written in what is supposed to be the form of fiction, but is not truly fiction, but rather a wholly unadmirable kind of wish-fulfilment on both an immature and a potentially destructive level, and be immediately successful on a scale far beyond average.

It would be a lot more fun (and a lot easier) to write a parody of these Mike Hammer books instead of an article, but the point to be made is a serious one, unfortunately, and the parody is limited in its application and has already been brilliantly done by Walt Kelly in his *Uncle Pogo So-So Stories* under the title of "The Bloody Drip by Muckey Spleen," about "Meat Hamburg, Private Eye, Ear, Nose, Throat, and Leg Man, in another Big Game of Corpse and Robbers."

I don't know what moved Spillane to write about Mike Hammer as he did. Certainly there is in none of the three books I have made myself read anything whatever to justify the assumption that the series was cynically begun merely as a way of creating a highly salable commodity; though the continuance of the series might be a cynical act on the part of both author and publishers. Cynicism implies a form of prior intelligence that is nowhere evident. Rather there is indicated clearly by these books something very like a necessity felt by the author to explain again and again, and to attempt to justify, the philosophy of the very central character of all of them, Mike Hammer, as though that philosophy were justifiable. Many an author has felt himself compelled to create a character who is evil, or sadistic, or immoral, or a combination of these (as is Mike Ham-

From *Saturday Review,* 37 (45), November 6, 1954, 11–12, 54–59. Reprinted by permission of the *Saturday Review* and The Oldwyck Trust, copyright © 1954 by The Saturday Review Associates, Inc. (Footnotes have been added.)

mer), and has been equally compelled to attempt to make some facet of that character sympathetic or even attractive to his readers, either through a genuine compassion or an intellectual conception of the variations possible within one human being. But it has never been my experience before to read of a sadist whose sadism was held up as a justifiable means to an admirable end.

What troubles me about this manifestation is that Spillane seems to have succeeded in making the character of Mike Hammer acceptable to a huge public. In this I believe he but reflects (and profits by reflecting) an attitude already held by that public—an attitude which has grown to an extent that is at the least inimical to the basic principles on which our country has so far operated. Mike Hammer is the logical conclusion, almost a sort of brutal apotheosis, of McCarthyism: when things seem wrong, let one man cure the wrong by whatever means he, as a privileged savior, chooses.

There is nothing new in history about McCarthyism, which has occurred again and again since recorded time, and reflects nowadays the human impatience of men at the necessarily slow movements of a government of laws, not of men. There is equally nothing new about the essential skeleton of a character like Mike Hammer, who represents in himself a one-man army of Vengeance and Retribution. In essence (but only in essence) he belongs to the Robin Hood tradition: the man who operates on the side of the Good but outside of, or in conflict with, Constituted Authority; and who (for whatever reasons) decides entirely for himself what is the Good and what is the Bad. He has even two recent forerunners in Edgar Wallace's "Ringer" and Leslie Charteris' "Saint"; and Erle Stanley Gardner's "Perry Mason," a lawyer, breaks the laws so that Right may Triumph. Hammer shares with all of these a willingness to take the law into his own hands, to bring to trial, to judge, to condemn (but in his case even personally to execute) those who he singly decides to have been of the Bad; and there is given to him, as to them, always some motivation, some purpose, that is in part laudable or, at least, popular. With them too he operates, as has Senator McCarthy, on the final philosophy that the end can justify the means: in this Hammerism and McCarthyism are similar.

We hear a great deal nowadays about witch-hunting, and this reflects the disgust of all truly liberal minds with the continuance of an old and bloody tradition in our country. The witch-hunt is still practised because we continue to have within us a strong residue of fanaticism, which operates to force us toward the elimination, rather than the alteration, of anything we disapprove, regardless of any balanced judgment and in conflict with all liberality of being; and because we are still close to the frontier days when it seemed necessary for men to take the law into their own hands, there being no other apparent alternative. The existence of the Vigilantes seemed to frontiersmen necessary, and such a system fitted into their impatience with what they saw as wrongdoing and the remoteness of the law. That such a system should ultimately spread from the elimination of cattle rustlers and brigands to persons whose moral, racial, religious, or political outlook was disliked by the majority of a community was inevitable. Its children have been the persecutions and intolerances, the riots and the lynchings that mar so much of what is fine and good in our historical growth as a nation.

It is well, in thinking of this (as we must to understand Hammerism's popularity), to add to it another modern factor. This is the huge, impersonal groupings of an industrial civilization, creating (almost by opposites) a frontier of overpopulation instead of isolated dwellings of scattered humanity. No system of law-enforcement has yet been devised which can operate successfully within an industrial complex composed of a packed humanity of diverse and disparate backgrounds, desires, income, needs, and social habits that does not seem to such people cold and impersonal and essentially hostile. To many overcrowded city men, infected with the impatient fanaticism which colors our historical tradition (or the tradition they stem from in other lands), Hammerism must appear to be a comprehensible and justifiable method, one that the individual can grasp. It is the dream of justice, however imperfect, meted out without delay, with fierce and wonderfully satisfying immediacy. Those who, in their massed anonymity, feel their own individual helplessness and isolation tend to see in all the slow process of law the corruption of justice by the privileged. Hammerism, like McCarthyism, seems to cut through to that swiftness of retribution, regardless of privilege, that they themselves (the unprivileged) despair of. That this can spell the ultimate corruption of a republic of laws is not realized by such people. But I shall have more to say of this, in illustration, later on.

Mike Hammer, like the stories in which he appears, also derives from the recent work of other writers in America, the so-called Tough School of Fiction. Spillane has simply carried further—I believe to a point beyond which it will, happily, be impossible to go—the work of such great or truly gifted writers as Ernest Hemingway, William Faulkner, John Steinbeck, and more exactly, Dashiell Hammett, James M. Cain, and Raymond Chandler. The interesting and significant difference here is that all of these men write with brilliance and ability and their characters, however hard boiled, have reality and three full dimensions. Mr. Spillane's writing is frequently and painfully bad by any standard; and none of his characters, including Mike Hammer, has any true reality whatever.

I do not think one can explain, even partially, the popularity of Mr. Spillane's bloody murder stories by saying that there was so much killing done by so many Americans between 1941 and 1945 that millions of them became calloused to death by violence. History doesn't support that thesis. Some men were much toughened by combat but the huge majority of them came off from the experience with a desire to put that side of war—and the brutal methods self-preservation taught them—as far back in their minds as possible. The truly toughened man who has actually fought in combat is more often able to afford psychologically to be gentle than the untried or the untoughened. Judging entirely from the evidence of these three books, one would say that Spillane had never been in actual combat and might, indeed, be somewhat compensating for that in these stories. (Since writing this I have learned that Spillane was in the Army Air Forces during the last war, but was kept in the U.S. as an instructor; and that he volunteered for active duty in Korea, but was not accepted.)

What then, is the explanation for the great popularity of the stories about Mike Hammer? Perhaps it will be well to see what sort of man he is, as Spillane presents him to his enormous public.

Hammer is a large man, described as extremely powerful physically. His physical prowess of all sorts is in no way impaired by heavy drinking and smoking, of course; and this follows a usual stereotype. He is irresistible to all the women he meets, and his effect on all of them is identical: they want to have physical intercourse with him at once, and often do. This occurs with frequency in the three books I have read, with the two notable exceptions of Velda, his secretary and female counterpart, of whom I shall say more later; and Charlotte (in *I, the Jury*), whom he later murders by shooting her in the stomach while she is unarmed. To both these women he becomes (in different books) engaged and, with a stereotyped nobility of character nowhere else evident in him, he refuses to sleep with them before marriage, though both of them urge him passionately to do so. This nobility of soul is faintly clouded by the fact that he is well supplied with a succession of women toward whom he doesn't have to be noble at all; and isn't.

All the women are identical physically (with the single exception of Linda Holbright in *One Lonely Night,* who is described as having a face that is not pretty), being young and full-bosomed, wide shouldered, with perfect bodies and legs. Their only differences are the color of their eyes and hair; and Mike Hammer is so perceptive that he can foretell an unbleached blonde from a photograph. They frequently wear nothing at all under their outer clothes (except for Velda, who packs a .32 automatic); these outer clothes are skin tight to show ALL; and they unzip these garments as soon as possible after meeting Mike Hammer. One can, perhaps, best form an estimate of the moral code of Mike Hammer both in relation to women and as a Reformer by his experience with the plain-faced (but not -bodied) Linda.

Linda is a member of the Communist Party. Hammer smiles at her at a Communist meeting. She gives him "the damndest look you ever saw."[1] "Just for the hell of it" he gives her "one back with a punch to it. What she made of it stopped her breathing a second." Because of this soul-shatter-ing experience, Linda follows the true Spillane pattern and arrives at Ham-mer's apartment, unbid, later that night; has a drink; is kissed; unzips her dress (which had nothing under it and "peeled off like paint") and offers herself—having never before (a) had a drink or (b) kissed a man or (c) had physical relations with a man. She simply asked of Hammer "nothing except to be shown how to be a woman." She was shown. She left then at once and most conveniently, wanting "to be part of the darkness and alone." Poor Hammer feels so like a heel that he can't finish more than half of his drink until he comes to this comforting conclusion: "Then it occurred to me that now that she had a little taste of life maybe she'd go out and seek some different company for a change." He stops feeling like a heel, pours another drink and is able to finish it, and goes contentedly to bed. It is an interesting though conceivably ineffective way to reform Communists. And of course provided One not entirely Lonely Night.

Velda, the secretary, is the Lilith conception: every immature or ado-lescent male's dream. She is beautiful, attractive, young, available, faithful. She will wait for her man forever, and forever want him wholly when he comes back from whatever absence or adventure including a lot of other women. She is simply cross with her man when he forgets to wipe off the most recent other woman's lipstick. Velda has, by the end of the latest book I have read, *Kiss Me, Deadly,* killed two men herself. She can and does beat up and disfigure permanently any man who makes improper ad-vances to her. Indeed, in these books the only persons who can safely make improper advances are women and to Hammer. Velda "could whip off a shoe and crack a skull before you could bat an eye." Whatever Mike Hammer says is so and true, that is so and true for Velda without further necessity of proof. It is for this that I have characterized her as Hammer's counterpart, because he needs no proof of anything beyond his own per-sonal judgment. Whatever violence Hammer may commit is right in Velda's eyes because he committed it. She shares with him his entire moral outlook on life.

What is that moral outlook?

In each of the three books I have read there is a Vengeance to be

1. From *One Lonely Night,* by Mickey Spillane. Copyright, 1951, by E. P. Dutton & Co., Inc., publishers, and used with their permission.

executed on the exact basis of an eye for an eye, a tooth for a tooth. In *I, the Jury* it is to revenge the murder of a man who was Hammer's war buddy and an ex-cop. In *One Lonely Night* it is to revenge the murders and thefts of secret documents of a Communist ring. In *Kiss Me, Deadly* it is to revenge the murders and acts of drug-peddling members of the Mafia.

In each case Mike Hammer sets out to solve the problem of who is doing these things—not with the intention of bringing the guilty to justice or even to the electric chair, but that he may personally find, judge, condemn, and kill these persons before the police can get them. Not only that: but also that he may act as executioner of his victims in a manner precisely as brutal and violent as the brutality and violence he judges them to have practised. This intention he also publicly proclaims.

It would be strange enough if a man in fact could do this in the United States at this time of its history and still be allowed at large with a permit to carry a deadly weapon. It would be even stranger if the police cooperated with him, worked with him, fed him information, and protected him. Yet this happens in all three books. Mike Hammer's best and most loyal friend is Captain of Police Pat Chambers. Oh, Chambers warns him from time to time that what he is doing is sort of illegal, this business of going around by himself and killing people he has decided need to be killed; but that is all. Chambers sees, as Hammer does, that the end— the destruction of evil persons or at least of those that Hammer decides are evil—justifies the means to that end. It's quicker that way. Add it to the brutality of the methods of revenge in which Hammer is allowed to indulge to his own entire and declared satisfaction, and you begin to get the moral picture clear. An example from *Kiss Me, Deadly* may help.

Hammer, disarmed by the FBI, his license as a private investigator temporarily revoked, publicly hunts for two professional killers, Sugar Smallhouse and Charlie Max, off Broadway at night. Both the police and the FBI know that these two are at large and that Hammer has passed the word around that he will get them. He has been told they are out to get him. He finds them in a bar. He renders Smallhouse unconscious by a sort of jujitsu hold from behind, "like a kid snapping worms." He gets Charlie Max, as Max reaches for his gun, by kicking him in the face so that "the things that were in Charlie's face splashed all over the floor." He then breaks Max's arm by kicking that. As he reaches for the gun that Max dropped three members of the FBI stop him, search him, register extreme surprise that he is unarmed, and—let him go. Of this Hammer says, "There wasn't a damn thing they could do and they knew it, so I turned around, walked back outside, and started crosstown to the Astor." He gets there, too, unmolested. This was necessary to the story, of course, as he is going to meet a woman at the Astor who has fallen for him so hard that she is going to betray her half-brother to him. It gives one an odd impression of the limitations of legal law enforcement as well as family feeling.

In *One Lonely Night* the book begins with Hammer irrationally upset because a Judge has excoriated him publicly as a killer. The Judge's voice, which had been righteous, says Hammer, "changed into disgusted hatred because I was a licensed investigator who knocked off somebody who needed knocking off bad and he couldn't get to me."

This makes Hammer think, to the extent that that process is possible to him, and he thus describes himself: "That was me. I could have made it sound better if I'd said it. There in the muck and slime of the jungle, there in the stink that hung over the beaches rising from the bodies of the dead, there in the half-light of too many dusks and dawns laced together with the crisscrossed patterns of bullets, I had gotten a taste of death and found it palatable to the extent I could never again eat the fruits of a normal civilization." This is the police-licensed Private Investigator.

Velda's comment on the Judge's words was, "Let's get out of here, Mike. I hate people with little minds. . . . Mike . . . that judge was a bastard. You're an all-right guy."

Another quotation from a later passage in the same book sums up the philosophy of Hammerism throughout all three books. Hammer is answering the Judge in his own thoughts, in the italics which are Spillane's. He is referring to Communists who have stolen secret Government documents of extreme value, but it applies as well to his other acts of vengeance. It is interesting to note how closely his description of Communist methods matches his own.

> My guts were all knotted up in a ball and my head felt like a machine-shop was going on inside it. Here I had the whole lousy situation right in my hands and I had to keep it there.
> Me, Mike Hammer. I was up in the big league now. No more plain and simple murders. I was playing with the big boys and they played rough. The end justified the means, that was their theory. Lie, steal, kill, do anything that was necessary to push a political philosophy that would enslave the world if we let it. Great!
> *Nice picture, Judge, a beautiful picture of a world in flames. You must be one of the normal people who get the trembles when they read the papers. A philosophy like that must give you the willies. What are you thinking now . . . how that same secret that was stolen might be the cause of your own death? And what would you say if you knew that I was the only one who might be able to stop it in time? Okay, Judge, sit your fanny in a chair and relax. I have a little philosophy of my own. Like you said, it's as bad as theirs. I don't give a damn for a human life any more, even my own. Want to hear that philosophy? It's simple enough. Go after the big boys. Oh, don't arrest them, don't treat them to the dignity of the democratic process of courts and*

law . . . do the same thing to them that they'd do to you! Treat 'em to the un-glorious taste of sudden death. Get the big boys and show them the long road to nowhere and none of those stinking little people with little minds will want to get big. Death is funny, Judge, people are afraid of it. Kill 'em left and right, show 'em that we aren't so soft after all. Kill, kill, kill, kill! They'll keep away from us then!

For anything that tries to be so tough, the last six words sound re-markably like a frightened small boy.

But Mike Hammer doesn't confine the statement of his attitude to his private thoughts. He declares it to Captain of Police Pat Chambers at the outset of *I, the Jury.* Like this, after viewing the body of his murdered friend: ". . . by Christ, I'm not letting the killer go through the tedious process of the law. You know what happens, damn it. They get the best lawyer there is and screw up the whole thing and wind up a hero! . . . A jury is cold and impartial like they're supposed to be, while some snotty lawyer makes them pour tears as he tells how his client was insane at the moment or had to shoot in self-defense. Swell. The law is fine. But this time I'm the law and I'm not going to be cold and impartial. . . . You're a cop, Pat. You're tied down by rules and regulations. There's someone over you. I'm alone. . . . Some day, before long, I'm going to have my rod in my mitt and the killer in front of me. I'm going to watch the killer's face. I'm going to plunk one in his gut, and when he's dying on the floor I may kick his teeth out."[2] (The killer turns out to be Charlotte and he does plunk one in her gut, but it doesn't say that he kicked her beautiful teeth out. Or in.)

So it goes in all three books. He shoots a lot of people in the gut and he kicks a lot of people's teeth out. It's all right because they are all Bad People and Deserve to Die Brutally. They are Bad because Hammer says so. It doesn't affect him at all (and in this he is also like Senator McCarthy) that he makes mistakes. In *One Lonely Night* he is being pur-sued by what he believes to be Communists, chasing him at night in their car. He checks to be sure his .45 is free and ready and prepares to "haul the wheel right into them" as they begin to pass him. The car that is following goes off the road and rolls over in a field. It turns out later that its occupants were members of the FBI, ditched by some Communists following *them.* (Don't ask me how; it is all very obscure and badly written and improbable.) But that they were members of the FBI wouldn't have saved them from Hammer if they hadn't been ditched by the Communists. No, no, to *him* and *then* the FBI men were Communists. He takes the woman who was in the car with him to her country retreat (he had pre-

2. From *I, the Jury,* by Mickey Spillane. Copyright, 1947, by E. P. Dutton & Co., Inc., pub-lishers, and used with their permission.

viously slept with her there) and tears her dress off and starts to beat her nakedness with his belt because he thinks she tipped off these men he thought were Communists to follow him; and the *real* Communists shoot her through the window. What she had tipped off was the FBI, thinking Hammer a Communist himself. Hammer the Infallible, the Judge, the Jury, the Executioner. But never forget that Communists are Very Bad People and the quickest and best thing to do to them (or members of the Mafia, or anyone you judge is ripe for it) is to shoot them in the gut, as a starter, of course.

Normally one would say that it was silly to write a critical article about a lot of books so very badly written, so essentially immature in their composition. That's what these books are. Their writing is turgid or grotesque or childish or simply the worst sort of lurid. Or it is plain revolting. A hunchbacked janitor from whom Hammer and his Velda rent a room (to go through it because it had been occupied by a suspect) offers them his own room because it is furnished with a bed and the other is not, and he misjudges their intentions. One can hardly blame him. Of this hunchback it is said: "He leered and looked somewhat dissatisfied because he wouldn't be able to sneak a look on something he probably never had himself." This comes from the mind of our hero, Hammer. One could multiply instances of mistakes in grammar and use of words ("they huddled in recessions of doorways"), inconsistencies (like the "cold, impartial jury" weeping) *ad nauseam*—and to no good end.

One can say that the readers of murder stories don't necessarily demand good English or even good writing, but simply what is usually described as "thrill-packed action." One can say that of the 24,000,000 persons who have bought or read Mr. Spillane's books many readers must be young and uncritical, and also that many must have got a vicarious satisfaction from the sexual passages reduced to such simple and unvarying animalism, either because their own lives provide no such satisfactions or because they'd like to think of themselves as having such physical prowess. One can say that in a tense world, full of hysterical shrillness, many, as I've attempted to suggest at the outset, isolated within the overlarge groupings of an industrial civilization, must derive from such writing a sort of satisfaction because the Bad get their comeuppance without need for the delays of lawful justice. If that were all it would not be very important. But it isn't all.

There is left the popularity of a Hero who, with such a character as has been described, mocks at and denies the efficacy of all law and decency, flouts all laws, statutory, ethical, and moral, delights in assault and murder that is brutally executed, sets his personal judgment always above that of all other men but in particular above that of those to whom gov-

ernment delegates law enforcement (which he thereby constantly dero-
gates), and makes the words *soft* and *honorable* synonymous. This is the
sort of philosophy, *mutatis mutandis,* that has permitted to Senator Mc-
Carthy his periods of extreme popularity throughout the nation: one man
will, beyond the normal processes, unhampered by the normal and accepted restraints, bring the Bad to his own form of justice. Mike Hammer's Communists and members of the Mafia are, of course, all Very Bad.
They are also described as soft, homosexual, stupid, gullible, childish,
or easily tricked; but at the same time as the Most Dangerous Thing in
the United States. *Any* means which will, with Hammer, lead to their extir-
pation and in particular their death by his hand are Good. With Senator
McCarthy, any means that will expose Communists, including the deroga-
tion of all Public Servants, the telling of lies, the irreparable damaging
of the innocent, the sensational and the unfounded charge, is justified so
long as he thinks it is the right thing to do. Each, then, reflects the other,
though McCarthyism kills but careers where Hammerism (perhaps in the
end more mercifully) kills life itself.

When one has fought for years against the many forms and many evils
of mistaken censorship one walks warily in asking the question, How
much responsibility lies at the door of the publishers of Mickey Spillane?
It cannot be possible to conceive of two firms as established as E. P.
Dutton and Company and the New American Library of World Literature
(which publishes Signet books) as being as naive as he makes himself
appear by his writings. Was there in them at first but the wholly un-
analyzed hope that this bloodier than the bloody, this tougher than the
tough product would sell like hot cakes? Did they ever, as they continued
to publish (but now with a full knowledge that they were exploiting a
rarely excellent gold mine), stop to consider what they were doing in
being the agents to disseminate books which would surely be read, and
which would hold up to contempt almost every form of human decency
in law and in life? Did they (incredibly) agree with the philosophy of Mike
Hammer? Or did they decide that it was none of their business to pass a
moral judgment on a man's books which had proved so financially profitable? Or did they perhaps generously plan to use the profits from the
Spillane gold mine for the furtherance of the cause of true literature—
even though that would be to accept the thesis that the end. did justify
the means? I do not know the answers to these questions.

If it were my responsibility now, I would neither censor nor ban the
published works of Mickey Spillane; for the most worldly reason: to do
so would be but to increase their sale. For another, a more difficult reason,
it is hard always to establish that the reading of any such books is in itself
a corrupting factor on any individual, no matter how young and callow

and impressionable. But one must ask a larger and more difficult question than those concerning the responsibility of Spillane's publishers. What has come to our country that it can support and applaud these attitudes toward our common life as a country? Have we in fact become so impatient with due process of law, which is inevitably slow both in its creation, its interpretation, and its execution, that we are willing to abandon ourselves to the apparent quick curative of the Vigilante, the One Man in Power, for whom all laws with their checks and balances are ultimately suspended? Is this what the popularity of Hammerism and McCarthyism point to? If so, we had better realize it before their popularity is shared by a majority of our citizens, who can make valid their system of government by men. McCarthy is a fact. Mike Hammer is but fiction. Yet even as fiction his popularity, his acceptance point to something we would do well to reckon with, and soon. Eternal vigilance, goes the saying, is the price of liberty. It would be disastrous to change the word vigilance to vigilante.

What a pity it is that Mike Hammer and Mr. McCarthy cannot appear on the same television program and swap reminiscences during the Children's Hour!

The Case of James Dean

Edgar Morin

James Dean starred in three movies—East of Eden, Rebel Without a Cause, and Giant—before he died in an automobile accident at twenty-four years of age in 1956. Some adolescents, to whom James Dean was a hero, refused to believe that he was dead. (One persistent rumor alleged that he had been disfigured and did not wish to face the public.) In his short career, James Dean acted out the frustrations of American youth. His death allowed him to avoid the ultimate fear of Americans—that of growing old—and thus his image remains untarnished. James Dean, not Elvis Presley or Marlon Brando, was the quintessence of rebellion in the 1950s.

Successful within a commercial system which he supposedly despised, Dean illustrated the ambivalence of many Americans who regarded themselves as rebels. Within his movies, especially Rebel Without a Cause, *a silly tale of juvenile delinquency, Dean sometimes looked as if he could not believe the lines he was called upon to speak. But mumble them he did, thereby earning the Porsche that sped him to his death.*

Edgar Morin reviews the mythological quality of Dean's life in his essay. Morin's study should be compared with Robert Warshow's "The Gangster as Tragic Hero" in this book. Both clarify the American view of success. Ezra Goodman's "Delirium Over Dead Star" analyzes the reactions to Dean's death.

The mythological hero is always abducted from his parents or somehow separated from them: James Dean was an orphan. His mother died when he was nine and he was brought up by an uncle, a farmer in Fairmount.

The mythological hero must forge his own destiny in a struggle against the world. James Dean ran away from the university, and he worked as an ice-breaker on a refrigeration truck, a stevedore on a tugboat, a ship's boy on a yacht, until he assumed his place under the dazzling rays of our modern mythical sun: he appeared on the Broadway stage in *See the Jaguar,* then in *The Immoralist.* He went to Hollywood and made *East of Eden.*

The mythological hero undertakes many labors in which he proves his aptitudes and also expresses his aspiration toward the richest, most nearly total life possible. James Dean milked cows, tended chickens, drove a tractor, raised a bull, played star basketball, studied yoga and the clarinet, learned something about almost every field of knowledge, and finally became what in the modern world incarnates the myth of total life: a movie star. James Dean wanted to do everything, to try everything, to experience everything. "If I lived to be a hundred," he would say, "I still wouldn't have time to do everything I wanted to do."

The mythological hero aspires to the absolute, but cannot realize this absolute in a woman's love. James Dean would have had an unhappy life with Pier Angeli, who married Vic Damone: legend or reality? In any case, the legend is anchored in reality. In front of the church which Pier Angeli left as a bride, James Dean gunned his motorcycle: the noise of the motor drowned out the sound of bells. Then he dragged violently and drove all the way to Fairmount, the cradle of his childhood. (We rediscover here the theme of the amorous failure, necessary to heroic accomplishment, as well as the theme of the feminine maleficence which every redeeming hero encounters.)

The mythological hero confronts more and more touchingly the world he desires to seize in its entirety. James Dean's destiny became increasingly breathless: he was obsessed by Speed, the modern ersatz absolute. James Dean, seeming disturbed and feverish to some, extraordinarily serene to others, after finishing *Giant,* drove off into the night at 160 miles an hour in his racing Porsche towards Salinas, where he was to enter an automobile race.

The mythological hero encounters death in his quest for the absolute. His death signifies that he is broken by the hostile forces of the world, but at the same time, in this very defeat, he ultimately gains the absolute: immortality. James Dean dies; it is the beginning of his victory over death.

Translated by Richard Howard for *Evergreen Review,* 2 (5), 5–12. Reprinted by permission of Éditions du Seuil through Georges Borchardt, Inc.

The "heroic" life and character of James Dean are not prefabricated by the star system, but are real, *revealed*. There is still more.

Heroes die young. Heroes are young. But our times have produced, in literature (Rimbaud, *The Wanderer*) and, decisively in recent years, in the cinema, heroes bearing the new message of adolescence. Since its origin, of course, the movies' greatest audience has been composed of adolescents. But it is only recently that adolescence has become conscious of itself as a particular age-class, opposing itself to other age-classes and defining its own imaginary range and cultural models. Which is as clearly revealed in the novels of Françoise Sagan and Françoise Mallet-Joris as in the films of Marlon Brando or James Dean.

James Dean is a model, but this model is itself the typical expression (both average and pure) of adolescence in general and of American adolescence in particular.

His face corresponds to a physiognomically dominant type, blond hair, regular features. Further, the mobility of his expressions admirably translates the double nature of the adolescent face, still hesitating between childhood's melancholy and the mask of the adult. The photogenic quality of this face, even more than that of Marlon Brando, is rich with all the indetermination of an ageless age, alternating scowls with astonishment, disarmed candor and playfulness with sudden hardness, resolutions and rigors with collapse. Chin on chest, unexpectedly smiling, fluttering his eyelashes, mingling ostentation and reserve, naïve and gauche, i.e., always sincere, the face of James Dean is an ever changing landscape in which can be discerned the contradictions, uncertainties, and enthusiasms of the adolescent soul. It is understandable that this face should have become an insignia, that it is already imitated, especially in its most readily imitable features: hair and glance.

James Dean has also defined what one might call the panoply of adolescence, a wardrobe in which is expressed a whole attitude towards society: bluejeans, heavy sweater, leather jacket, no tie, an unbuttoned shirt, deliberate sloppiness are so many ostensible signs (having the value of political badges) of a resistance against the social conventions of a world of adults. Clothes are a quest for the signs of virility (the costume of manual laborers) and of artistic caprice. James Dean has invented nothing; he has canonized and codified an ensemble of sumptuary laws which allows an age-class to assert itself, and this age-class will assert itself even further in imitation of its hero.

James Dean, in his double life, both on and off the screen, is a pure hero of adolescence: he expresses his needs and his revolt in a single impulse which the French and English titles of one of his films express: *La Fureur de Vivre* (*A Rage to Live*) and *Rebel Without a Cause* are two aspects of the same virulent demand, in which a rebellious fury confronts a life without a cause.

Because he is a hero of adolescence James Dean expresses with a clarity rare in American films, in *Rebel Without a Cause* and *East of Eden,* the rebellion against the family. The American film tends to mask parent-child conflicts, either in the familiar idyl (*The Hardy Family)* or else by alto-gether suppressing the parents' existence and transferring the father's image to an insensible, cruel, or ridiculous old man (half-senile judge or employer). *East of Eden* presents the characters of an uncomprehending father and a fallen mother; *Rebel Without a Cause* presents the characters of an uncomprehending mother and a fallen father. In both these films appears the theme of the adolescent's combat against the father (whether the latter is tyrannical or pitiful) and the theme of his impotence to relate meaningfully to his mother. In *Giant* the framework of the conflict ex-plodes: it is against a family exterior to himself and, by extension, against all social norms that James Dean will do battle with such ferocious hatred.* But in all three of these films appears the common theme of the woman-sister who must be snatched from someone else's possession. In other words, the problem of sexual love is still enclosed within a sororal-maternal love, has not yet broken out of this shell to launch itself in a uni-verse of pin-ups external to family and age-class alike. Upon these imagi-nary movie-loves is superimposed the love, itself also mythical perhaps, which Dean is supposed to have felt for Pier Angeli with her ingenuous, sister-madonna face. Beyond this impossible love begins the universe of sexual "adventures."

In another sense, James Dean expresses in his life and his films the needs of adolescent individuality which by asserting itself refuses to ac-cept the norms of the soul-killing and specialized life that lies ahead. The demand for a total life, the quest for the absolute is every human individ-ual's demand when he tears himself from the nest of childhood and the chains of the family only to see before him the new chains and mutilations of social life. It is then that the most contradictory requirements come to a ferment. Truffaut expresses it perfectly (*Arts,* 26-9-56): "In James Dean, today's youth discovers itself. Less for the reasons usually advanced: vio-lence, sadism, hysteria, pessimism, cruelty, and filth, than for others in-finitely more simple and commonplace: modesty of feeling, continual fan-tasy-life, moral purity without relation to everyday morality but all the more rigorous, eternal adolescent love of tests and trials, intoxication, pride, and regret at feeling oneself 'outside' society, refusal and desire to become integrated and, finally, acceptance—or refusal—of the world as it is."

* George Stevens tells how it was James Dean himself who asked to interpret this role: "It's a part for me, Mr. Stevens."

The essential contradiction is the one that links the most intense aspiration to a total life with the greatest possibility of death. This contradiction is the problem of virile initiation, which is resolved in primitive societies by terrible institutionalized tests of endurance; in our society it is
effected institutionally only by war (and vestigially by military service);
lacking war or collective subversions (revolutions, underground resistance), this initiation must be sought in individual risk.

Finally, the adult of our middle-class bureaucratized society is the
man who agrees to live only a little in order not to die a great deal. But
the secret of adolescence is that living *means* risking death; that the rage
to live *means* the impossibility of living. James Dean has lived this contradiction and authenticated it by his death.

These themes of adolescence appear with great clarity at a period when
adolescence is particularly reduced to its own resources, when society
allows it no outlets by which it can engage or even recognize its cause.

It is not by chance that a James Dean has been able to become an
exemplary figure in these years of the half-century. To the fervent partici-
pations of the war and (in France) of the Resistance, to the immense
hopes of 1944–1946, have succeeded not only individualist withdrawals
but a generalized nihilism which is a radical interrogation of all official
ideologies and values. The ideological lie in which contemporary societies
live, pretending to be harmonious, happy, and uplifting, provokes in return
this "nihilism" or this "romanticism" in which adolescence both escapes
and discovers the reality of life.

It is at this point in the Western middle-class world that adventure,
risk, and death participate in the gunning of a motorcycle or a racing car:
already the motorcyclists of *Orpheus* left death's fatal wake behind them.
Already Laszlo Benedek's *The Wild One* traced bitterly and tenderly too
the image of the adolescent motorcyclist. Marlon Brando, roaring arch-
angel, like an imaginary John the Baptist heralded the real James Dean
because he himself was the imaginary expression of thousands of real
adolescents whose only expression of their rage to live as rebels without
a cause was the motorcycle gang. Motorized *speed* is not only one of the
modern signs of the quest for the absolute, but corresponds to the need
for risk and self-affirmation in everyday life. Anyone behind a wheel feels
like a god in the most biblical sense of the term, self-intoxicated, ready to
strike the other drivers with thunderbolts, terrorize mortals (pedestrians),
and hand down the law in the form of insults to all who do not recognize
his *absolute priority.*

The automobile is escape at last: Rimbaud's sandals of the wind are
replaced by James Dean's big racing Porsche. And the supreme escape

is death just as the absolute is death, just as the supreme individuality is death. James Dean drives into the night toward the death from which the contract to make *Giant* could protect him only temporarily.

Death fulfills the destiny of every mythological hero by fulfilling his double nature: human and divine. It fulfills his profound humanity, which is to struggle heroically against the world, to confront heroically a death which ultimately overwhelms him. At the same time, death fulfills the superhuman nature of the hero: it divinizes him by opening wide the gates of immortality. Only after his sacrifice, in which he expiates his human condition, does Jesus become a god.

Thus amplified in the character of James Dean are the phenomena of divinization which characterize but generally remain atrophied in the movie stars.

First of all, that spontaneous, naïve phenomenon: the refusal to believe in the hero's death. The death of Napoleon, Hitler, of every superman (good or evil) has been doubted and disbelieved because the faithful were never able to believe these heroes were entirely mortal. The death of James Dean has been similarly doubted. There is a legend that he miraculously survived his accident, that it was a hitch-hiker who was killed, that James Dean was disfigured, unrecognizable, perhaps unconscious: that he has been shut up somewhere in an insane asylum or a hospital. Every week 2,000 letters are mailed to a living James Dean. Living where? In a no man's land between life and death which the modern mind chooses to situate in insane asylums and sanitariums but which cannot be localized. Here James Dean offers himself to the spiritualist concept of death: James Dean is among us, invisible and present. Spiritualism revives the primitive notion according to which the dead, who are corporeal specters endowed with invisibility and ubiquity, live among the living. This is why one young girl cried out during a showing of *Giant:* "Come back, Jimmy, I love you! We're waiting for you!" It is the *living* (spiritualist) presence of James Dean which his fanatics will henceforth look for in his films. This is why spiritualist séances to communicate with James Dean have multiplied. This is why the little dime-store salesgirl, Joan Collins, took from the dictation of the dead James Dean the extraordinary spiritualist confession in which he declares, "I am not dead. Those who believe I am not dead are right," and in which he asserts he has rejoined his mother. This is why *James Dean Returns* by Joan Collins has sold more than 500,000 copies.

Thus a cult has been organized, like all cults, in order to re-establish contact between mortals and the immortal dead. James Dean's tomb is constantly covered with flowers and 3,000 people made a pilgrimage there on the first anniversary of his death. His death mask will be placed beside those of Beethoven, Thackeray, and Keats at Princeton University. His bust in plaster is on sale for $30. The fatal car has become a sacred object. For a quarter you can look at the big racing Porsche, for an additional quarter you can sit behind the wheel. This ruined car, which symbolizes the Passion of James Dean, his rage to live and his rage to die, has been dismembered: bolts and screws, bits of twisted metal, regarded as sacred relics, can be bought at prices starting at $20, according to size, and carried about like amulets to impregnate the wearer with the hero's mystic substance.

In death, by means of death, James Dean has recovered the forgotten prestige of the movie stars of the great epoch who, nearer gods than mortals, aroused hysterical adoration. But from another point of view his death authenticates a life which firmly fixes him among the modern stars, within the reach of mortals. The modern stars are models and examples, whereas the earlier ones were the ideals of a dream. James Dean is a real hero, but one who undergoes a divinization analogous to that of the great stars of the silent films.

And the immortality of James Dean is also his collective survival in a thousand mimetisms. James Dean is indeed a perfect star: god, hero, model. But this perfection, if it has only been able to fulfill itself by means of the star system, derives from the life and death of the real James Dean and from an exigence which is his own as well as that of a generation which sees itself in him, reflected and transfigured in twin mirrors: the screen and death.

The Fans

Jerry Hopkins

Elvis Presley's recording of "Heartbreak Hotel," "Hound Dog," and "Blue Suede Shoes" in 1956 may not have constituted a turning point in American culture, but it would be difficult to defend that judgment from the perspective of 1970. Rock music was ostensibly the most momentous creation of the last twenty-five years. And, although he did not originate rock, Elvis Presley transformed it from mere music into a stance for dissident youth. In the fifties Elvis was considered dangerous—even subversive—by some elements of the right wing. All he said was "don't you step on my Blue Suede Shoes," but "the Pelvis," along with James Dean, drew the first rudimentary lines between the "hip" and the "square," lines that a generation spawned by Presley and Dean would clarify in the sixties.

The cataloguing of fan-club activities by Jerry Hopkins in his comprehensive study, Elvis: A Biography, *from which this essay is taken, provides an insight into the substructure of the rock culture. Hopkins is also author of* The Rock Story, *and editor of* The Hippie Papers. *Stanley Booth's "A Hound Dog, To the Manor Born" is another useful essay. Jon Landau's astute analysis of Presley's current stage performance, "In Praise of Elvis Presley," is essential to an understanding of his continuing popularity.*

Mrs. Virginia Coons welcomed the visitors to her modest Redondo Beach, California, home. With her in the living room were her daughters, Elaine, sixteen, and Nancy, twelve. Her husband, Arthur, a lathe operator, was out for the evening and her son, David, fourteen, was playing in the neighborhood.

"Usually we watch films first," she said, almost before everyone had exchanged names and found seats. She nodded toward an eight-millimeter projector at one end of the small room and as her son entered asked him to put the screen in place in front of the television set. On nearly every piece of furniture in the room was a framed picture of Elvis.

"We're quite proud of these films," he said. "This one was shot by a friend."

Suddenly the room went black and the first of the home movies in color began with a shaky shot of Elvis's Trousdale gate. The gate swung open and a huge black limousine drove out, Joe Esposito at the wheel, Elvis seated next to him. The scene lasted under a minute and was followed by another that had the same limousine coming back. Now it was the end of the day and Elvis was returning from work at the studio, Mrs. Coons explained. This scene lasted a bit longer, as Elvis had Joe stop the car long enough for him to sign a few autographs for the fans clustered outside his home. And then the car disappeared through the gate. The next scene showed the limousine coming back out again. It was another day—at least Elvis had changed his clothes—and with a wave Elvis was gone. This lasted under thirty seconds. Then there was another return home at the end of the day, and once more Elvis signed a few autographs.

With the sputtering sound of film whirling loose on the reel, the first movie ended.

"This next one's more exciting," said Mrs. Coons. "It was taken by a fan when Elvis was in Houston. I'm afraid it's all out of focus, though."

The second film began.

Halfway around the world, in England, Rex Martin, the president of the Gloucestershire branch of the Official Elvis Presley Fan Club of Great Britain and the Commonwealth, was preparing a list of tape recordings he had for exchange or sale. Some of the items:

> Elvis on the Frank Sinatra TV Show 1960. Live! about 6 min. Starts "Its very nice to go travelling" into: Fame & Fortune; Stuck On You: Quality good! $1.50

> Elvis/Sinatra Show Extras: about 5 min. Rare. El & Frank joke around on stage. Then Frank sings a line of Love Me Tender, & El sings a line of Frank's hit song "Witchcraft" alternating between the 2. At the end, they both duet together on the ending of Love Me Tender. (Fantastic tape!) $2

Elvis on the Ed Sullivan TV Show. "Live" 1957 about 6 minutes. Talks & Sings
Hound Dog: Then a medley of Love Me Tender/Heartbreak Hotel/Hound Dog/
Peace in the Valley/Love Me/& Too Much. Quality fair only. $1.50

Annette Day Talks about Meeting Elvis: and filming with him for Double
Trouble + a USA interview with Annette & a short scene from Double Trouble.
50¢

Vancouver Radio Show on Elvis: Includes 1956 interview talking about people
who called him Elvis the Pelvis: 1957 Vancouver Press Conference about 12
minutes: Talking about how he got started, his first Memphis show: Touring,
making films & TV shows. Col. Parker etc. etc. Very interesting stuff. $2

In Portland, Oregon, a college senior named Carl Obermeier was
hastily filling orders for bumper stickers imprinted Elvis Master of Rock
'n' Roll (fifty cents), blue T-shirts with white letters that boast I'm an Elvis
Fan (three dollars, plus twenty-five cents mailing), pencils with Forever
King Elvis cut on the sides (six for a quarter), combs that say I'm an Elvis
Fan Club Member (six, in assorted colors, for a dollar), and a wide range
of rubber stamps for the fan to cover his or her correspondence with
messages such as Music that Will Be New Tomorrow, Our Elvis Is Singing
Today! and Yes, I'm an Elvis Fan and Proud of It! Carl says business is
good.

As long as there have been heroes and heroines there have been fans,
and the Elvis Presley fan probably is in many ways like all who came before. He or she contributes dependable career support, usually economic,
less often emotional. Certainly most of Elvis's fans are those who buy his
records, perhaps see an occasional movie, and if convenient see him in
concert, and let it go at that. But however important this large amorphous
mass of followers may be, it is the *avid* fan who has contributed so much
to the myth. This is the fan who makes it abundantly clear that the word's
origin is in "fanatic."

It is difficult to say how many there are. Colonel Parker's office
claimed there were upward of three thousand fan clubs in 1970, although
the figure probably was inflated and many were marginal operations with
limited memberships. Still, Carl Obermeier says he has 750 members in his
"Hound Dogs" Elvis Fan Club ("A 100% Elvis Organization"); and Sean
Shaver, the twenty-seven-year-old photographer who is president of the
"El's Angels" E.P.F.C. in Kansas City, claims a roster of 950 in twenty-
five countries. In Germany the International Elvis Presley Club Göttingen—
whose address was printed on the record sleeve of a recent single released in Germany—has nearly three thousand members. In England,
where Elvis fans have a crusading zeal not even surpassed by vegetarians,
Seventh Day Adventists and, currently, women's libertarians, the Elvis

Presley Fan Club of Great Britain and the Commonwealth boasts four thousand members and once mustered no less than a hundred thousand signatures on a petition to get Elvis to do a concert there. (The Colonel was reported impressed but unmoved.) Certainly there are a sizable number of fans, more perhaps than are attracted to any other single personality. (The Beatles may have had more fan club members in 1964–66, but where are they today?) Perhaps the Colonel was correct when he said there were a quarter of a million he could count on.

It is, of course, the Colonel who has cultivated the fandom, regarding the clubs as the money in the bank they represent. The letters he sends the club presidents may be mimeographed, but they're full of news and come often; and RCA is instructed to send enough calendars, photographs and record catalogues for all the members. Whenever Elvis fans gather in convention, as they do in many parts of the world, the Colonel sends a telegram. Even more care is directed toward those with newsletters, magazines and bulletins, of which there are, apparently, several hundred.

One of them is *The King's Scepter,* official organ of the Kissin' Cousins International E.P.F.C. It is headquartered in Spokane and lists Elvis Presley as honorary president; Judy Palmer, president; club song, "Kissin' Cousins"; club colors, royal blue and gold; club dues, two dollars a year. In recent years it has run between two and six letter-sized pages, all crammed almost to the borders with record reviews, effusive praise of Elvis's Las Vegas shows, plugs for other fan clubs, shorter news and gossip notes, and a number of nicely reproduced photographs. Judy signs her periodic report "Elove."

About half the size and considerably more commercial is the slender bimonthly publication that serves the "El's Angels" E.P.F.C. In part this is because the club's president and newsletter editor, Sean Shaver, also runs the Elvis Presley Record Club of America, through which members can buy any of Elvis's records, new or old, at discounted prices. Sean also peddles sheet music and other memorabilia, and signs the newsletter "Till next time, Keep Elvis King."

A more ambitious journal was the last assembled and distributed to special friends of the Elvis Presley Fan Club of Southern California—club motto: "Perpetrators Perpetuating Presley Platters"—whose joint chiefs, Linda Webster and Nancy Ambrose, lived in Mar Vista. This publication, stapled inside a manila file folder, reprinted articles from several metropolitan newspapers and one national magazine, and included five radio request forms, a letter from "Colonel Parker's Office," a section devoted to a disc jockey in Chicago who had stuck with Elvis through the years, a special report written by Virginia Coons, a Xerox copy of an Elvis movie ad, two color and two black-and-white photographs, four calendars from four different years, two different Easter cards and—for the collector—one bubble-gum card from 1956.

Clearly, the most professional of the American Elvis publications does not represent a club but is, rather, a monthly five-and-a-half-by-eight-inch magazine run on a break-even or just slightly profitable basis. This is Rocky Barra's *Strictly Elvis,* which Rocky edits in his Livonia, Michigan, home. It is now in its fourth year and costs six dollars for twelve issues. Like others in the field, it publishes articles written by fans and carries the texts of press conferences and rare interviews, most of them from the 1950s. Excellent graphics are the *Strictly Elvis* high point. And Rocky is himself a rock singer, bearing a marked resemblance to his idol.

Many of Elvis's fans resemble him, or try to. Some are teenagers like Steve Miller, a junior in a Spokane high school. He says it was in 1960, when he was eight, that he first heard one of Elvis's records. "When I played the record I flipped," he says. "I thought, Man, I gotta look into this Elvis guy! So straight to the drugstore I went and bought a teen book with Elvis stuff and I read up on him. I bought a bunch more Elvis records and ditched my Ricky Nelson ones. I cut out a lot of Elvis pictures and plastered them on my wall and then I put my hair up in a pompadour just like Elvis. My friend Dave Kirkingburg and I would get our Elvis records together and imitate him hours on end. The first movie Dave and I saw was *Loving You.* After the movie Dave and I went all over the place grinning like Elvis. We also tried to talk like him. The main Elvis habit I copied —and I still do it—was putting my shirt collar up." And several older Elvis fans, including a twenty-five-year-old California dentist, are the hit of private parties they give when they stand in front of their record players pantomiming to Elvis songs. Says a friend of the dentist: "For that moment, as long as he is pretending to be Elvis, he *is* Elvis."

It is a religious fervor many of the fans manifest in trying to explain how they feel about Elvis. Says Julie Montgomery, a twenty-three-year-old student from Polson, Montana: "Since October 1955 so many of my experiences, dreams—not daydreams but sleep dreams—and memories involve Elvis that they'd fill a book. I've had no control over and have not attempted to control these experiences. I believe that there are powers and forces working to pull me toward Elvis. These forces are so strong that at this point in my life I couldn't pull away from Elvis if I desired to do so." Irene Feola, who is twenty-seven and a housewife and mother of two from Carmel, New York, is another in whose dreams Elvis has been cast in the starring role. "I have to tell you about a dream that came true one year ago," she says. "I flew to Las Vegas to see Elvis at the International. Me! I left Sunday, August tenth, and stayed with a girl friend that lives there. I saw him Monday and Tuesday night. But you wouldn't believe this. I had front-row seats and I kissed him! He stood in front of me and I called him. He looked at me and walked over and bent down and whispered that I was sweet and then he kissed me on the lips. Every time I talk about it now I wish I were there. No one will ever understand how I feel. I love him! He has given me happiness and excitement in my life that will never die. This is my dream come true. Elvis kissed me! For that moment, it was just me." What does Mr. Feola say? His wife says he understands.

The fans sew the names of Elvis's movies on their skirts and shirts, the names of the characters he's played on their bedspreads.

They save their money for pilgrimages to Graceland and Tupelo, where they shoot up dozens of rolls of film, mostly of the gates, houses and each other.

They send request cards to radio stations—often using the cards provided by the fan clubs, an idea of the Colonel's—to insure broadcast of Elvis's records, and then vote, and vote often, in all readership or audience surveys to insure Elvis his usual number one position.

They inundate Elvis and Priscilla—whom they seem to love rather stoically—with Christmas, birthday and anniversary gifts, send dolls and clothing by the truckload to Lisa Marie, pile fresh flowers on Elvis's mother's grave, and mail get-well cards when anyone is sick.

They write letters to one another, sign them "Elvisly yours" and "Proud 4 Presley," and cover the envelopes with stickers and rubber-stamped messages or stamps showing Elvis's face.

They track Elvis relentlessly, hoping to get a snapshot and have the picture duplicated by the score to trade for other almost identical snapshots taken by other fans, all of which they keep in huge scrapbooks along with newspaper clippings, postcards, calendars and the buckets of promotional literature mailed by RCA and the Colonel each year. One fan boasts sixty-two scrapbooks, another thirty thousand photographs.

They collect anything they can get their hands on—taking leaves from the Tupelo trees, grass from the Graceland lawn, bricks from the Trousdale patio. A thirty-one-year-old cashier in Honolulu has some of the sand Elvis walked on. Several have glasses he drank from in Vegas—preserving the water in bottles—and napkins stained by his sweat. One fan in Australia claims even to have some garbage taken from one of Elvis's trash cans. When asked what she had in her Elvis collection, a girl named Mary, who lives in Cleveland, said, "Everything except for the real thing. And oh, what I could do with the real thing." Mary is thirteen.

They decorate entire rooms, creating Elvis environments, covering the walls of bedrooms as completely as the Colonel has covered his office walls. A teenaged fan in Indio, California, has a photograph in the glove compartment of her car, another laminated in plastic so it won't get wet when she takes it into the shower. "I sleep under an acre of Elvis photos," says a twenty-year-old typist from Miami, "and the record player never stops."

They join clubs the way aspiring public office holders join civic organizations. Many clubs take their names from one of Elvis's songs or films. Besides those mentioned, there's the Ready Teddy E.P.F.C. (in Quebec), the Stuck on You Forever Elvis Fan Club (West Malaysia), The Blue Hawaiians E.P.F.C. (Beverly Hills), the Love Me Tender E.P.F.C. (Monroe, Louisiana) and the Sound of Elvis Fan Club of Australasia, whose members call themselves Roustabouts. Others describe the members' collective state of mind: the Forever Faithful E.P.F.C. (Mount Holly, New Jersey) and the For Ever for Elvis Fan Club (with branches in Miami, Memphis, Mexico City, Australia and Brazil). The list goes on and on. There are clubs in every major city in the U. S., where any traveling fan is sure to have a place to stay the night.

Some fans even name their children for Elvis. Stephen Toli, a twenty-eight-year-old construction worker from Somerville, Massachusetts, is one of these. Steve and his wife are among the most active and prolific American fans, members of nearly a dozen clubs and correspondents for several British fan publications. Says Steve: "I have a boy four years old named Stephen Elvis. And my other son, who is two years old, is named Lonnie Glen—Lonnie from *Tickle Me* and Glen from *Wild in the Country.*

When Elvis was hit with a paternity suit in 1970, several fans called the Colonel's office, and although they said they didn't believe the charge for a minute, they wanted to adopt the baby.

Being an Elvis Presley fan is not inexpensive. Glenn D. Hardin, Elvis's pianist in Las Vegas, tells one story: "There was this little ol' girl from Chicago and her father was a lawyer. We did about sixty shows and she made forty-five of them. She sat in the same seat twice a night. She told me in the bar her pop paid eighty bucks a night for that, for tips and all. Like, they gave them eighty bucks a night and she got that chair. She was a groovy little girl. Her father took a bunch of us out to dinner one night. The boys in the band. It was a thing like: If my little girl likes Elvis, we'll take the band to dinner; if we can't get Elvis, we'll do the next best thing."

Most fans don't have rich poppas, however, and are like Judy Palmer, the twenty-two-year-old president of the Kissin' Cousins E.P.F.C. in Spokane. "I've been very lucky and have met Elvis and seen him several times," she says. "I spent a month in Memphis, February 1968. Then I was part of the audience at Elvis's live TV special tapings in Burbank in June 1968. I saw him at his Los Angeles home last April 1969 and have seen six shows, each trip to Vegas, August 1969 and February 1970. I imagine that from this list of travels you'll assume I'm a millionairess. I work as an assistant manager at a photo-camera shop and make two dollars an hour. But I spend all my vacations in Elvis country."

On that salary, she says, it is difficult for her to cover club operating expenses. "I get from thirty-five to fifty letters a week," she says, "and the majority of them don't enclose a stamp for reply. I spend about twenty dollars a month on postage, plus another twenty dollars every two or three months to mail the newsletters. And the newsletters themselves cost another forty dollars or so. It's costly having a club, but I enjoy it, so I feel it's worth the money I put into it. It's fun to share Elvis with other fans."

By far the biggest Elvis spenders are two fans who divide their time between Memphis and Los Angeles. Sue Wiegert, who is twenty-four, with a college degree, and Cricket Mendell, who is twenty-one, are the dynamic duo of Elvis fandom; they are, almost all of every day, within sighing distance of Elvis. This means that when Elvis is in Los Angeles the girls begin each day outside his house, wave to him as his limousine appears and then lead the car to the studio, where they will wait until it is time to escort him home again. If Elvis flies to Memphis, Sue and Cricket point their Dodge Dart in that direction and get there as fast as possible. If he goes on location, or to Las Vegas, or Houston, or anywhere else they can drive, that's where they go too. When Elvis is at the International, they go to every show, charging everything to their credit cards.

Occasionally the girls do take jobs, of course, working as temporary secretaries in whichever city they're in so they can make the payments on the credit-card charges, pay for food and rent. But most of the time their vocation is Elvis, their avocation more of the same. As a consequence, the apartments they have shared, and continue to share, in both cities are less than sumptuous, usually containing little more than a bed and a record player. Often they sleep in the car.

Cricket, a plain little blonde with a lot of energy and girlish enthusiasm, became an "Elfan" in Canton, Ohio, where by 1963 she had joined upward of thirty fan clubs and, figuring she could do as well, formed her own, the Elvisites. The club motto is "King Elvis Reigns Supreme." Sue is a brunette, less garrulous than her partner. She first saw Elvis on one of the Sullivan shows in 1956, finished college at her mother's insistence and after forming *her* own fan club, Blue Hawaiians for Elvis, started hanging on the Graceland gate. That's where the two girls met in 1967. They've been inseparable since.

Sue and Cricket are reluctant to talk with writers these days, fearing what they call—without using the word—"exploitation." They permitted themselves to be interviewed for an article in *West* magazine the summer of 1970 and began threatening lawsuits even before the story appeared. Asked why, they said they were afraid Elvis would think they were paid for the interview, that they were taking advantage of their friendship (that was the word—friendship) with Elvis.

If Sue and Cricket are the champs of Presleymania, England is where most of the runners-up live. In Great Britain there are Elvis fans in sufficient number and heat to support a slick newsstand magazine devoted to him, *Elvis Monthly*. In its sixty-four pages are many familiar features— record raves, assorted discographies and other statistical compilations, letters to the editor, a personal testimonial titled "Discovering Elvis" (usually carrying the conviction and verve normally found only in a fresh religious convert), columns of gossip and news, and occasional poems. There are monthly reports from Memphis on what Elvis has been doing day to day, provided by Gary Pepper, whose father works the Graceland gate; a column of club news edited by Albert Hand, a printer who founded the International Elvis Presley Appreciation Society; dozens of photographs; and a few advertisements such as "The Jordanaires Sweater—from the Jordanaires' own ladies' dress / sweater shop in Nashville. Usual Price: twenty-five dollars. For Elvis fans: a fifteen-dollar international money order." *Elvis Monthly* also is responsible for an *Elvis Special* yearbook and offers badges, records, notepaper and envelopes.

It was on this five-by-seven-inch magazine that the *Beatles Monthly* was based, but while *Elvis Monthly* is now in its eleventh year, the Beatles publication folded in 1969, after five.

Most important function of the *Monthly* is communication, for it is through this publication that most of the biggest Elvis "do's" are supported, planned and announced. (Title of a recent article: "Presley Parties Pack Power.") In honor of Elvis and Priscilla's third wedding anniversary, for example, Maureen Fricker planned an all-day celebration party that promised screenings of *Roustabout, Follow That Dream* and selected short subjects including three Warner Pathé news films, one of them of Elvis's wedding. Additionally there was a "Question Half Hour" and a "Discussion Half Hour." Tickets: 18/- (about two dollars), including tea, biscuits and assorted sandwiches.

A larger Elvis "do" is the annual Elvis convention, now in its sixth year, organized by the *Monthly,* and usually held in London, but in 1970 all over Europe. "Fans travelling on the eight-day Elvis fans' holiday will be treated to an Elvis Party in Brussels, when films of Elvis' Las Vegas engagement, taken by a fan will be shown," said Todd Slaughter, president of Britain's Official Elvis Presley Fan Club, in a recent issue. "In Holland, two feature films are planned, and when fans move on to Koblenz, the German Fan Club promises a screening of the Elvis Presley NBC-TV Show. And don't forget, in addition to the Convention [in Luxembourg], we are hoping to arrange with a Luxembourg cinema for the screening of *Live a*

Little, Love a Little and *Charro."* It was enough to make any Elvis fan drool with anticipation.

The organization is fantastic. Says Maria Luisa Davies, the club's branch leader in Liverpool: "What happens here is that the country is divided into areas which have an area leader. It is my job to keep in touch with the members who live in the locality, answer their queries—to save Todd from being snowed under with questions—to organize trips to other towns to see Elvis films, etc. Because we are such a small country we can get about meeting other members. I think it is the spirit of companionship and the wonderful feeling of being of one accord which makes these events so successful."

Many of the European events take their cue from Elvis's philanthropy and are used as a vehicle to raise money for some charity, in England usually for guide dogs for the blind.

Elvis Monthly is not the only Elvis publication in Europe. In Italy there is the *Elvis Times,* a full-sized newspaper published monthly, half in English, half in Italian. In Holland a fan, Hans Langbroek, spent ten years researching—largely by mail—Elvis's early life and published an attractive and generally quite accurate if highly personal and chatty biography that takes Elvis through 1955, *The Hillbilly Cat.* And in England and Ireland there are dozens of regularly issued newsletters and fan magazines.

It is unfair to generalize about what the "average" Elvis fan(atic) is like in terms of background, age, occupation and so on. But polls have been taken, one of them by *Elvis Monthly,* and fragmentary pictures are formed. In England, apparently, nearly half the *Monthly* readership is between nineteen and twenty-two, with the young men claiming a slight edge in numbers over the young women, the rest fairly equally divided between under-eighteens and over-twenty-threes. Clerks, white-collar workers and professions (43 per cent) placed well ahead of factory workers and tradesmen (30 per cent) and students and housewives (22 per cent). In the U. S. there seem to be two essential types of fans, differentiated largely by age, with twenty serving as a boundary. The older fans remember Elvis from the 1950s; those twenty and under became fans during his post-Army days. Clearly two-thirds of all fan club members are in their teens or younger, not a surprising finding except that it leaves one-third twenty or older, a large number of them in their late twenties and early thirties. Females have the edge in the U. S., but for all fans the education level is—compared to England—low, closer to the national average. Although college registration has more than doubled in the past twenty-five years, the median education level for white Americans is short of a high school diploma, while only about 20 per cent of the U. S. work force is professional or proprietorship, the rest being sales people, laborers, farmers and the like. Discounting for the moment the students, it is, generally, from the lower to middle economic classes—those who work rather than think for a living—that Elvis gets his most vigorous fans. There are, for example, an astonishing number of IBM keypunch operators, with factory assemblers and clerks following.

Of course many fans are teenagers going through the normal stages of hero worship. There is nothing odd about that. But many—the most zealous—do show character traits of interest to psychologists. These are the ones who are so possessive and so paranoid they deny Elvis human frailty. Thus they write obscene and threatening letters to anyone who attacks him or so much as criticizes a film or performance. Similarly, when a critic reviews Elvis favorably, he is flooded by letters and cards of thanks. And when stories of trouble between Elvis and Priscilla persist, if the fans believe them at all (which is doubtful), they are convinced it's Priscilla's, not Elvis's, fault. And as for all the bad films and weak sound-track recordings, they were the Colonel's doing; said the *Elvis Monthly,* noting that 44 per cent disapproved of the Colonel's policies: "A defeat of Elvis's management even after 1969's successes is a startling condemnation of the 1963/7 policy. Had this question been asked in 1967 the noes would have numbered at least 75%."

Psychologists say this exaggerated adoration often is a reflection of some identity crisis within the fan, that he (or she) is often so poor or so unpopular among his peers he must select someone glamorous through whom to live his life vicariously. Said one psychologist: "By affixing himself to an established star and devoting so much time to worshiping that star, in Elvis's case collecting scrapbooks and photographs and so on, he can develop—at least in his own mind—a *relationship* with the star, which by itself seems to be enough to make that individual 'better' than the peer group that rejects him. It is an old insecurity, self-treated in an old and generally harmless fashion."

But just why Elvis attracts so many of these people remains a mystery. Perhaps it is because they're made to feel so welcome.

Whoever they are, and whatever their motivations, the "Elfans" are fascinating creatures, upon whose backs much of the Elvis success story rests.

In Hollywood, Ann Moses, the pretty twenty-three-year-old editor of *Tiger Beat,* a newsstand magazine for teenagers, was trying to convince her publisher that her readers really do want more Elvis features, that it wasn't just her own prejudices. She, like most Elvis fan "leaders," has a better education than many—with two years of college—and also like many others says she became an Elvis fan through her husband. "I think being an Elvis fan is like being in love," she says. "You can't explain *why,* or *how,* it happened, but that feeling is just there and unmistakable."

In Morningside, Maryland, Bill Kaval, a twenty-seven-year-old police officer with three small children, was working on one of his discographies and film lists. Bill corresponds with fans over much of the world (England, Japan, Italy), is a member of several fan clubs, believes he has one of "the most complete Elvis Presley collections in the world" and is one of the more serious students and statisticians of the Presley phenomenon.

In Chicago, Lana Kotenko, twenty-two, entered her office for the filing and typing assignments that provide money for periodic visits to Memphis and Las Vegas. She is an attractive girl who covers much of her clothing with Elvis pictures and slogans. "Is he ever beautiful and sexy!" she exclaims. "And when he saw me with all my Elvis buttons and an Elvis blouse which I wore, he just couldn't believe his eyes. And I was so nervous I started crying." It was Lana, friends say, who later bit Elvis on the neck during one of his performances in Las Vegas.

("I think Elvis is genuinely amazed by some of his fans," says Stan Brossette. "I've seen looks in his eye that say, 'Man, you're weird.' I mean, how could he take it all seriously after all these years?")

And in Redondo Beach, Mrs. Virginia Coons was threading another Elvis film on her projector. Mrs. Coons, one of the truly big collectors, has approximately 25,000 photographs of Elvis in her collection and as she brings them out, book after book after book, she likes to comment on how Elvis stands with his right foot turned just so; it is obvious she has studied these pictures countless times.

"There," she said, patting the projector and reaching for the light switch. "This was one taken from the balcony at the International."

The film lasted only a few minutes and then Mrs. Coons ran it backward.

Halloween and the Mass Child

Gregory P. Stone

The ways in which American holidays and traditional celebrations are acknowledged have evolved with American society. Rapid changes within the twentieth century have caused a decline in participation in such events as Groundhog Day, April Fool's Day, and St. Valentine's Day. Valentine's Day was a major holiday in the nineteenth century; sentimental greeting cards trimmed with lace and imitation jewels were exchanged by all age groups. Elaborate parties for adults were inspired by the legend that birds chose their mates on Valentine's Day. Couples dressed as birds and the dining table was set to resemble a bird's nest! Today, despite the merchandisers of candy and cards, Valentine's Day survives mainly as a children's celebration.

Most of the major holidays have retained their relative importance in the twentieth century but have changed in meaning and ritual. A few researchers have attempted to elucidate the underlying determinants of these changes, but most of them have simply decried the commercialization and secularization of traditional customs. Gregory Stone provides an example of how more thoughtful studies can illustrate basic changes in American life in his pioneering article on Halloween. George R. Stewart's chapter on "Holidays" in American Ways of Life *is a starting point for further reading. Another useful reference is George William Douglas's* The American Book of Days.

I set these notes down with a sense of *déjà vu*. Certainly it has all been said before, and I may have read it all somewhere, but I cannot locate the sources. I have often thought about these things in the past. Then, too, as a sociologist, I like to think I am providing observations as well as impressions for my audience. I cannot recall any other counts and tabulations of the very few facts and happenings that I counted and tabulated this year in a small "near southern" town on the traditional hallowed evening.

In brief, I found that Riesman's "other-directed man" may have exported his peculiar life style—tolerance and conformity organized by the prime activity of consumption—from his suburban northeastern habitat to areas westward and southward perilously close to the Mason-Dixon line. The town I speak of is a university town. As such, it has undoubtedly recruited "other-directed's" from the universities of the northeast. For example, I have been there. Moreover, the part of town in which I carried on my quantitative survey (properly speaking, a "pilot study") is a kind of suburb—a sub-village, perhaps an "inner-urb"—the housing section maintained by most large universities where younger faculty are segregated from the rest of the community in World War II officers' quarters. "Other-directed's" are younger and better educated than "inner-directed's."

You will recall the main theme of *The Lonely Crowd:* the very *character* of American life has been revolutionized as the fundamental organizing activity of our waking hours has shifted from production to consumption. We used to work—at least ideally and Protestantly—because work was our life. By our works we were known. Max Weber, among others less careful and profound, has attempted to explain this in his *Protestant Ethic and the Spirit of Capitalism,* showing how a vocabulary of motive was required to consolidate the spread of capitalism in society and arguing that the sheer dialectic of class antagonism was not always sufficient to account for the institution of pervasive economic change. *Every social change requires a convincing rationale.* Protestantism supplied this in part, and its persistence may still be seen in the contrasting attitudes toward gambling (*gaming*), for example, held by Protestant and Catholic churches. Only in the 1920's did the American Protestant churches relax their bans on such games, and then it was with the stipulation that they be played for amusement only. Risk and gain were cemented in the context of work; never in the context of play. The place of consumption in the "old" society—the industrial society—may be caricatured by referring to Marx's view that the cost of labor was the money

From *American Quarterly*, 11 (3), Fall 1959, 372–379. Reprinted by permission of the author and the *American Quarterly* of the University of Pennsylvania. Copyright 1959 by Trustees of the University of Pennsylvania. (Footnotes have been omitted.)

and goods required for laborers to exist and reproduce themselves. Abbreviated: we consumed so that we might work. Today, for the most part, we work to live and live to consume. Abbreviated: we work to consume.

"Trick or Treat" is the contemporary quasi-ritual play and celebration of Halloween. Characteristically, the "trick-or-treater" is rewarded not for his work, but for his play. The practice is ostensibly a vast bribe exacted by the younger generation upon the older generation (by the "other-directed's" upon the "inner-directed's"?). The doorbell rings and is answered. The householder is greeted by a masked and costumed urchin with a bag—significantly, a *shopping* bag—and confronted with dire alternatives: the unknown peril of a devilishly conceived prank that will strike at the very core of his social self—his property; or the "payoff" in candy, cookies or coin for another year's respite from the antisocial incursions of the children. The householder pays.

In his *Psychology of Clothes,* J. C. Flügel has noted that the mask and costume free the individual from social obligation by concealing his identity and cloaking him in the absurd protective anonymity of a mythical or legendary creature—a clown, a ghost, a pirate or a witch. The householder must pay. For, by "dressing out," the urchin is symbolically immunized against those punishments that might ordinarily inhibit the promised violations of property and propriety. Punishment presupposes the identity of the offender.

Nonsense! This conception of "trick or treat" is clearly and grossly in error. In the mass society, the "protection racket" seems as archaic as the concepts of psychoanalysis. To revive either in the analysis of contemporary life betrays the nostalgia of the analyst. Both are but the dusty wreckage of long dead romances. Moreover, as we shall see, the mask invites the ready disclosure of the wearer's identity. Instead of protecting the urchin, the costume is more akin to the Easter bonnet, designed to provoke the uncritical appreciations of the audience.

Even so, we can apprehend the "trick" as a production; the "treat" as a consumption. Just twenty-five years ago, when I was an urchin, Halloween was a time set aside for young tricksters—a time for creative productions. Creativity, I might remind the reader, is inevitably destructive, as it pushes the present into the past. Of course, it is never merely nor exclusively the destruction of established forms. Our destructive productions were immense (I wonder at my adolescence, as Marx wondered at the *bourgeoisie*!). I don't know now how we managed silently to detach the eave troughs from the house of the neighborhood "crab," remove his porch steps, then encourage him to give chase by hurling those eave troughs, with a terrifying clatter, upon his front porch. I do know it was long, hard and careful *work.* The devices of Halloween were also artfully and craftily produced, like the serrated spool used to rattle the windows of more congenial adults in the neighborhood. We had no conception of being treated by our victims, incidentally, to anything except silence which we hoped was studied, irate words, a chase (if we were lucky), or, most exciting of all, an investigation of the scene by the police whom we always managed to elude. Our masks, we believed, did confound our victims' attempts to identify us.

In sharp contrast to these nostalgic memories are the quantitative findings of my "pilot study." Being a sociologist, I must apologize for my sample first of all. An editorial in a local newspaper warned me that between seventy-five and one hundred children would visit my home on Halloween. Only eighteen urchins bedeviled me that evening, a fact that I attribute to two circumstances. First, I unwittingly left my dog at large early in the evening. A kind animal, a cross between a Weimeraner and some unknown, less nervous breed, she was upset by the curious costumes of the children, and, barking in fright, she frightened away some of the early celebrants. Second, I think that our segregated "inner-urb" was neglected in favor of more imposing, perhaps more lucrative, areas of town. My eighteen respondents ranged in age from about four years to about twelve. Half were girls and half were boys. Two of the six groups— one-third—were mixed. Twenty-five years ago the presence of girls in my own Halloween enterprises was unthinkable.

Was the choice proffered by these eighteen urchins, when they whined or muttered, "Trick or treat?" or stood mutely at my threshold, a choice between production and consumption? Was I being offered the opportunity to decide for these youngsters the ultimate direction they should take in later life by casting them in the role of producer or consumer? Was I located at some vortex of fate so that my very act could set the destiny of the future? Was there a choice at all? No. In each case, I asked, "Suppose I said, 'Trick.' What would you do?" Fifteen of the eighteen (83.3%) answered, "I don't know." The art of statistics, taken half-seriously, permits me to estimate with 95% confidence that the interval, .67–1.00, will include the proportion of children who don't know what a trick is in that "hypothetical universe" for which the eighteen constituted a random sample (this is a ruse employed by some sociologists who find out belatedly that the sample they have selected is inadequate). Yet, it seems that at least two-thirds of the children like those who visited my house on Halloween probably have no conception of producing a trick! They aren't bribing anybody. They grace your and my doorsteps as consumers, pure and simple.

What of the three—the 16.7%—who did not respond, "I don't know"? One said nothing at all. I assume he really didn't know, but, being a careful quantitative researcher, I cannot include him with the others.

> Interviewer: Hello there.
> Respondent: (Silence)
> Interviewer: What do you want?
> Respondent: Trick or treat?
> Interviewer: Supposing I said, "Trick"?
> Respondent: (Silence)
> Interviewer: What would you do, if I said, "Trick"?
> Respondent: *I don't know.* (Long pause.) I'd *probably* go home and get some sand *or something* and throw it on your porch. (Emphasis mine.)
> Field Notes: The porches of the old officers' quarters are constructed from one-by-three slats so that about an inch of free space intervenes between each slat. In short, the porch simply would not hold sand, and the "trick" of the urchin could never be carried off!
> Interviewer: O. K. I'll have to treat, I guess.

The third answered, without prompting, that he'd go home, get a water pistol and squirt my windows (which could have used a little squirting). The "tricks" did not seem so dire, after all! Moreover, the "means of production"—the sand and the water pistol—were left at home, a fact that reminds me of one of Riesman's acute observations to the effect that the home has become a workshop (work is consumed) and the factory, a ranch house (consumption is work).

Did the masks and costumes provide anonymity? To the contrary! I asked each child who he or she was. Happily and trustfully each revealed his or her identity, lifting the mask and disclosing the name. Had they ripped off *my* eave troughs, I would have had the police on them in short order! "Trick or Treat" is a highly personalized affair so that even its ritual quality is lost (for their persistence, rituals depend upon impersonal enactments), and my earlier use of the term, "quasi-ritual," is explained.

On the possibility that the costume might have been a production or a creation, I noted the incidence of ready-to-wear costumes. Two-thirds had been purchased in their entirety. Four of the others were mixed, consisting of homemade costumes and commercial masks. Two were completely homemade: one a ghost outfit, consisting of an old tattle-tale gray sheet with two eye holes; the other, a genuine creation. It was comprised by a mesh wastebasket inverted over an opening in a large cardboard box with armholes. On the front of the box, printed in a firm adult "hand," were the words: Take Me to Your Leader. Occasionally, adults produced, but only to ratify or validate the child in his masquerade as a consumer.

To ascertain the part played by adults in "Trick or Treat," I must, unfortunately, rely on recollections. In preparing my interview schedule and observational data sheets, I had not anticipated the adult, thinking that the celebrants of Halloween would be children. This impression was confirmed by my local newspaper which published the rules of Halloween, stipulating its age-graded character. "Trick or Treat" was set aside for the preadolescents of the town, while teen-agers were obliged to celebrate the event at parties. The rules were apparently enforced, as this news item on the November 1 front page shows:

> Police yesterday afternoon arrested, then released, a youth they said was dressed in a Halloween costume and asking for tricks [sic] or treats at downtown stores.
> They said the youth was about 17. He started the rounds of the stores early, he said, because he had to work last night.
> Police said they lectured the youth and explained the traditional [sic] trick-or-treat routine is normally reserved for children.

What adults were to do was not clarified by the local press. What many did do was to ease and expedite consumption by clothing their preadolescent children for the role, providing them with shopping bags and, in many instances, accompanying them on the rounds. At least three of the six groups of urchins that called at my house on Halloween were accompanied by adults (the father was always there, one alone!) who lurked uneasily and self-consciously in the darkness where night was mixed with the shadowed shafts cast by my porch light. In one case, a peer group of adults lurked in the shadows and exceeded in number the peer group of children begging on my porch. There they were: agents of socialization, teaching their children how to consume in the tolerant atmosphere of the mass society. The "anticipatory socialization" of the children—accomplished by an enactment of roles not normally played at the time, but roles that would be assumed in the future—was going on before my eyes. I wondered whether the parental preoccupation with the child's adjustment in the larger society could not have been put aside just for Halloween. Perhaps the hiding in the dark allegorically comple- mented my wish in the tacit expression of shame.

They were teaching a lesson in tolerance, not only a lesson in con- sumption, encouraging their children to savor the gracious and benign acceptance of their beggary by an obliging adult world. My questions made them nervous. The lone father was silent. He turned his face sky- wards, studying the stars. One couple spoke rapidly in hushed whispers, punctuating their remarks with nervous laughter. In another couple, the mother said sheepishly, "I wonder what they'll say? They've never been asked that." All the parents were relieved when I tactfully rescued the situation from deterioration by offering to treat the children with (pur- chased) goodies. Consider a typical protocol.

> Field Notes: The bell rings. I go to the door. On the porch are three children between five and nine years old, two boys—one in a clown suit, the other in a pirate suit—and a girl in a Japanese kimono, holding a fan. On the sidewalk are a mother and a father whose faces are hidden in darkness.
> Interviewer: Hi!
> Respondents: (Silence.)
> Interviewer: What do you want?
> Respondents: (Silence.)
> The clown: Candy.
> Interviewer: Why?
> Field Notes: The married couple giggles. They shift their feet.
> Japanese girl and clown: (Silence.)
> Pirate: I don't know.
> Field Notes: I look questioningly at the girl and the clown. Each is silent.
> Interviewer: What are you supposed to say?
> Japanese girl: I don't know.
> Interviewer: Have you heard of "Trick or Treat"?
> Clown: No.
> Field Notes: The married couple is silent. They lean forward expectantly, almost placing their faces in the circle of light arching out and around my porch and open front door, almost telling me who they are.
> Interviewer: Well, I guess I'll have to treat.
> Field Notes: I get a handful of corn candy from the living room, and divide it among the three outstretched open shopping bags. All the respondents laugh in an appreciative, relieved manner. My study is passed off as a joke. The world has been tolerant after all.

I am reminded of Ortega's remonstrances against the Mass Man, for whom *privileges had become rights.* Standing there, existing, it was the clown's right to receive the treat, the candy. The treat or gift was at one time an act of deference in recognition of esteemed friendship. Herbert Spencer wrote of it in that way—the gift was a privilege. On Halloween, the gift has become the right of every child in the neighborhood, however he or his family is esteemed. Now, rights are not questioned. That such rights would be questioned was hardly anticipated by those who claimed them. It made them ill-at-ease and nervous, perhaps lest the questions betray an indignation—a state of mind more appropriate to an age when people were busy, or perhaps busier, more productive.

Yet, this is not a plea for a return to the "good old days"—ridiculous on the face of it. Certainly, the farther south the tolerance of the mass society creeps, the happier many of us will be. It seems to be unquestionably true that the younger people of the south are less opposed to segregated schools than the adults. There is nothing morally wrong with consumption, per se, as production was often the setting for ruthless destruction. The conformity of "other-direction" (no trick-or-treater came to my door by himself) need not disturb us. Each society must secure conformity from a substantial majority of its members if that society is to persist. Instead, I have tried to show only two things. First, Reisman's character type of "other-direction" may, indeed, be a *prototype* of American character and not some strange mutation in the northeast. Consumption, tolerance and conformity were recognizable in the Halloween masquerade of a near-southern town. Production, indignation and autonomy were not. Second, national holidays and observances may have been transformed into vast staging areas for the anticipatory socialization of mass men. By facilitating this change in life style, they can give impetus to the change in character conceived by Reisman (and many others). I am being very serious when I say that we need studies of what has happened to all these observances—the Fourth of July, Thanksgiving, Christmas and Easter—in all parts of America. After reading this report, you will agree that we need a study of Halloween.

It is not only as a sociologist, however, that I ask for these studies. Something does trouble me deeply about my observations—the "I don't know." Here is the source of our misgivings and dis-ease with respect to the mass man. It is not that he consumes, but, to the profit of the "hidden persuaders," that he consumes, not knowing why or just not knowing. It is not that he is tolerant, but that he is *unreasonably* tolerant. It is not that he conforms, but that he conforms for conformity's sake. *The mass society, like the industrial society, needs a vocabulary of motive—a rationale—to dignify the daily life.* That's what troubles me about my findings on Halloween. It was a rehearsal for consumership without a rationale. Beyond the stuffing of their pudgy stomachs, they didn't know why they were filling their shopping bags.

Pueblo Baseball:
A New Use for Old Witchcraft

J. R. Fox

From their initial encounters, the European stereotyped the native Ameri-can. Both the concept of the "noble savage" and that of the "brutish savage" served in differing ways to dehumanize the American Indian; without any doubt both were powerful within American civilization. These contradictory images produced within white thinking an ambivalence which helped to create a shifting and confused Indian policy. Sometimes assimilation was encouraged, at other times the reservation system of separation was stressed, and at times, it must be admitted, the govern-ment's policy was genocide. During the periods in which assimilation was emphasized, American culture made inroads into the traditional culture of native tribes. However, the process was never completed and the primacy of tribalism and traditional customs in the current Red Power movement indicates that the assimilation process may be reversed.

J. R. Fox's article provides a humorous insight into the results of introducing an American sport into native American culture. It provokes general questions about the role American popular culture plays in other societies, as does James Thurber's "Wild Bird Hickok and His Friends" also in this book. Thoughtful current studies of the American Indian also include Vine Deloria's Custer Died For Your Sins *and* We Talk, You Listen, *and Stan Steiner's* The New Indians.

The ideals of harmony and cooperation and the outlawing of competition among the Pueblo Indians have become an anthropological commonplace over the last few decades.[1] Benedict's confusion of institutions with personality traits which led her to believe that the Puebloans were "harmonious" people has since been corrected. Such books as Sun Chief[2] have shown vividly the amount of hate, aggression and suspicion which lies behind the conscious harmony of Pueblo social life. If one could characterize the content of interpersonal relations in the Pueblos with one word, I think "cautious" would be that word. One has to be careful in dealing with others for fear of "what people will say." The power of public opinion in these crowded little communities is the strongest force for social conformity, and manifests itself in the extreme fear of witchcraft accusations. Indeed, the fear of being accused is greater than the fear of actual witchcraft. Informants are vague about the powers and practices of witches and often complain that they have forgotten what witches are supposed to do—"only the old people remember what the kanatya do."[3] But everyone is agreed that the most terrible thing that one can say of another is "everyone knows he (or she) is a witch." Thus, while the cultural trappings and elaborations surrounding witch behavior have largely been forgotten, the motivational basis for this projective system remains strong. It exists, as it were, in the raw.

Everyone is suspect. The Sun Chief of Oraibi even suspected his own mother on her deathbed of being a "two-heart." All interpersonal relations are fraught with danger and there are few people one can wholly trust. In particular women do not trust each other. The Don Juanism of the males and the relative promiscuity of the women means that no woman can be really sure that any other is not her husband's lover, or has not been at some time. A woman can trust her sisters, more or less, and of course her mother, primarily because it would be difficult for members of the same household group to carry on affairs under each other's noses.[4] Affines are very much mistrusted and often with good cause.

What is involved is not so much sexual jealousy as, again, the fear of "talk." This also is not just fear of gossip. Words have power and are not to be used lightly. "Bad thoughts" have tremendous repercussions and are believed to have effects in the real world. Bad words, as the manifestations of bad thoughts, "poison the air of the Pueblo."[5] The real repercussions of accusation and insults are in fact disturbing to Pueblo peace. In societies based on extended kin groupings one cannot insult one person at a time. Thus any accusations may lead to a widespread split-up of the village, and this fear of internal dissension provides strong motivation for not making open accusations, or at least for toning them down. In the

From Journal of American Folklore, 74 (291), January–March 1961, 9–16. Reprinted by permission of the author and the editors. (Footnotes have been placed at the end of the text.)

case of a philandering husband caught *in flagrante delicto,* relatives on both sides will try to patch the matter up or at least persuade the pair to part quietly and without fuss. In "the old days" a woman could be rid of her husband fairly easily by ordering him out of her house. This is becoming more impossible today as men are now more likely than women to be houseowners. In the Eastern Pueblos the Catholic Church complicates matters by forbidding divorce and remarriage. A wronged woman will often go to live with her sister or mother, taking her children, but life becomes hard because she cannot remarry and she risks priestly censure if she takes another mate.

The frustrations consequent upon these limitations to direct action cause much bitterness between women, and witchcraft accusations are more likely to be female affairs than male. In the old days the War Captains, ceremonial police of the Pueblos, would have dealt with the witches once sufficient proof had been gathered of their activities. Death or banishment would have been the punishment. Today, however, and often in the past, nothing would be done about it. "People just got mad and didn't speak to each other or they left the village." Today also the relatively sophisticated Cochiti realize that white people think these beliefs silly, and tend to shrug off or deny them. Some members of the ultra-Catholic progressive faction share the white man's contempt for these beliefs. But beneath this air of careless disbelief and denial there lies the motivational and social basis for the interpersonal fear that has not changed.

Formal Pueblo institutions, then, as a counter to, rather than an acting out of, personality forces, stress harmony and cooperation. People must dance together, work together, play together. They are enjoined to think good harmonious thoughts so as not to spoil the air of the Pueblo. Bad thoughts are as dangerous as bad deeds and conscious effort should be made to eradicate them. Drunkenness is feared, as it lets loose all the aggressive impulses which one must constantly work to damp down. All forms of overt hostility are taboo.

In Cochiti, the intricate criss-crossing of clans, societies, Kivas (dual ceremonial organizations), extended families, church and other groups helps to ensure that no permanent oppositions and cleavages can occur which would channel hostilities into armed camps. The factional split (conservatives and progressives) came nearest to open war, but the cross-cutting of these divisions by others (particularly extended families) saved the village from complete disintegration. As long as any two groups continue to exchange women in Cochiti, it is difficult for them to remain in hostile opposition. All formal divisions within the village have been divisions of labor and not of enmity or opposition. The cooperation of the two Kivas is essential to the proper performance of public ceremonies and they in no way compete with each other. All medicine societies complement each other's work—there are never two societies for one cure. A careful political balance is struck so that every group is evenly represented on the council. As the village is small, the result is a series of overlapping roles with a consequent impossibility of permanent conflict, despite the fact of continually recurring conflicts.

The old competitive games of the Pueblo followed this principle and were never played between any two formal groups. For races and shinny games the categories of "married" versus "unmarried" were employed, or teams were picked from the young men on a count-out method. There was never a competitive alignment in terms of the existing social groupings and teams were not permanent affairs. Since the advent of baseball in Cochiti, however, and particularly within the last decade, a new and unique situation has arisen. Cochiti now has two baseball teams playing in the same league (Inter-Pueblo Baseball League)[6] and in open competition with each other. The original team, now called the Redskins, was formed many years ago and old photographs testify to the long-standing interest in baseball in the Pueblo. Support comes from all sections of the population including the old medicine men and the ceremonial heads of the Kivas. Baseball is not thought of as alien. Most men now playing grew up in a society which was already enthusiastic about the sport. The present *cacique,* the religious leader of the tribe, was for a long time a pitcher for the second team. On his assuming office the medicine men forbade him to continue, as playing ball was not consonant with the dignity of his office—but he is the sole exception. The original team, first known as the Eagles, was the sole focus of interest for many years, but with the return of servicemen to Cochiti after the Second World War, interest grew and a second team, the Silversmiths, was formed. This team, now known as the Braves, claimed independent status, built its own ball park and entered the league in competition with the Redskins. They were immediately successful and won the championship three years in succession. Thus a new and potentially dangerous situation occurred—these two teams had to meet each other in the village and fight it out twice a year. The situation was wildly at variance with the whole Pueblo ethos.

What happened was interesting. The first game was played and while all went reasonably well on the field there were fights on the sidelines and these between the *mothers* of the players. As the momentum of the game increased these ladies began to abuse each other, to brawl, and finally to do open battle. The horrified Pueblo council immediately banned all future games between the teams in the Pueblo.

An examination of the original membership in the two teams shows that, because of the voluntary nature of their recruitment, they were a perfect breeding ground for factions. One was not constrained by kinship ties, initiation, or any other automatic factor to join either team, but could choose. The Braves, when they broke away from the Redskins, broke away by family groups, i.e., several families of players left the one and formed the other. Thus the choice was made, not by individuals, but by families. It seems from the statements of informants that there have always been, within living memory, two ill-defined groups of extended families which formed opposing "blocks" on the basis of quarrels now forgotten. Previously these two blocks had never had occasion or excuse to come out in opposition to each other, as there had been no basis for such an oppositional grouping, and the two groups even cut across the conservative-progressive factional boundaries—but in the baseball split there was a unique opportunity for the old latent hostilities to come to the surface. Allegiance to the team is patrilineal as with the Kivas, but the two teams are by no means coterminous with the Kivas. Thus the two teams represent a dual alignment of families for purely competitive purposes. Families which mistrusted or disliked each other could readily line up on opposite sides of the fence and even to uncommitted families the infection spread. The crosscutting tendency in Pueblo institutions of course works to mitigate this as it did with the factions, but here the essential factor of the exchange of women has not had time to work itself out. What is more, the away games of the teams have increased the chances of young men to meet girls from outside the village and hence increased the number of outmarriages. The wives of these marriages, having no female relatives in Cochiti, tend to become assimilated into the husband's mother's extended family and this increases the gap between the two sides. Out of eight marriages in one year, three were to San Juan girls—results of the popular away game at that Pueblo. It is not the young wives, however, but rather the older women who are the "trouble-makers." These women who would formerly have had little chance to attack other women they disliked without invoking the frightening subject of witchcraft, now have excuse and opportunity to do battle royal over the bodies of their sons and grandsons. The epithet *cheater* has become a virtual synonym for witch.[7]

The council ban was effective in preventing open war in the village for a time, but it only served to drive the feelings underground. Suspicion and hostility grew until this year (1959), when they broke out again into the open. By this time the antagonism had spread to the players. Previously the teams had made strenuous efforts to be fair and play the game, but the noise from the sidelines had made this difficult. This year the Braves had indulged in a series of rulebreaking episodes which flared into open quarrels. These were accentuated by the fact that after a trial game last year which rumbled but went off without incident, the council had reluctantly decided that the annual games could be played again. Significantly the games were placed at the beginning of the week during which the annual corn dance was to take place, on the feast day of the village saint (St. Bonaventure). Thus they should come at a time when "all hearts are in harmony" and everyone is bending his efforts towards the success of the great communal dance for rain, good harvest and long life.

The Braves, according to their opponents, had not been in with the spirit of the thing. A Redskin commented, "Rules don't mean nothing to them; they don't care." It seems that the Braves had gone to town with the rule book. They had: 1) played people in the finals who had not played five consecutive games; 2) failed to turn up for games but refused to forfeit the points for them; 3) played men who had previously played for other sides and refused to relinquish them even after threats of suspension; 4) cheated in the games; 5) threatened umpires (unspecified); 6) attempted to maim opponents. A rule which was not in the official book but which, I was told, the Braves and their female supporters broke most often was to influence the course of the game by occult means—witchcraft. Particularly, it seems, they attempted to cause "accidents," to make the ball hit a runner, etc. To any enquiries as to why they hadn't been suspended or denied the replays, I was told, "they get their own way because the other teams are scared of them." San Juan had a good claim to two forfeited games but gave in because "they were scared." The manager of the Braves is a feared man in being the *Kwirena Nawa,* head of the powerful *Kwirena* society, one of the "managing societies" in Pueblo ceremonial. He is also head of the Pumpkin Kiva. Some of the Redskins spoke out against the Braves' conduct at meetings of the league, and in a confused bit of political maneuvering the Braves were alternately suspended, reinstated, quit the league, and rejoined. By the time of the Cochiti games they were in again but had lost points for two games the league decided they must forfeit.

The Cochiti games, set on Sunday, were to have made up a doubleheader—the first game in the morning after Mass and the second in the afternoon prior to the Kiva practice for the corn dance. For some reason I was never able to fathom, the Braves failed to show up for the morning game. The Redskins, in an attempt to be friendly and keep things on an even keel, agreed to play the lost game on the following Saturday. Several female relatives of the Redskins muttered that the game should have been claimed; "the men are too soft." But the men were making a conscious if nervous effort to keep things going smoothly. Several men said they would not watch the game: "they'll only fight, those ladies;

they'll just yell and shout and upset everybody; people don't forget easily."
"They don't care about the game, they just want to fight and upset other
people." Sometimes, "they don't speak to each other for a year or more."
Other times, "they are just mad in the season, they forget it in the winter."
The Redskins' supporters could name only one Braves family which was
consistently friendly with any Redskin family. Asked why this antagonism
didn't exist between Kivas, they told me, "Why should it? They don't have
nothing to fight about." But no one could explain why the antagonism was
there in the first place, or rather no one was willing to risk the analysis
for fear of reaching conclusions too unpleasant to bear about his beloved
village. All the men agreed that it was the fault of "them old ladies. I
guess they just like fighting."

The afternoon game was played in a fit of nerves and deliberate
efforts were made to keep things calm. To lend weight to the authority of
the council, both the Governor and the Lieutenant Governor came and sat
together, and the War Captain and his assistant were present, strate-
gically placed between the supporters of the two sides. The men of the
village deliberately chose a neutral spot behind the wire and huddled
there while the women of the teams stood around their respective dugouts.

The game progressed in a lively fashion and the women gathered
force as it went on. The comments, at first mild—"Get him glasses, he
can't see," "He can't hit what he can't see; he's blind"—became bitter,
personal and obscene.[8] The men meanwhile made polite comments and
factual observations and differences of opinion were glossed over. At one
point the comments of the women became so noisy that the Redskins'
manager, at his team's request, hurried over to the female supporters
and gave them a lecture. This had no noticeable effect. However, the
game passed off without any really unruly incident, although the nervous-
ness of the players led to a phenomenal number of errors. Two factors led
to a relaxation of tension: there was a neutral umpire (a colored boy from
Virginia), and the game was never in doubt. The Redskins went into an
early lead and finally won eighteen to eight. Everyone left the ball ground
quickly and irate old ladies were hustled away by sons and grandsons.

During the following week tension mounted towards the second game.
Many people declared they would stay away, while others were equally
sure they wouldn't miss it for anything. The latter were usually women.
"There's going to be a lot of accidents," I was told by a Redskin mother,
" 'cause them Braves is sure mad they lost last Sunday." The corn dance
served to lessen the tension somewhat in midweek, and opposing families
had to dance together in the communal prayer for harmony and happiness.
But by the Saturday morning the tension was high again. The intention
to stay away was carried out by many people. Those that came, perhaps

lacking the feeling of safety in numbers, stayed mostly in their pick-ups and cars and watched from inside. The Lieutenant Governor, not himself a regular fan, placed himself between the two blocks of women and invited me to join him. Some Redskins had been to the local Spanish-American town of Pena Blanca and returned drunk and excited. Twice in the previous week I had been cautioned to "watch out for their (the Braves') magic."

I did not have long to wait. After the game had been tied up at one-one for four innings and the tension was increasing, the skies suddenly darkened, lightning flashed and thunder rolled, but no rain fell. A huge pre-storm wind swept across the valley and lifted clouds of sand many feet into the air. The field was obliterated and players crouched down to avoid being blinded by the stinging dirt. I took refuge in a Redskin car, where it was pointed out to me that had the other ground been used (the Redskins') this would not have happened as there was less loose dirt there. But the Braves had insisted on using their own inferior ground, "so that they could work more of their magic." How this complete stoppage of play was to the Braves' advantage, I failed to see.

The game should have been halted until the sand cleared but the Braves insisted on continuing to play. So play went on sporadically between sharp bursts of wind, swirling sand-storms and the crashing of thunder. And still no rain fell. Sun Chief describes how if, instead of rain, at the end of a Katsina dance only a strong wind blew spreading sand, then this showed that those who sent for the Katsinas had bad hearts and had done evil. This feeling was present at the Cochiti game. Thunder, lightning and storm clouds which bring only the dead dust and no life-giving rain are the worst of portents. One Redskin going out to bat fell on his knees, crossed himself and muttered a prayer.

Things were complicated by the presence of a non-neutral umpire. He was in fact of the Redskin faction, but was courting the daughter of a prominent Braves family (Q*). The only reason he was made umpire was that he was on leave from the Navy and hence would be returning taking any bad feelings with him. He gave a faulty-seeming decision which cost the Redskins a base. Immediately insults were flung at him by the Redskin women. Out loud they called, "Some of the Q* dirt has rubbed off on you!" and "She's got you under her skin, that Q* girl." Amongst themselves they used other epithets than girl, and muttered about "influences." Complications were added by the fact that the umpire was the son of the Lieutenant Governor, and no one wished to offend the much liked and respected official. This served in some ways to prevent more trouble.

In between the sand-storms the game continued and the score levelled to two-two at the bottom of the eighth inning. In the final innings the Redskins seemed to go to pieces as the sand lashed their faces, while the Braves hit two runs to win the game four to two. The players ran to shake hands, although some refused—an unheard-of thing in previous games. The male participants by and large tried to keep things calm. The Braves women were screaming with delight at the success of their side, while the Redskin women went away tight-lipped and furious, convinced of dirty work. That dirty work was involved was obvious to these women. The storm, the influenced umpire, the unaccountable reversal of the Redskins (an admittedly superior team under "normal" conditions), all added up— to witchcraft.

In the weeks following the games, tension remained high, with rival families not speaking. About three weeks after, however, an incident occurred which brought the whole thing out again. The Redskins had just lost a game and were returning home disconsolate, when a Braves mother accosted one of them as he entered his house. The burden of her remarks seemed to be that he had lost the game because his love life was sapping his strength. All this was said in the presence of the Redskin's wife, who was furious but mute. The Redskin hurled a few replies and went indoors. The Braves mother had not finished however; she stood on her own roof top and hurled insults across at her neighbor. The Redskin took his whole family to the Governor's house and asked for the council's protection against these onslaughts. That evening a council meeting was called, and in typical Pueblo fashion the combatants were told to shake hands and apologize to each other. An announcement was made to the Pueblo to the effect that this baseball antagonism must cease or the sport would be stopped. This was a desperate measure and a test of the council's authority that may only serve to weaken it, as the council has precious few sanctions left at its disposal. The young people are not at all likely to give up baseball whatever the council may say, and the antagonism is likely to continue. However, as harvest and winter approach and the baseball season draws to a close, hard feelings tend to soften and some wounds to heal. This factor obviously helps to preserve harmony, as there is time during winter to forget the summer's quarrels.

Competitive Western games that have been introduced into primitive societies have usually been substituted for some more violent forms of competition. For example, football in New Guinea replaced intervillage spear fighting. Baseball in the Pueblos is a competitive intrusion into essentially non-competitive social systems. While competition is between villages, no untoward events occur, as this is in line with tradition, but within villages, it is, as we have seen, potentially destructive. Pueblo institutions act as a counter to aggressive tendencies in the Puebloans and are so constructed as to eliminate and nullify aggressive conflict between people by placing them in automatically determined overlapping role situations. The baseball teams, based on voluntary recruitment and stressing competition, allow for the acting out of aggressive and competitive tendencies. Various steps are taken by the Pueblo to neutralize this effect but the participants seem bewildered in the face of the turn of events. Resort to naked authority in the settlement of interfamilial disputes is a new thing to Cochiti and in a way a confession of weakness in the social system, previously so ingeniously adequate to deal with conflict. It looks for the moment in Cochiti as if the male forces of authority and order may be able to keep the peace for the time being. But the women especially have married the old witch fears to the new sport and thus directed a whole body of deep-rooted motivations into new and pertinent channels. When the tension is high and feelings rise, the old cries of "witch" fly from the women and the suppressed rages are given full vent. It may even prove therapeutic.

NOTES

1. The research on which this paper is based was made possible by the Social Science Research Council and the Laboratory of Social Relations, Harvard University. It was carried out largely in the Pueblo of Cochiti, New Mexico (approximate population in 1959: 500, of which 300 were actually resident in the Pueblo).

2. *Sun Chief: The Autobiography of a Hopi Indian*, ed. Lee W. Simmons (New Haven: Yale University Press, 1942).

3. Full descriptions of witch beliefs in Cochiti are to be found in Noël Dumarest, *Notes on Cochiti, New Mexico (Memoirs of the American Anthropological Association*, VI, No. 3, 1919), and E. S. Goldfrank, *The Social and Ceremonial Organization of Cochiti (Memoirs of the American Anthropological Association*, No. 33, 1927).

4. The number of actual matrilocal households is declining in Cochiti, but as Fred Eggan says of the Hopi, "... the *conceptual* unity of the household group still remains" (*The Social Organization of the Western Pueblos*, Chicago, 1950, p. 30).

5. "Breathing" and "blowing" are two common ritual gestures and there is a whole system of beliefs concerning the taking in and giving out of power by breathing. Thus the importance of "the air" of the village.

6. The teams are: Cochiti (2), Santa Ana, San Felipe, Santa Clara (2), San Juan, San Ildefonso, Tesuque, Santa Fe Jays (based at the Santa Fe Indian School).

7. There was a chance that the "Little League" team, formed in 1958, would pull the two teams together by drawing on children of both parties. This failed to happen and such was the bickering and dispute over the children's team that this year it was discontinued. No one wanted the responsibility for it, as there was too much fighting between the mothers.

8. "Baseball talk" is all in English. See my "Note on Cochiti Linguistics," in Charles H. Lange, *Cochiti: A New Mexico Pueblo, Past and Present* (Austin: University of Texas Press, 1959).

Here's HUD in Your Eye

Larry McMurtry

No matter how many times they have seen Roy Rogers and John Wayne reenact the western saga, Americans are never satiated. Television producers make it available every night. Recently movie producers have turned to "adult" westerns and to variations and reversals of the formula with no loss of audience. Apparently the appeal of the western transcends the victory of good over evil; the black and white hats have been replaced by gray with ease, and the cowboy who loved only his horse has become a full-fledged heterosexual.

The western movie fulfills a unique role in present-day western communities where many males work at jobs similar to that of the mythological cowboy. There, the western movie is taken seriously and influences standards of conduct. Larry McMurtry notes the resulting effects on one small Texas town in his essay. His description of the filming of Hud *documents the torments that the cinema "dream factory" has fostered in the hinterlands of America. The estrangement of male and female by the popular culture has never before been so vividly depicted.*

Larry McMurtry is known primarily as a novelist of Texas; in addition to Horseman, Pass By *(which was the basis for* Hud*) he wrote* The Last Picture-Show, *another merciless portrait of small-town Texas, which has recently been made into a movie. William K. Everson's* Pictorial History of the Western Film *is a comprehensive introduction to the western movie.*

In 1961 I published a first novel called *Horseman, Pass By,* a title I felt sure the world would remember. To my surprise, the world quietly overlooked it, and even the few staunch friends who read the book seemed to experience the gravest difficulties with the title. Some called it *Horseman, Goodbye,* others *Horseman, Ride By,* still others *Passing the Horseman.* One colleague took to calling it *So Long, Horseman,* but since he customarily speaks of my second book, *Leaving Cheyenne,* as *Leaving El Paso* I have decided that perhaps his memory is unusually whimsical. The nadir was reached one day when a kind but doty old lady asked me if I was the man who wrote *The Four Horsemen of the Alamo.*

One evening several months after the novel was published I was sitting in Ft. Worth eating my Sunday supper when the phone rang and an excited Hollywood voice informed me that Paramount Studios was about to film my book. The title, of course, would have to be changed—it was much too poetic. Could I suggest an alternate?

Offhand, I couldn't, but I cheerfully agreed to try. I had begun to feel that my devoted readership deserved something simpler in the way of titles. A few weeks later Mr. Lloyd Anderson, the genial Paramount location manager, came to Texas to look for a film site. One evening over dinner I asked him if they had decided what the picture would be called.

"Well, not definitely," he said, poking his steak with sudden embarrassment. "They're thinking of calling it *Wild Desire.*"

After a moment of silence we went gamely on with our meal. "Write them if you've got any suggestions," Mr. Anderson said. "Don't hesitate. They'd be glad to get your ideas."

I mulled the matter over for a few days and then sent Paramount a list of about a dozen titles; the best, as I recall, was *Coitus on Horseback,* a title I had long hoped to fit onto something. In the rush of production that and the rest of my suggestions somehow got brushed aside—the next report I had, Paramount was going to call it *Hud Bannon Against the World.* At that point I decided to give up on titles and concentrate my hopes on the location committee.

If they weren't going to call it *Coitus on Horseback,* I hoped they might at least find it possible to make the film in Archer County, where I was raised. Archer County is not particularly scenic, but I was all primed to observe the impact of Hollywood on my hometown. Black humour was just being invented and I could think of no easier way to get in on it. Mr. Anderson obligingly took pictures of Archer County all one northery winter

From Larry McMurtry, *In A Narrow Grave: Essays on Texas* (Austin, Texas: Encino Press), pp. 3–19. Copyright 1968 by Larry McMurtry. Reprinted by permission of the author and the Encino Press. (Footnotes have been numbered.)

day, but all he got for his trouble was frozen hands and shots of several thousand denuded and uncinematic mesquites. Archer County clearly would not do.

In late March, 1962, Mr. Anderson informed me that a location had been chosen near the town of Claude, in the Texas Panhandle. Claude (population 895) lies thirty miles southeast of Amarillo, a city I have always regarded as Ultima Thule. Most of the filming was to be done around an old, abandoned ranch house a mile or so from Claude, but the pasture scenes would be filmed near the hamlet of Goodnight, in the rugged country bordering the Palo Duro Canyon.

When I saw the locations I had to admit that Archer County had been fairly defeated. In addition to the topographic advantages, there was a certain fitness in having a film which was in some sense about the end of ranching filmed so near the place where Old Man Goodnight had established the first Panhandle ranch. Goodnight drove the first herd into the Palo Duro in 1876 and built the great JA, the cattle ranch whose present headquarters are only a few miles from where *Hud* was filmed. No doubt the Old Man—as he is still called in that country—would have been disgusted by *Hud* if he could have seen it, but then if he were ranching today he would scarcely need go to the movies to find things to disgust him. Certainly he left the mark of his personality on the Panhandle as no other man ever has or likely ever will. The local cowboys who worked around the movie set knew a great deal more about Charles Goodnight than they knew about Paul Newman or any other movie star.

Often, during lulls in the filming, as I watched the white June thunderheads roll southward over the plains, I thought of the Old Man—a vigorous, irascible, lonely figure. In that country, looking at the weathered ranch buildings or out across the grassy, shadow-flecked plains, it was easier to believe in the ghost of Old Man Goodnight than in the costume-department darling in huaraches and yellow silk shirt who crossed and recrossed one's path.

Because of teaching duties in Ft. Worth I missed the first month of filming. I made the drive to Amarillo one evening in early June, a cool, windy evening with distant lightning and the rumble of spring thunder on the plains. Just before midnight I passed through Claude—its streets deserted, its houses dark. I didn't even slow down, there was only a yellow blinker light where the highway cuts across the main street, but I noticed as I passed through that the name on the water-tower had been changed: it read Thalia, the name of the imaginary town in my novels. It was one of the finer moments I've had as an author.

The cast and production crew were staying at the huge Ramada Inn in Amarillo. It was midnight or after when I drove up, but a stream of traffic was circling the motel like Indians supposedly circled wagon trains. I broke through only with difficulty and checked in. Two policemen were standing by the swimming pool, morosely watching the traffic.

"If it was teenagers I could see it," one said. "But it ain't. It's grown women too, hopin' Paul Newman will come out and dive off this here divin' board. Somethin' like this comes to town you find out just how crazy the public is."

It appeared that the two officers were supposed to keep the town women from swarming over the motel and breaking into the actor's bedrooms, a task they found spiritually wearying.

"I'd rather be out chousin' Meskins," one officer said. "You can't stop all these women. Funny thing is, I grew up in this town and I don't remember there being so many women around. I wouldn't a thought there was this many women in the whole Panhandle."

The other officer seconded that. Only the week before, for all their vigilance, a bulky matron had managed to get through Newman's window in the early morning, and after that he and Brandon de Wilde had shifted rooms every two or three days, to confuse enemy intelligence, as it were.

"Never seen anythang like it," one officer said.

I hadn't either, so we all three stood at the edge of the pool and watched the circling ladies for awhile. Diversion is not to be sneezed at, in Amarillo.

Paramount had rented a small flotilla of cars to transport the crew to and from the set, and the next morning one was made available to me. A publicity man offered to be my guide. When we started out he was very cheerful, but on the way the sky began to cloud over and the man's mood darkened accordingly. Rain meant lost time, and time was selling for thirty thousand dollars a day.

We turned off the highway just south of Goodnight and were immediately stopped by a man with a walkie-talkie. The road was in camera, and since they were shooting, we would have to wait. The wait lasted an hour. We listened hopefully to the hum of the walkie-talkie and watched the thickening grey clouds spume toward us out of the northwest. Just as I thought we were about to be allowed in, the guard hurried over and hastily motioned us off the road. The movie people were coming out. A huge truck with a camera boom on it came first, followed closely by about thirty cars in tight formation. The dust they raised on the dry road was sufficient to obscure whatever celebrities may have been inside.

We followed, and happily managed to park before the interceptors with the walkie-talkies got set up. As luck would have it we parked only a few yards from the car containing Paul Newman and Brandon de Wilde. They had just finished a round-up scene and were dressed like working cowboys: brown chaps, spurs, dusty boots, Levi jackets, and well-broken-in straw hats.

Their dress was perfectly authentic, indistinguishable from that of the dozen or so real cowboys who worked as extras in the cattle scenes, but even so they didn't particularly look like cowboys. De Wilde looked like someone a millionaire oil man might invite to his ranch for a weekend. He was enjoying the fantasy that he was a real cowboy, a man of the soil, but he walked like a young executive, and showed no hint of the characteristic slouch most cowboys adopt when they are afoot. On a horse he was even worse, as the film abundantly documents.

Newman came a great deal closer. He had picked up the cowboy's habit of cocking one hip higher than the other when he was standing still, and one could almost have taken him for a young, aggressive rancher, someone just beginning to make his pile. One could have, perhaps, had it not been for his eyes. His look was introspected and self-occupied, though not egotistical; he simply looked more curious about himself than most young ranchers look.

In the next hour I met a great many movie people, but the only ones from that hour that I remember well were Martin Ritt, the director, and Harriet and Irving Ravetch, the screen-writers. I am not sure how I expected to be greeted, but I was certainly ill-prepared for the barrage of apologies I faced. For the first two hours no one did anything but apologize to me, presumably because they had wrought changes in my book. I had quite expected the changes and didn't care at all—by that time I didn't think much of the novel anyway. I told them as much, but no one seemed to believe me, and my mild assurances of good will merely served to increase the general uneasiness at having an author on the set. I think they would have welcomed some display of temper. As it was, my quiet confusion was taken for Olympian disdain.

Fortunately, lunch soon came and everyone loosened up a bit. The Ravetches and I made our way to the end of the chow line and were soon joined by Newman, who had a copy of a Durrenmatt play in his hand. Harriet Ravetch was attempting to protect herself from the wind and the abrasive dust with a formidable hat and a curtain of scarves; she succeeded rather well, but others were suffering considerably. Most of the crew had adopted the dress of the region; only the art director could have been considered sartorially eccentric. He wore high-topped safari boots, heavy duck clothing, and an Australian bush hat.

Lunch was served each day by the late Walter Jetton of Ft. Worth,

who was soon to become barbecuer to the President. Whatever one may
think about Mr. Jetton's barbecue, his organization had to be admired:
the 110-man crew plus guests were stuffed with professional dispatch. The
fare was a sort of family-reunion special: pinto beans with chili pepper,
potato salad, beef, chicken, ribs, ham, coleslaw, stewed apricots, cobbler,
iced tea and coffee. Tables were ranged along the long porch of the old
ranch house, and people ate there or on the ground. Those so fastidious
as not to like Panhandle sand in their iced tea ate inside the house, which
was completely bare except for a table piled with photographs.

I have no fondness for sand and chose to eat inside. There was no
place to sit, so I stood up and idly looked through the stills as I ate. I noticed there seemed to be an awful lot of photographs of buzzards, and
when I went outside to get some more beans I asked the Ravetches how
the buzzard scene had turned out. I had merely thought to make conversation and was a little taken aback by the number of stricken looks that
turned my way. "Oh, those fucking buzzards," someone said, in a tone
that discouraged further discussion.

Later I managed to get a version of the buzzard story from some extras, who thought it hilarious. There was to be a scene in which a number
of buzzards sit around waiting for the people to leave so they can consume a dead heifer. Newman roars up and in his wild way shoots one of
the buzzards, whereupon the others fly away. The first difficulty turned
out to be getting the buzzards. There are no professional buzzard-trappers
in the Panhandle, and the few birds that showed up of their own accord
were skittery and unphotogenic. It was necessary to arrange for someone
in the vicinity of Laredo, roughly a thousand miles away, to round up a
dozen buzzards and fly them by jet to Amarillo. The plan was to wire the
buzzards to a dead tree until they had been photographed; then when
Newman shot the gun they could be released electronically and photographed again as they soared into the blue Panhandle sky.

In outline it was a good plan, but it quite failed to take into account
the mentality of buzzards. As soon as they were wired to the tree they all
began to try and fly away. The wires prevented that, of course, but did not
prevent them from falling off the limbs, where they dangled upside down,
wings flapping, nether parts exposed. It is hard to imagine anything less
likely to beguile a movie-going audience than a tree full of dangling buzzards. Everyone agreed it was unaesthetic. The buzzards were righted, but
they tried again, and with each try their humiliation deepened. Finally they
abandoned their efforts to fly away and resigned themselves to life on their
tree. Their resignation was so complete that when the scene was readied
and the time came for them to fly, they refused. They had had enough of
ignominy; better to remain on the limb indefinitely. Buzzards are not with-

out patience. Profanity, fire-crackers, and even a shotgun full of rock salt failed to move them. I'm told that, in desperation, a bird man was flown in from L.A. to teach the sulky bastards how to fly. The whole experience left everyone touchy. A day or so later, looking at the pictures again, I noticed a further provocative detail. The dead heifer that figured so prominently in the scene was quite clearly a steer. When I pointed this out to the still photographers they just shrugged. A steer was close enough; after all, they were both essentially cows. "In essence, it's a cow," one said moodily. No one wanted those buzzards back again.

As it happened, I was not the only McMurtry connected with *Hud*. The cattle used in the film belonged to my cousin Alfred, whose ranch adjoined the land where the film was made. During the many lulls in shooting I visited with Alfred and his cowhands, hoping to find out how the cowboys reacted to the whole thing. It is not every day that cowboys get the chance to assist in creating an illusion about themselves.

When I first arrived, the cowhands were all looking forward to a scene in which Brandon de Wilde was to be kicked into a fence by a cow. De Wilde's stand-in was the one who would actually be kicked, a local boy whom all the cowboys knew. He was not exactly unpopular, but it was clear that the men thought stardom had gone to his head a bit—getting kicked through a fence ten or fifteen times would probably do him good.

On the whole, the cowhands derived a great deal of amusement from the film-making. They got on famously with the production crew, most of whom were as down-to-earth as they were. The hierarchy—stars, director, screen-writers—they regarded with tolerant incredulity. They clearly felt that what was going on was beyond the reach of ordinary human comprehension, and were consequently as diffident as they would have been with a company of Martians. "I'm just working from the shoulders down," one said, summing it up for them all.

On the third day of my visit a scene was prepared in which the cattle were put through the chutes and vaccinated. To hold them for inspection, the moviemakers were proposing to use a device called a dehorning gate —a heavy gate with a number of levers and bars which lock an animal's head firmly in place. A dehorning gate is painful enough for cattle, but it is deadlier far to the man who operates it, unless the man is an expert. He must catch the thrashing animal at just the right moment as it emerges from the chute; if his timing is off and the animal kicks just right the operator may catch one or both levers in the face. Even experienced gate men miss every now and then, and a broken jaw is one of the milder results. The movie-makers, unaware of this danger, were planning to have Paul Newman operate the levers himself. De Wilde could much more safely have been kicked through the fence a few times. The cowboys all knew this, but none of them made a move to mention it to the director. I mentioned it to him, and when I asked the cowboys why they hadn't, they just shrugged. Ritt was the *director*. For all they knew he *wanted* Newman to get hit in the jaw.

Like most visitors to a film-set, I soon discovered that my curiosity about filming was more limited than I would have supposed. It seemed a slow, repetitious, tedious business, no more so to me than to the people engaged in it. Except for Martin Ritt and James Wong Howe, almost everyone connected with the movie seemed bored. Half the crew was always inactive, and this half spent its time in one of the equipment sheds, gossiping, drinking coffee, gawking and being gawked at, and talking about sex. Ritt and Howe were the only two whose attention was fully and continuously engaged by the filming: the rest killed what time there was to kill as best they could. Newman did it most sensibly, by staying in his dressing room and reading. Others did it by titillating the crowd of local visitors. De Wilde practiced riding. Melvin Douglas reminisced about the stage.

The fellow who got the biggest kick out of dazzling the locals was a sort of Westian cowboy, a lineal descendant of Earl Schoop in *The Day of the Locust.* His mannerisms were updated and his idiom was closer to Stoney Burke than William S. Hart, but he was still very clearly a marginal man—a creature of the fringe. His nickname was S.C. (for Super Cock), and his stock-in-trade was sex. He talked, thought, knew nothing else. He had an official position, but I never saw him exercise it. Had it not been for his ability to keep the idle members of the crew amused, he would have been dead weight.

Whether his nickname flattered him I cannot attest, but I did observe that he had a way with women: he might not have been able to take them in, but he could certainly draw them out. Several times I saw him introduce himself to a group of farm women, none of whom had probably uttered ten words about sex in their entire lives. His candor seemed to hypnotize them; doubtless in their experience it was unprecedented. Within twenty minutes he would have them talking about their orgasms, those of them, at least, who had had any to talk about. Many were put on the defensive and found themselves attempting to defend their husband's performances, an awkward and unaccustomed task. Whatever the defense, S.C. always managed to be pleasantly derisive, pointing out to this or that little lady that she probably lacked a valid standard of comparison.

Later, in Hollywood, I saw S.C. lurking outside the studio in a four-year-old car, waiting to try his luck with the secretaries when they emerged at five o'clock. He looked much diminished. To the little ladies of Los Angeles he was just another cowboy shirt.

In Texas, as a general rule, money comes into the conversation much oftener than sex: on the movie set the reverse prevailed. Millions were being spent, but were seldom mentioned. Sex got mentioned constantly— the tedium of location work had to be relieved some way. At one point we were out on the plains shooting a scene with two longhorns when a heavy rain shower hit. Everyone piled into cars to wait for it to pass over, and I landed in a car with Martin Ritt and several of the actors. Someone mentioned a Richard Burton doll, the latest in Hollywood toys. You wound it up and it did incredible things to Elizabeth Taylor. This reminded someone of something that lady was rumoured to have done during the filming of *Giant,* which in turn reminded someone else of a disease Marlon Brando was rumoured to have caught in Tahiti, while doing *Mutiny on the Bounty.* Things went on in this vein for several minutes and I suddenly noticed that the back of the driver's neck had grown very red. I don't know what spades are called in California, but I have noted that the copulative act is usually called fucking, mixed company or no. We were mixed company, and the driver, a local man, was most probably a deacon in the Baptist church. None of the movie people even noticed that he had turned red.

On this particular day, Brandon de Wilde was feeling gloomy. It was clear that he was struggling hard to leave adolescence behind, but it wasn't always clear whether he was winning or losing. The most distasteful part of movie-making, he complained, was that strange women kept trying to crawl in bed with him. He was an engaged man, and he had scruples. Some locations were worse than others: during the filming of *All Fall Down* his scruples had been overcome some eighteen times. A nightmare. A colleague unkindly pointed out that his scruples were of about the consistency of toilet paper, but I don't think de Wilde heard him. He was trying to decide whether to fly to El Paso that weekend, to test his scruples against the fleshpots of Juarez.

I was only around the set a few days, but that was quite long enough. The presence of the Californians set the life of the Panhandle in an odd perspective, one that I won't soon forget. I remember the stringy, hard-handed farm women giggling at S.C.'s indecencies; the solid, silent driver turning red; the wives and daughters of Amarillo, circling the Ramada Inn at night. In retrospect, the reactions seem perfectly predictable. The men of the area felt directly threatened: here was an energy and a masculinity that seemed stronger than their own. Women, on the other hand, felt expectant. Hollywood with all its money and its possibility was finally there. Anything might happen. Their leaden lives might be made golden, somehow.

When the movie was released, West Texas reacted ambivalently, but

---

along much these same lines. It was said to be profane, and members of the hard-shell sects stayed away. A lady of my acquaintance offered to stay home and pray for her family while they went. Despite its taint, a great many people did go see it, and most of them came away enthusiastic. It was generally regarded as an accurate, even flattering picture of the area. The Panhandle preened itself for a time, and a baby or two was named Hud.

Any number of people assured me they knew someone just like Hud. *Their* Hud was a real hellion, they told me—if they were men their tone indicated that he was the sort of man they almost wished they had been: tough, capable, wild, undomesticated.

Invariably they would hasten to add that, so far as acting went, Melvin Douglas took the cake. Hud might tempt them, but they knew well enough that old Homer was the sort of man their fathers had wanted them to be. Hud had made terms with the twentieth century, whereas Homer was unwaveringly faithful to the nineteenth, and in those parts the nineteenth century ideal has not yet lost its force. That Homer was a dreadfully sentimentalized version of the nineteenth century cattleman was apparently never noticed, except by Pauline Kael. Her excellent essay provides all that is needed in the way of criticism of Hud.[1]

If the men of the area wavered and were ultimately unable to identify either with Homer or with Hud, the women had no such problem. Most of them probably identified with the unseen woman whose bed Hud leaves when the movie opens. You don't find many Texas women willing to identify with a ranch cook, not even one that looks like Patricia Neal. Women seldom mentioned Miss Neal to me until after her illness, when tragedy had placed her clearly in a domestic context.

To date I have seen *Hud* six times, twice on my own and four times due to circumstances beyond my control. One showing was a bit unusual: it was to a college film group and the young projectionist had neglected to bring his cinemascope adjuster. Since the screen was only twelve feet wide the distortions that resulted were bizarre. The verticals were elongated, the horizontals squashed. Hud's Cadillac became a fat Volkswagen. The beautiful proportions were lost and one was left with nothing but the drama.

The sixth time around I decided I couldn't bear to watch it again, so I sat outside and listened. Again, I was left with the drama.

Those two showings did much to bring home to me what was excellent in the film and what was poor. The camera work of James Wong Howe

1. *I Lost It At The Movies*, pp. 78–94.

was very fine, and the acting of Newman and Miss Neal equally so. The camera was completely faithful to the beauty and pitilessness of the Panhandle: it showed what is there, a land so powerful that it is all but impossible to live on it pleasantly. Newman and Miss Neal took advantage of their roles as brilliantly as the camera took advantage of the terrain; between them they saved what was otherwise a weak and badly shaped dramatic vehicle.

The first time I saw the film I thought the screenplay was superb. All I heard was the wit, and there is wit. By the third showing I had begun to wince, and by the sixth it seemed to me clear that the screen-writers had erred badly in following my novel too closely. *Horseman, Pass By* has its moments, but they do not keep it from being a slight, confused, and sentimental first novel. The screen-writers had the good sense to shift the focus from Lonnie to Hud, but otherwise they were content to follow the book, and as a result most of the confusion and all of the sentimentality were carried over. Touches which were overpoetic in the novel become merely awkward in the screenplay; occasionally a line of description from the book would be turned into a line of dialogue, but with no change in the adjectives, a practice hardly recommendable. Worst of all, they chose to stick with the novel's faulty structure, which meant that old Homer collapsed as pathetically and unconvincingly in the movie as he had in the book.

Still, I am grateful to the screen-writers for inadvertently pointing out to me where my story should have gone; and I am even more grateful to them for bringing home to me how careful one must be of the lyric impulse when writing about the Southwest. Prose, I believe, must accord with the land. The forests of East Texas reach to Yoknapawtapha—someone like William Humphrey can occasionally get away with the Faulknerian density. For the West, it doesn't work. A viny, tangled prose would never do for a place so open; a place, to use Ross Calvin's phrase, where the sky determines so much. A lyricism appropriate to the Southwest needs to be as clean as a bleached bone and as well-spaced as trees on the llano. The elements still dominate here, and a spare, elemental language, with now and then a touch of elegance, will suffice. We could probably use Mark Twain, but I doubt we're yet civilized enough to need a Henry James.

Since the movie was released, I have not been through the town of Claude. I imagine they have put the correct name back on the water-tower, and now the name Thalia is on no water-tower anywhere. In June, though, the thunderheads will still roll south, across the JA and the Palo Duro; and in Claude and Clarendon, Muleshoe and Quitaque (Kitty-quay) the old timers at their whittling still tell stories of the Old Man, Charles Goodnight. The stories slowly alter, become local myths. Some remember that the Indians called him Buenas Noches. They can tell the sad story of the last running, about the ragged band of Comanches who came all the way from their reservation in Oklahoma to Goodnight's ranch on the Quitaque, to beg a buffalo of him. At first he refused, but in time he relented and gave them a scrawny young bull, thinking they would drive it back to the reservation and eat it. Instead, whipping up their thin, miserable ponies, they ran it before him and killed it with lances and arrows, then sat looking at it for a time, remembering glories and centuries gone.

Such a story catches a whole people's loss, but only a few old men and a few writers tell it today,[2] and the old men, for that matter, usually tell it as a story about the craziness of Indians.

The Old Man has become a local god, his legends recounted in a few ranch houses, a few courthouses, and the domino parlors of a few West Texas towns. The old timers and the cowboys know about him, but the youngsters of Texas don't: they know Hud, that keen, hard, attractive bastard who drives a Cadillac. Since the youngsters have never heard of the Old Man they don't know that Hud is his descendant, and the few who know both are so partisan to the Old Man that they would adamantly deny that the two are related. But related they are, though they knew different times, and put their powers to different uses.

---

2. See John Graves, *Goodbye to a River*, pp. 62–63.

Remember Bomb Shelters?

Roy Bongartz

The hula hoop, electric toothbrush, and football stadium reveal much about America in the 1960s, but the individual bomb shelter may prove to be the artifact most intriguing to future scholars. An attempt to explain the popularity of the shelters would go far beyond the fear of nuclear war. The shelters might indicate an optimistic attitude, a belief that people could survive a nuclear war, and that life would be worth living after such a conflict. Certainly the do-it-yourself quality of many of the shelters would seem to have implications for an understanding of American individualism. Or the shelters may, on the contrary, divulge nothing more than conformity to a passing fad. Certainly, as Roy Bongartz implies, the most fascinating question is why they suddenly went out of style.

Numerous scholars have commented upon the effect of the cold war and the possibility of nuclear war on American culture. Two different but equally worthwhile essays probing this subject are Christopher Lasch's "The Cultural Cold War: A Short History of the Congress For Cultural Freedom," and Norman Mailer's "The White Negro." Susan Sontag's study of science-fiction films in this book, "The Imagination of Disaster," also contains pertinent insights.

Come, my people, enter thou into thy chambers, and shut
thy doors about thee: hide thyself as it were for a little
moment, until the indignation be overpast.—Isaiah 26:20

It is only ten years now since that ancient time we panicked and tried to
crawl into safe primeval dust and built all those bomb shelters in our
cellars and threatened to shoot off the head of any intruding neighbor.
Somehow it all seems very far away from us, as remote as the French
Maginot Line of the Thirties, which also briefly provided a cozy sense of
security for the good guys. The great shelter boom, although well within
range of the childhood memories of our newest teen-agers, is dead as a
mackerel and gone from our minds. As if some secret all-clear signal had
called out an "Ally-ally-infree!", all those elaborate cement-block dog-
houses with their stocks of survival crackers and ammunition have been
abandoned, or turned into junk boxes or wine cellars or tool sheds or
lawn-mower garages.

What happened was that the upstanding citizen—the frustrated
rugged individualist, of limited imagination, perhaps, yet invincible anyway,
like Skeezix—unhumorously and heroically defended his family by digging
in when his government began seeing Russian bombers behind every
cloud. He had, however, a short attention span. The bomb never dropped,
and he soon said the hell with it. But if he thought that hiding in the cellar
was a good idea ten years ago, he ought to take another look around
today. The fact that newer threats to his environment are coming more
from general cosmic carelessness than out of any enemy's malice would
not make much difference in shaking off an accidental attack of nerve gas
or bubonic plague. Maybe he needs more than just a shelter—a new
planet, possibly.

It did take the American some considerable time, during the Fifties,
to build up to an acceptable level of terror, where he was ready to bur-
row. Postwar Europeans had been saying all along that it was too bad the
U.S. couldn't have experienced a few sample bombs, on the ground that it
would have made Americans more sympathetic to the torn-up other half
of the world, made them more human, more jumpy. In May, 1955, when a
flight of Russian bombers was spotted heading for the Pacific Coast, and
a real alert was sounded in the streets of Berkeley and Oakland, nobody
paid it the least attention. The identity of the planes had been mistaken, of
course, but the alert was real, and a team of sociologists set to work on a
monumental study of this indifference to danger, which eventually proved
only the obvious fact that people weren't really worried yet. In November,

From *Esquire*, 73 (5), May 1970, 130, 198, 200–204. Reprinted by permission of Esquire Magazine
and the author; copyright © 1970 by Esquire, Inc.

1958, telephone lines accidentally tied in with the Civil Defense system set off air-raid warnings all over Washington, D.C., and only five percent of the people tried to find shelter. In September, 1959, when the Chicago White Sox won the pennant, air-raid sirens were sounded in Chicago for five minutes. It was the standard alert signal, but only a third of the population thought it might have been that, and comparatively few took it seriously. Two percent did believe it meant "something bad," though—the panic was just beginning.

Then the cold war chilled and suddenly everyone had to have a shelter in his house. Schlock outfits installed phony "blast-proof" rooms with "100-PF," a hard-to-disprove "protection factor" supposedly a hundred times safer than no shelter at all. The Federal Trade Commission had to regulate shelter ads against false claims and switch selling; one rule was, "Scare tactics such as the employment of horror pictures calculated to arouse unduly the emotions of prospective shelter buyers shall not be used." A shelter salesman's manual was published by an outfit called Nuclear Shelter Consultants, and a booklet called "Mr. Atom and his Sinister Blanket" was issued by the National Concrete Masonry Association. Mail-order houses sprang up all over the country to provide such items as a thermoelectric generator to power a transistor radio with a kerosene flame, a "family radiation-measurement kit," a pen-sized Geiger counter called "Chirpee" that chirped to radioactivity, and wallet-sized preparedness cards with such printed instructions as, "If you cannot reach a shelter lie flat on the ground face down, or crouch on the floor of a car." A copy of "What to do until the Doctor Comes," by William Bolton, M.D., was also stocked in many shelters.

The mania brought with it a moral issue that split the country: in a bombing, should intruders into a shelter be shot? Civil Defense coordinators officially instructed residents of Beaumont and Bakersfield, in California, to arm themselves against the hordes of refugees who would pour in upon them from Los Angeles in a nuclear attack, and immediately Nevada began arming its border against the same threat. Novelist Pat Frank threatened to shoot anyone he found in the emergency food supply in his Florida house, especially since he had in it some vacuum-packed cigarettes and some liquor, for trading. "I have a hunch that one year after the outbreak of nuclear war a pound of tobacco will be worth more than a pound of gold," Frank wrote. "If you don't have a gun and are concerned about protecting your home, I'd recommend the Remington 66, a .22-caliber automatic rifle with nylon stock, so light that your wife can easily handle it. And if there is no war, it is a fun gun."

Some religious spokesmen thought differently. Billy Graham said, "I feel a primary responsibility for my family, but I don't believe I myself could stay in a shelter while my neighbor had no protection." Another clergyman said, "Christian believers ought to greet today's almost morbid interest in fallout shelters with a smile and a tear—a smile, because it challenges the popular fallacy that death is always a tragedy, that the essence of human life lies in mere physical survival; a tear, because man seeks refuge from atomic radiation more than from the fallout of evil." Dr. Edward L. R. Elson of the National Presbyterian Church predicted: "Some very sturdy Christians will decide to live dangerously, to ignore preparation of shelters and to die with dignity as part of the brightly colored cloud. No Christian or any other citizen should be asked to provide an individual shelter for himself or his family."

But thousands of home shelters were built nevertheless. A Harvard group mocked anti-shelterists in a Committee for a Sane Navigational Policy that came out against lifeboats in ships on the ground that these would undermine passengers' confidence in the captain. A private shelter in Sylvan Shores, Florida, sold rooms for just twenty-five families, four in a family, at $1500 a room. The underground complex had a decontamination room for late arrivals, although only the immediate families of the original subscribers would be admitted inside. The residents would be equipped to live forever, having supplies of farming tools and seeds for fast-growing vegetables, and they could stay down in the shelters for six months by bringing in filtered air with foot-powered generators. The place was quickly sold out, and the occupants were sworn to secrecy; the caves were hidden under an orange grove. The long-range planning included three crypts with the latest plastic "body bags" for anyone who might want to die of natural causes during a bombing. In Danvers, Massachusetts, a motel put in a shelter that could double as a nest for the beginning of a whole new (and intriguing) population after an attack. Besides sixty transient motorists, the proud parents would include fifty locals: doctors, nurses, machine gunner, veterinarian with cow, bull, chicken, rooster.

In Milwaukee, the installation of shelters created tensions in some neighborhoods where certain houses weren't going to get them, so contractors pretended to be television repairmen, and delivered materials in unmarked trucks for secrecy. A Connecticut engineer designed a "poor man's shelter" that could be built for $30. Dairyman Gordon Roberts built a shelter for a hundred cows on his farm at Elk Horn, Iowa.

As for the problem of what to do with pets, writer Pat Frank had this advice: "The quick and simple way is a .22-caliber bullet in the cortex of the brain." Frank also suggested: "You certainly should lay in a supply of sunburn lotion. Even if the nearest explosion is miles away, it is likely that someone in your family will be burned or crisped." He warns of possible toothache, so be sure to store a pair of pliers.

Another sort of shelter would be boats moving slowly up and down the coastline; fifteen or more feet of water depth would protect from fallout, except for that dropping on deck—this would have to be washed off constantly with special pumps provided for the purpose. A Long Island boatyard planned to launch all stored boats in any emergency. A New York State expert foresaw a great number of barges loaded with people, moored in the canal system—but if the canal froze over, the fallout could not sink to the bottom, and you'd be in trouble. One improvised shelter that could be set up in a hurry was made of dresser drawers full of bricks, to be stacked on a table: "Be careful not to overload the table to the point where it will collapse," read the official instructions. In another, you dug a hole, pulled two doors off your house and lay them over the hole, piled the dirt on top, and hopped down inside.

After the home-shelter craze, interest in public shelters also began to grow. Local Civil Defense officials had some special problems: how to get building owners to cooperate by lending their basements to the cause, who was to put up the "Shelter" signs, and how to make the arrows fit into the interior decor. One official, worried about responsibility for the storing of emergency rations and equipment, said, "We will have to put them in vaults. And the next question will be who will have the keys to the vault, and that will be a big headache. When you get out into some sections where they will knock you in the head for a nickel, they won't hesitate to steal the supplies also." A Federal Civil Defense Guide faced and solved, all in one paragraph, a problem that had arisen in Civil-Defense training: "The medical kit contains phenobarbital tablets. These are not considered necessary or desirable for training purposes and should therefore be disposed of in a safe manner. . . . It is recommended that the tablets be disposed of by flushing them down a sink or other drain in the presence of a witness. An affidavit should be prepared, to be signed by both the person who disposed of the tablets, and by the witness. The original should be sent to the Office of Civil Defense regional director for retention in official records." An emergency radio network called Conelrad was set up to transmit without revealing the location of transmitters, thus preventing radio targeting by an enemy; the system was soon scrapped when it seemed obvious that the Russians had already found out where New York is. Some towns installed outdoor loudspeakers; Salina, Kansas, for example, boasted that it could reach almost all of its 45,000 people through only thirteen units of a system called "Big Voice."

In 1961, when the Berlin crisis and Soviet nuclear testing exacerbated American fears, home shelters seemed to many righteous folk a faint hope for survival, compared to the suicidal official policy of evacuation. Then, in 1962, President Kennedy proposed construction of separate public shelters. It was too late. Abruptly the national obsession with self-burial died away. Congress killed the Kennedy program, and Civil Defense was left to hunt for an odd spare basement in unfashionable parts of town, and to issue reports to itself. But Civil Defense could still learn, from its richer brothers at the Pentagon, the Monte Carlo Technique, as the rules of mathematical probability are known when playing Missile Argle Bargle or Blind Battalion's Buff. Stated simply, you take a number, any number, then add, subtract, divide, or multiply to, from, or by any given number of megatons. Before you know it, you're playing Permutations, and, all these eight years, that is what Civil Defense has been doing, on a steadily reduced diet of money (from $257,200,000 in 1962 to $61,000,000 in 1969).

A cardinal rule of Permutations is to take nothing for granted. One Civil Defense gamester named David W. Johnston won't even assume that down is the right direction to dig until he looks it over carefully: "There are only three ways to go to avoid the explosion: up, sideways, and down. Up is obviously impractical, although some airborne persons might survive. Sideways (or evacuation) is good if there is time for it. The only remaining direction is down." From this modest start he works it out that for a twenty-megaton bomb your shelter ought to be about 600 feet deep; for a hundred megatons, make it 850 feet below the surface of the earth. Another ace player, William M. Brown, who wrote a tremendous report on "Optimum" Blast Shelter Programs for Civil Defense, beautifully describes ways of using special shorthand in the game:

"It turns out that the results can generally be expressed in terms of a simple vulnerability criterion, β, which represents the maximum number of fatalities expected from a 1-MT explosion. . . . For a program with a given β, for any attack consisting of an array of megaton weapons [Wj] the number of blast fatalities among the sheltered is given by the equation:

$$\text{Fatalities} = \beta \, \Sigma j \, Wj$$

Brown gives sample problems at the end: "Assume threat is 300 10-MT bombs. Assume maximum mortalities allowable: 40,000,000 or 133,000 per 10-MT bomb. . . ." In most of his brainteasers he gets nearly everybody into a shelter, except those in Manhattan. "Either leave one quarter to fate or plan to relocate balance of a half million Manhattanites." The only way to stay in Permutations is to think up clever new variables, such as this gem by Brown:

"If we had an acceptable trade-off between lives and property values, as seen by us or the enemy (e.g., suppose he deemed one life equivalent to $20,000 of property), then our sheltering plan could be reoriented to reflect this trade-off. For some designs the population vulnerability might be made relatively smaller than β in areas where property damage is apt to be greater, thus leveling somewhat the combined value of the target to the enemy in terms of people plus property. This approach may only be partially satisfactory, however, because any hypothetical dollar value assigned to a person by us as the enemy's view has a basically large uncertainty...."

One who quickly soured on Permutations was Gerard Piel, publisher of *Scientific American,* who said, "A primary responsibility for this hoax on public opinion must be attributed to those authors of fraud by computer who produced the literature that argues the feasibility of thermonuclear war." But the smart Rand Corporation played a sort of Russian Permutations in a report on Soviet civil defense, inferring, from a foggy photograph of a mysterious closed door in a Moscow subway, the existence of a vast underground shelter system. The Rand writer, Leon Gouré, reports that the Blackout Service operates from the electric-power department and is always ready for "a successful blackout," even though the Russians realize that modern missiles don't need lights to find their targets. "The effort is apparently still considered worthwhile, especially as it is cheap and simple," says Gouré, making the Russians seem terribly familiar.

Back home, the earlier ostrich mentality of the public finally, by 1966, filtered down (or up, or sideways) to Top Permutations Headquarters. The North American Air Defense Command dug itself into a 9500-foot mountain near Colorado Springs, occupying eleven two- and three-story buildings sitting on 937 heavy springs, where 1250 technicians watch the world's horizons through radar eyes that span the earth from Greenland south in all directions, ready to send a bomb or missile to any foreign address. The elaborate communications circuits bring in an annual phone bill from the American Telephone & Telegraph Company and the Mountain States Telephone and Telegraph Company for $85,500,000. A Civil Defense center rents a room in here that is connected with 16,000 warning centers around the U. S. There is even a space-defense center here, with a staff of seventy men who keep their eyes on all the satellites for any false moves, prepared to knock them out of the sky with Thor missiles. The personnel—there are sixty-six women among them—in the mountain could give the world another kind of choice in its type of descendants in case everybody else was killed in the final Permutation; we'd have either a race of traveling salesmen, from the Danvers motel, or a race of troglodytic electronic-screen watchers from Colorado Springs.

Recently, in Washington, Civil Defense officials have had to rely on a resolute cheerfulness in the face of decreasing funds and warnings of doomsayers that the mega-death-balancing act is an unfunny joke. They produce such optimistic thoughts as the prediction that even if Country A (the fifty-three major U. S. cities) was totally destroyed, Country B (the rest of the U. S.) would not only be okay, but could easily rebuild Country A in ten years, if it wanted to. Meanwhile, "surviving wealth per capita could be greater than it is now," says an official. But there is reason to believe that Country B would leave well enough alone. The provinces never liked New York anyway, and there is no proof the yokels would build another one. Civil Defense people pass over the fact that Country B has most of the strategic airfields in it, so that it would be as likely to be wiped out as Country A would be, and there is no use arguing with them about it, because they see the bright side as if their lives depended on it, and, anyway, as soon as you accept such ploys as the "Country A" and "Country B" that they've made up, you're playing Permutations, and it's their game, and it's fixed.

Civil Defense busies itself with ever-hopeful paper studies of blown-up power systems, water supplies, oil fields, sewage plants, and railroads, and it plans airlifts (without planes) and "local assessments of conflagration potential of urban areas" (without fires). Its exhibit called "Maintaining Life in a Hostile Environment" concludes manfully that if man can survive on the ocean floor, in space, and on the moon, then by George he can make it on earth as well. Its tests of blast overpressure on walls "have been encouraging" and its movie *Once to Make Ready* won an honors award in the American Film Festival. By adding together the measurements of many public buildings, Civil Defense concludes it has 187,000,000 shelter spaces right here, not counting another 31,000,000 found in a home survey of twenty-six states. These last are just ordinary basements, mostly, but a computer in Jeffersonville, Indiana, has been sending advice to surveyed homes on how to make shelters out of them. "Because no follow-up is planned to determine how much of the advice is actually followed," Civil Defense says, "the value of the survey is unknown." But already half of the public shelters have received emergency supplies, including fiber-drum portable toilets made for Civil Defense by workshops for the blind, and medical kits "adequate to serve emergency needs generally of normal, healthy persons." In case other types should turn up, Civil Defense is working on a non-addictive painkiller.

Civil Defense is looking forward to hooking in with the Navy's Project Sanguine, a hundred-mile-long stretch of low-frequency radio transmitters in Wisconsin, costing $1,500,000,000, that will be able to reach any point on earth, including submarines. It will tie in all U. S. strategic forces, and Civil Defense as well; and already, in tests, the system has kept all the local telephones ringing, charged wire fences, and screwed up railroad signals and television reception. The Navy has recently given $700,000 to the telephone company to help find a way to avoid this interference. But the juice won't be turned on until late in 1970, and there are people who think that, in spite of all its programs, Civil Defense could never be much of a help in a nuclear attack. Walter Cronkite said last year, "If there are enough of us left after a nuclear war to carry on our government, one can safely forecast that the first order of business will be the gosh-darndest investigation this nation has ever witnessed. Subject? What Ever Happened to Civil Defense?"

What happened is that the people have abandoned civil defense. A Massachusetts doctor says that people thought he was a fool when he built his shelter. "Now I guess I was," he says. The rusty cans of food and moldy biscuits have long ago been thrown out of most of them, and the shelters serve such various uses now as mushroom farms and teenage dance areas (soundproof!). Rare exceptions are Douglass and Ruth Walker, who live in Safe City, a cave a hundred and fifty feet under the ground eighty miles from New York City. It all began when Walker started a business for storing duplicates of vital records for city firms, but he got to like it down there, and fixed it up, with orange-painted walls, false windows, and a winding staircase. "I wanted to get away from the usual idea people have about caves—that they're cold, dark, damp places," Walker says. He and his wife enter their apartment past an armed guard, through a seven-ton steel door. Inside, Walker keeps busy over a collection of stamps and guns, while his wife arranges her ceramics pieces, and an old music box plays *Dream of Heaven.*

Also cold now is that once-raging moral question: Who is to be let into your shelter? Consider just briefly what happened at Hiroshima and you can see that the question was never complete anyway. A thirteen-year-old girl said: "My face was so distorted and changed that people couldn't tell who I was. After a while I could call others' names but they couldn't recognize me." In such a case, how can you be sure it's really your daughter you're letting into your shelter? In a like manner, many of the logical moves people are supposed to make, according to instructions on paper, in a bombing, just aren't made; in *Hiroshima Diary,* Dr. Michihiko Hachiya writes: "Those who were able walked silently toward the suburbs in the distant hills, their spirits broken, their initiative gone. When asked whence they had come, they pointed to the city and said, 'This way,' and when asked where they were going, pointed away from the city and said, 'That way.' They were so broken and confused that they moved and behaved like automatons."

Over the years, official policy has had to shift around as its aims collapsed for lack of factual support. The evacuation idea gave way to shelter; the shelter hope was then downgraded to mean only fallout protection. Now, speaking of the shelter policy in his own state, a Rochester, New York, scientist, Dr. Everett M. Hafner, said, "It stopped talking about the radiation levels at two weeks. But it did give the interested citizen the opportunity to extrapolate, if he could do calculus. To our horror we discovered that the official policy does not protect the people. You are dead a few weeks after you come out of the shelter." A more cruel threat, rarely mentioned by Civil Defense people either in Russia or in the U.S., is the fire storm, such as killed 300,000 persons in Dresden in one night, and 200,000 persons in Tokyo. People in blast-proof shelters were simply cremated. Publisher Piel says that a thousand-megaton bomb at satellite height could set afire six Western states, and though this may look like a move in a Permutations game, the fact that retina burns were suffered 345 miles away from a Pacific nuclear explosion in 1958 shows that the power of these new weapons is beyond the strength of a dresser drawer full of bricks. The current response of Civil Defense to fire has been to produce some "dimensionless equations" by burning potato-starch distillate, and to set up some fan-type anemometers in forty acres of piñon trees on the California-Nevada border and set the woods on fire.

For any amateur of black futures, two other forms of world murder should be his dish of tea: chemical and biological warfare. Civil Defense has no intention of getting itself involved with such hopeless threats as these, and summarily writes them off thus: "Chemical agents are not considered a major strategic threat. . . . Although the possibility of employment of biological agents against U.S. population centers cannot be ruled out, neither a chemical nor biological threat against the continental U.S. warrants, at this time, the attention and priority given to defense against the effects of nuclear weapons."

Civil Defense limits itself to some circumspect advice on these unwelcome weapons. Soap and water is generally best for washing off toxic gases, or lye can be used for nerve gas and bleaches for blister gas. A publication entitled *Personal Preparedness in the Nuclear Age* advises, "Explosives can be used to blast paths through contaminated vegetation such as high grass." But the best protection from gases is, "Avoid a contaminated area, or an area likely to be contaminated." Detection of gases is hard; a special crayon shows a color change in the presence of mustard gas. A nerve-gas detector has to have its chemicals changed every day, and gives a lot of false alarms anyway. In any case, shelters are not supplied with any of these, nor with gas masks, nor with atropine, the antidote for nerve gas that has to be administered within one minute of exposure, or death results. Artificial respiration, or mouth-to-mouth resuscitation, is indicated for nerve-gas victims, but rescuers are warned to blow *small puffs* when saving an infant: "You may rupture his lung if you blow in too much air at one time. Watch his chest rise to make sure you are giving him the right amount of air with each puff."

The booklet says of biological weapons, "Decontamination of large areas and the exteriors of most buildings is not considered practical. . . . " It suggests breathing through a filter in case of attack, should there be any way of detecting it, which there is not: "Common household items that would be useful as filters are a large wad of absorbent cotton, a man's handkerchief (eight layers), a bath towel (two layers), or toilet tissue (three layers). These items must be used dry to be effective, and be held tightly over the nose and mouth to eliminate air leaks." The advice goes on: "Safe food and water is essential for protection against biological-warfare agents." Another Civil Defense adviser says, "Unfortunately, immunizing agents have not been perfected for some of the potential biological-warfare agents. This is a characteristic which can influence the selection of a biological agent for an attack. Likewise, immunity levels obtainable with the accepted antigens and methods may not hold against the challenge of high dosage and unusual organisms. It does not seem practical to immunize the entire population against all of these agents simultaneously." So there we are. It may be worth noting that the American Chemical Society, meeting at the height of the nuclear jitters a decade ago, reported, "Our emphasis throughout is on keeping the individual threats from chemical, biological, and radiological agents in proper perspective. . . . All are major threats. Each must be regarded as on, or nearly on, a par with the other two." Of course, the chemists might be accused of bias in favor of chemicals and germs, while Civil Defense, finding the nuclear threat more understandable, plumps for bombs. The rest of us will just have to sit back and wait to see who was right.

Before that happens, though, we may get it in the neck from a cloud of nerve gas wafting by error across U.S. 40 out in Utah. Mistakes similar to the one at Dugway Proving Grounds, in Utah, in the spreading of a teacup of anthrax bacteria fifteen years ago, causing permanent contamination of an eight-mile piece of land there, may prove our own government experimenters to be the most terrifying danger. When they get busy, we could all use a shelter. Of these germs that are supposed to be ready to go after our enemies, Dr. Gustave L. Davis of the Committee for Environmental Information, in St. Louis, says, ". . . their fate in the environment is not well understood. We do not understand how or why natural epidemics start, spread and maintain themselves. Therefore, the fate of biological agents in the field is unknown and uncontrollable."

With this wild array of malevolence on all sides, it's probably natural on some days for us to feel like an ant an inch under the lowering sole of a giant shoe. A snug, warm place would be awfully welcome, especially for the young kids, who after all have got to outlive us somehow. The U.S. Army has just the thing, an Infant Protector, that maybe the Civil Defense people could be lobbied into procuring for us all. Its description reads: "This pup-tent-like device has a strong aluminum frame upon which is fastened a tough vinyl plastic covering with two large filter pads in the rear. There is a clear panel window for observation of the child by its parent. The flap is lifted, and the child is placed in it with its food, toys, etc." Now we tiptoe down cellar—there's a shoulder strap included on the Protector—and we carefully place Baby under some boards piled high with concrete blocks. The filters will keep out anything from mustard gas and nerve-gas agents to South African tick-bite fever, rickettsiae and bubonic plague bacteria. You're safe, safe, old Baby Bunting, old kid— just as safe as anybody can be these days.

Love and Sex
In the Romance Magazines

David Sonenschein

While modern America has witnessed the destruction of some distinctions based on sex, many aspects of the popular culture continue to survive by appealing to one sex. A significant commercial market for popular entertainment is still based on traditional concepts of the "female mind." The modern gothic novel produces a comfortable income for its authors (some of whom are males writing under female pseudonyms), the celebrity magazines persist in following the alleged exploits of a mythological figure named "Jackie," and the soap operas appear to be permanent fixtures on daytime television. One of the most mystifying products for women is the "romance" magazine. Seemingly based on formulas involving illicit sexual relations, deviant sex, unwed mothers, and rape, romance magazines continue to have a large following in an age when more explicit treatment of these matters can be found in any movie theater. Apparently, their popularity does not derive from the mere use of sex but from the specific context in which it is depicted.

David Sonenschein has analyzed the content of romance magazines. His article should be compared with the work available on the soap operas; the best study is Mary Jane Higby's Tune in Tomorrow. *Joan Barthel has written an amusing report of one of the most successful soap operas in "The World Has Turned More Than 3,200 Times."*

It is fairly common to say that the mass media and popular culture contain suggestions as to many of our culture's values. There may be some disagreement as to the exact boundaries of these systems, but a general consensus among social scientists on this seems to exist. The anthropologist in particular is prone to examine textual material for value and symbolic content, for it is within this realm that he sees the very essence of culture. This area is our concern here.

Two major interests have motivated the present analysis: one in cultural conceptions of "pornography" and the other in forces of cultural socialization. A great deal of the mass media has been identified with, even defined as, "pornography," "obscenity," or "objectionable" material. Hard-core erotica (the sole, specific depiction of sexual action) has been referred to as "the mass media of sex," but now we find sex permeates much of the media around us; items readily available on the market that deal directly (girlie magazines) or indirectly (advertising) in erotica have been called "soft-core" pornography. Thus, the traditional and perennial question of obscenity—what are its effects?—is asked of a far wider range of material than before; in fact, many are asking that question of what they see to be no less than their total environment ("it's all around us!").

In addition, however, to the mere mention of acts, an extremely crucial aspect of erotica is the way in which sex is described with attendant values. It is this total configuration that becomes the major variable in socialization. Through this process of "social scripting," acts, contexts, and consequences are spelled out as behavioral alternatives in various interpersonal settings. It is this that determines for the observer or reader whether the sex is arousing or not, moral or immoral, and consequently, pornographic or not.

Beyond the immediate action in the stories, we find that sexual behaviors and attitudes are inseparably linked to broader cultural symbol systems, and it is within these that we begin to find and understand what it is that may be "wrong" with certain kinds of activities. We know that sexuality, previously thought of as a monolithic "drive" that motivates and determines a number of behaviors and dispositions, is in fact much more diffuse in human personalities and social systems. We may gain a sense of this linkage in the ways sex is connected to non-sexual values and activities in the lives and thoughts of people in the magazine stories.

With regard to socialization interests, it is known that many of the readers of confession magazines are adults, usually younger married lower-middle or lower class housewives, living in the Midwestern United

From *Journal of Popular Culture*, 4 (2), Fall 1970, 398–409. Reprinted by permission of the author and the editors. (Footnotes have been omitted.)

States. On the other hand, there are indications from initial observations by this author that many readers of the magazines are of a different sort: younger girls of preteen years, usually from ages 9 to 12, are also attracted to the magazines. This population needs further definition in terms of its motivations and characteristics, but the need for socialization considerations for an age group younger than previously thought is established.

Eight different romance or confession magazines with a total of 73 fictional stories form the basis of the analysis. They were purchased from a downtown Austin newsstand and represent *all* of the magazines available on the stand at that time (one month's availability). While they are a "universe" of material at that point in time and space, they are a "sample" of a larger universe of published magazines. In 1966, there were 32 different confession magazines available; total readership was about 13½ million. The magazines used here were published by five different publishers though there seems to be little difference among them with regard to editorial policies. Each magazine averaged about nine stories per issue.

An initial survey of their content was made by coding for aspects of format, characteristics of the narrator and main partner, sexual events and situations, and other factors that figure in the plots of the stories.

For those who have seen the magazines, it is clear that the most salient characteristic of them is sex. Throughout all of the format features, the themes of sex and the physical nature of people are heavily played upon. The immediate and initial appeal, however, is to the femininity of the potential buyer, an image with which she may most readily identify. For example, six of the eight magazines carry cover pictures of young females of a very wholesome sort; even those depicted in a "seductive" kind of pose (i.e., facial expressions, body postures, clothing arrangements and types suggesting eroticism) may still retain a look of innocence.

Surrounding the picture are the titles of the magazine itself and of the stories for that month, but, upon inspection, one is struck by the apparent incongruities of the two sets of images. The names of some of the magazines in the sample were such ones as *Real Confessions, Secrets, Intimate Story, Daring Romances,* and so on. The titles imply what is to be the nature of the stories. They promise to be stories of an intensely personal sort, the kind that one would confide only to one's closest friend. There is a strong element of wickedness and even sinfulness about the relationships to be described inside. Such large-type statements as

One Night A Week We Were Wicked—We Were
Single Girls on the Prowl For Men!

I Lost My Virginity—And Reputation—In The
Boys' Locker Room!

He Left Sex Out Of Our Dates—If He Loved Me,
Why Didn't He Show It?!

all serve to heighten the anticipation for sex in a way that finds some
correspondence with many popular judgments of what is seen to be "obscene": *illicit* sex. Such activities as abortion, premarital sex, incest, and
adultery are explicitly mentioned on the covers of the magazines.

In the table of contents, the stories are listed with a short statement
of what is to be the basic theme, a kind of "abstract" of the story. Again,
these statements serve to set up the reader for access to an illicit affair
of the narrator. Some examples are:

"When I Say It Baby, You Do It—Anything And Everything!" His Vile Commands Ring In My Ears, And There Is Nothing I Can Do To Escape His Ugly
Desires!

"My Stepfather Taught Me Sex!" It's My Wedding Night—I'm In My Bridal
Bed. But The Arms That Hold Me, The Lips That Seek Mine, Belong To My
Mother's Husband!

There begins to appear a message that the narrator seems to have little
control over the situations she finds herself in. All in all, however, 77%
of the story titles directly implied some sort of *sexual* activity as the *main*
theme for the story.

For each story, there is an accompanying photograph supposedly
depicting some main event in the story. These were coded in a broad
way for the kind and style of posing in the picture. Photos of couples predominate, with 22% involving kissing (some with partial undress), and
15% depict the couple in a situation that can be described as "erotic,"
that is, there is a salient sexual intent between the two individuals. In
most of these latter cases, the couple is touching or is in some kind of
physical contact. Consequently, 37% of the format pictures involve a
sexual or at least physical relationship. Thirty-three percent of the pictures
represent some kind of fight, argument, or anguish, usually between a
couple or in a family setting. This latter theme becomes significant as we
shall see in the content of the stories.

Advertising was also coded for simple content and kind of appeal. Ads
selling material of a mail-order dime store variety comprised a large category, 37% of all ads. However, the general category of "improvement"
was the largest and most significant. In this there were two varieties. One
was labeled "appearance improvement," and included such things as
bust development, weight losing aids, fashions, and beauty aids; this
comprised 36% of all the ads. Other kinds of ads based on a direct appeal
to the improvement of one's self and position, such as loans, medicine,

and religion, comprised 27%. In total, "improvement" advertising amounted to 63%.

The values of oneself as a physical being, more so as an appealing and in some ways a marketable physical being, are thus played upon heavily from the beginning. But we also start to get a sense of some of the risks that simply being a woman may entail. The relationships that await one, and the path through them that one must necessarily take, begin to seem more and more difficult. To what extent merely living life and being a woman means enduring punitive experiences are themes further elaborated upon in the texts of the stories.

Story types were classified into four general categories according to a classification set up by the editors of *True Story* magazine (one from 1958—not included in the sample) as a guide to potential authors. The resultant distribution on this basis was as follows:

Marriage story types	36%
Love story types	30%
Family story types	20%
Teenage story types	14%

It may be noted that the stories that deal with home life, marriage and family stories, total over half of the sample: 56%. The contextualization of the activities in the stories (recall the titles) are not as exotic, or erotic, as originally anticipated; they turn out to be settings that involve the basic values and symbols in our culture: the Home, Family, and Love.

Overwhelmingly, the narrator is female (90%), young in age (teenage, 36%, or in her twenties, 22%), fairly religious (34% of the narrators mentioned a Christian affiliation or a "general belief in God"), and usually a housewife, 41% (other occupations are secretarial/clerical/sales: 22%, or student, usually high school, at 16%). Race was, with one exception, unspecified but implied white. Fifty-one percent were married, 38% were single with no previous marriage. Married women usually had a small family of one or two children. The settings of the stories were usually in small towns, but if set in a large city, the narrator was mentioned as having come from a small town or rural area. The depiction of the narrator then is that she is just "average." Even her physical appearance is not especially gorgeous, but she is explicitly described many times as being "pretty." She is at the same time like all other girls, yet like all other girls want to be.

The life of the narrator is also "average," with problems that arise in any family which are not of a totally disabling sort. Money problems, for example, occur in 25% of the stories, housing problems in 21%, health difficulties in 16%, and occupational troubles in 14%. The complications in the lives of the narrators, however, derive not from aspects of a larger world or "society" (indeed, there is little that can be called social consciousness in the stories), but rather problems come from the people in life, especially those close to the narrator, and from within the narrator herself. Life is a series of personal involvements, the management of which constitutes "life" or "living," and the existence of which "makes life worthwhile." Satisfaction comes from having a loving mate and having a supportive environment of "people you can get along with."

To return to the characters of the stories, the main partner of the narrator usually had fewer specified qualities. The main "other" was usually a male (69%), older in age, either the narrator's spouse (34%) or a previously unmarried single male (25%). His religion and race are unspecified but he appeals less to religion or the name of God, and no question ever arises over miscegenation. His occupation is given in general terms but usually set in skilled jobs or middle class office work.

Given the anticipation for sex as set up by the format, the actual incidence of activities was not as frequent as expected. Coitus is the most frequently occurring singular activity (63% of all stories) but more diffuse in its setting, "scripting," and consequences. Kissing occurs in second place (60%) but with more partners than coitus. Heavy petting is mentioned least of all in its specifics but occurs in 18% of the stories. Other kinds of sexual activity are rare. Incest is mentioned in only a few of the stories, homosexuality hinted at only once, and oral-genital activity never considered. Extra-marital sex occurs in less than 5% of the married cases. It is of note that the partners with whom the narrator has sex are either the spouse (27% for coitus) or a single male (i.e., only one: 25%). In most of the cases, therefore, sex takes place within the boundaries of an emotional relationship with one male. Despite the lure of the titles, promiscuity in the sense of frequent and indiscriminate sexual behavior does not occur as a behavioral mode. In those few cases where it does happen, the punishments for indiscriminate sex are swift and severe; they are dealt out in an almost destructive fashion so as to indicate that those kinds of consequences were what was to be expected anyway.

The disruptive troubles that beset the stories are those that have personalistic references; that is, as we indicated before, "people" are the causes of trouble and the kinds we see in the stories are of a particularly damaging sort. Relationships are volatile, hostile, and even dangerous; in contrast to male-oriented erotica, it is trauma, rather than sex, which is "just around the corner." In those relationships where sex occurs, the results for the people involved were destructive. In relations where sex occurred, 54% of the relationships worsened because of the event. Much of this, of course, happened in cases of premarital sex, but even in many instances of marital sex the message was that when sex is attempted to be used as a solution for a problem, or the basis for forming a relationship, it became evident very quickly that it was not the answer. According to the stories then, guilt, anxiety, and personal difficulties for the narrator as well as damages to others are the costs of misusing or even just having sex.

Other themes of disruption occur significantly and regularly. Some are as follows:

Fight or argument in stories	70%
Mention of violence of any kind	53%
Loss of partner	36%
Guilt felt by narrator for coitus	34%
Loss of virginity by narrator	33%

Each of these, of course, may be elaborated upon separately, but we may mention here only how they cumulatively contribute to the feeling of uneasiness underlying each story. In nearly all the stories, the narrator goes through some sort of crisis; the crux of each, and the attraction for the readers, seemingly, is the *consequences* of events and their resolutions. This is in itself a separate topic for investigation, but story endings give us a clue. Forty-eight percent end on a note of the narrator having mixed feelings of guilt and hope, punishment and salvation. This derives from the narrator having gone through a basic and fundamental crisis that seems to involve one's psychological self, particularly as felt through the emotions of love and sex. Nineteen percent of the stories end on a completely sad tone, where punishment has come about with the tacit admittance by the narrator that she deserved what she got in the end. Even though others are in the environment who will, perhaps by their very nature, take advantage of the narrator, the burden of villainy is assumed by her. She has misused or misapplied her self and her sex in a way that brings not only punishment but retribution.

We noted that the crucial and emotionally involving aspect of the stories is not so much the sex itself but the "social scripting" of the sex, the perception of the partner and the narrator as "responsible" (as opposed to "responsive") beings, and the consequences of interpersonal commitment. The emphasis in the stories is that the purpose of life is the establishment of a series of dependable and stable sets of interpersonal relations, ideally to be founded upon that most stable and enduring of all forces, Love. To this, sex is only secondary; sex can be generated by love but love may be degenerated by sex. When we spoke of the "misuse" of sex, we were referring to the settings in the stories where relationships were attempted to be founded and sustained by sex. It couldn't be done.

We spoke of sex as being "diffuse" in both personality and sociocultural systems. We wish to place particular emphasis upon the latter and suggest that in addition to sex being connected to such things as roles, preferences, and activities, sex is at least distributed through, and at most generated by, a broader system of values which contains views of the world and the social order. It is this latter set of orientations that determines the place and propriety of sex. From the scriptings in the romance magazines, a very explicit sense of what that value and symbolic order is can be obtained.

The basic theme of each story is the stabilization of one's personal life. This may occur in a variety of settings (as with our story types on marriage, etc.) and with a variety of results (getting married, getting divorced, getting pregnant, etc.), but the essence of life is the search for continuity through dependable relationships. It is very obvious in the stories that the most desired manifestations of this essential quality for life are marriage, a family, and love. These are the stable blocks on which daily life, and hence our culture and society, is built. These institutions are the resources for the relationships that allow for the expression of our "real nature." The crises in our stories all seem solvable by recourse only to love; love is the overriding context of sex and any use of sex beyond this is taboo and destructive.

Here are the links between the values of legitimate versus illegitimate behavior. The condemnation of sexual activities and relationships is discussed not so much in terms of themselves but in terms of their consequences. Thus, activities and attitudes that threaten or violate the symbols and values of love, marriage, and the family are acts which endanger their very existence. The stability of these institutions is threatened by the volatile nature of sex itself and the enduring values of the institutions are threatened by sexual and emotional exploitation, "taking" rather than "giving." Sex cannot occur without love; by itself it is immoral, illicit, and even "obscene." Outside the institutions of the family and marriage, it is even worse: it is "unnatural."

What we are led to is the conclusion that the condemnation and negative sanctioning of sex occurs when the continuity and stability of basic cultural institutions is perceived to be threatened or denied as valid and necessary. "Obscenity" and "pornography" in this sense are those acts and attitudes which violate fundamental and symbolic realms in our culture. We know historically the perception of this has varied with time and place, but we may explain the great variety of judgments that have occurred in the past on this basis.

The issues of obscenity and pornography are basically symbolic issues; they are connected to what is perceived to be the essential traditions of our society in its cultural values and social structures. Violations of these are what call forth the cries of the impending End of Civilization As We Now Know It. Judgments of obscenity and pornography can be applied to a wider variety of things and behaviors, many of them non-sexual in nature. It is believed that widespread and continued indulgence in "obscene" and illicit acts creates a "moral collapse" and social destruction. The family is the fundamental sociocultural unit and the institution of marriage through love is necessary for its origin and continuance. "When these go, what else is there?" ask the magazines.

Contrary to our initial expectations, then, the romance magazines really appear to be paragons of virtue, arguing with a traditional, cultural morality for the necessity of love and the family and the minimizing of sex if one is to survive personally or socially. The effects and consequences of acting outside these values are spelled out in a fashion that explicitly details the risk. For the reader, the result is not a pretty picture.

Contained in the romance magazines and their explicit treatments of sex is the argument for the continuity of the American mode of life. Obviously, one of the main ways of establishing cultural continuity is to define the borders of deviance and state the consequences for going over. This is done by imbuing specific areas of interpersonal relations with an aura of heavy negative sanctioning. If a young female reader acquires the language of sex in the punitive terms that are portrayed in the magazines, we may wonder what the cost is of maintaining cultural continuity. The alternatives are limited for us in the media and the penalties are severe for the wrong choices. Yet the social order continues to be questioned and challenged. The problem is one that is demanding attention by its very protestations.

Come Alive, America

Charles and Bonnie Remsberg

From the first promotional letter extolling the wonders of the New World to the latest football player testifying to the magical powers of a shaving cream, the advertisement has been a potent force in America. Highly educated admen spend their working hours in search of methods that will compel children to persuade their parents to buy them certain toys—a situation that apparently does not appear unusual to most Americans.

Despite the supposed sophistication of the advertising industry, the old-fashioned "giveaway" has long been a favorite gimmick. Companies have given away trips around the world, "dream houses," bath towels, and balloons in order to stimulate the sale of products. Recently, some firms have dropped sweepstakes, perhaps because of governmental regulations requiring that all prizes offered must actually be given away. However, it is unlikely that the giveaway will disappear entirely in the near future; the concept of "something for nothing" is too deeply embedded in the American ethnos.

Charles and Bonnie Remsberg graphically detail the effect of a sweepstakes campaign on a midwestern family and community. For a comparable portrayal of ordinary people overwhelmed by popular culture, see Larry McMurtry's "Here's HUD in Your Eye" in this book. An entertaining but uncritical chronicle of advertising is Frank Rowsome's They Laughed When I Sat Down: An Informal History of Advertising in Words and Pictures.

In the World Headquarters of the Pepsi-Cola Company, an eleven-story glass-and-aluminum structure known to New Yorkers as the Joan Crawford Building, a group of executives met not long ago to discuss a new idea for product promotion. Their goal was to sell more Pepsi-Cola and also to gain for the soft drink a larger place in the hearts and minds of the American people.

What they proposed was a contest. They planned a national sweepstakes of the just-fill-in-the-blank-nothing-to-buy-no-jingle-to-write variety. The grand prize of the contest was to be the *ne plus ultra* for enterprises of this sort, and a discussion of it consumed much of the creative energies of the sales-promotion staff. The gift of a South Sea island was ruled out ("too unreal for general public identification"). So was an around-the-world cruise for two (too few promotable opportunities).

A Pepsi-Cola spokesman said, "We're going to hit people where they live. And what hits them hard, *really* hard? Groceries!"

The winner of the contest and his entire family, wearing roller skates if they so desired, would be turned loose in a supermarket and permitted to keep all the foodstuffs they could take from the shelves and deposit on the check-out counters in the space of thirty minutes. Pepsi executives would pick up the tab on the spot, handing the store manager a negotiable check and a "photogenic" five-foot-long nonnegotiable blowup that he could "keep forever."

According to the press release announcing this event, there would be children and adults "scurrying helter-skelter through the empty aisles of a store, racing against the clock ... the blur of sprinting slacks and maybe even shorts ... perhaps a relay system, using basketball tosses to get food from the shelves to the check-out counter ... the facial expressions on the family's faces as they try to make split-second decisions on the most dollar-rewarding food choices to make ... the looks on their faces as the check-out tape records higher and higher totals ...."

The press release was delivered to newspaper offices wrapped around a six-pound sirloin steak.

The papers printed stories of the promised event. There were television commercials that showed gasping families furiously grasping for packaged foods while crowds of spectators cheered. The word began to spread.

Very little was required of the people who entered the sweepstakes. They had to print their names and addresses (and the name and address of their "favorite retail outlet that sells Pepsi-Cola") on an entry blank and drop the blank into collection hoppers in supermarkets. Within two

From *Esquire*, 63 (2), February 1965, 102–105, 128. Reprinted by permission of Esquire Magazine and the authors; copyright © 1965 by Esquire, Inc.

months, Pepsi-Cola had received 61,000,000 entries, thereby reportedly quadrupling the biggest response from any previous sweepstakes. From the entries, local Pepsi bottlers drew various low-echelon winners. They were guided in this by a Publicity Exploitation Kit which had been sent them by the home office. Many of the bottlers tumbled their group of entries in a cement mixer.

Most of the prizes at this stage consisted of gift certificates. But several entrants in each of the 525 Pepsi franchise areas were permitted "individual shopping sprees" in which they were allowed five, ten, or fifteen minutes to grab as many edibles and potables as possible.

After this prelude, the local bottlers shipped all the entries to the offices of D. L. Blair Corporation, an impartial contest-management company in New York. There, anonymous judges drew the names of fifty state grand-prize winners, each of whom reaped a year's supply of groceries, automotive service and accessories, and Pepsi, 2,496 full bottles of it, or, as one Pepsi official put it in an unguarded moment, "whatever the bladder can take."

Then finally, last July, when the nation's appetite had been properly whetted, Blair officials went back to the pile of entries and plucked out the name of the "top national winner."

It was Opal Miller, forty-seven, a seamstress who lives with her husband, Sharol, a paper-mill roustabout, and three of their nine children in Taylorville, Illinois, population 8,801. Before the selection was announced to the public, a private investigator reported to Pepsi headquarters that Mrs. Miller was a brown-haired, bespectacled woman of "medium build," white, neat, clean, a "friendly neighbor" in an "average" neighborhood.

Mrs. Miller was called upon to make a statement. She took a pill to help curb her excitement and said, "I just can't believe I'm top. It musta been God's hand leading the hand that picked my entry. It's that miraculous."

Taylorville lies amid the cornfields and soybean patches of central Illinois. On the day before the Millers were to claim their winnings, the town was adorned as if for a holiday. Banners were hung in the courthouse square. They said: "Congratulations Opal Miller" and "Welcome to the Pepsi-Cola Capital of the World." Bunting draped the light poles. The bank displayed a sign calling Mrs. Miller its "Luckiest Customer." The clothing store where she works set forth in red letters this message: "Look! We're Bustin' with Pride for Opal Miller!"

At the intersection of Pepsi Boulevard and Miller Drive (the two major thoroughfares had been renamed for the occasion), visitors could inspect the modest supermarket where the event was to take place. There, drinking a Pepsi-Cola and surveying the new street markers from under an awning, was a greying, crew-cut man who resembled W. C. Fields. He was the mayor of Taylorville. He said that Taylorville was in the midst of "a volcano, a goodwill volcano."

"Nobody gets anything bad out of something like this, that's what's important. People here are thrilled. They realize this is the only time in their lives and the lifetime of Taylorville that they'll see something like this shopping spree come to pass. Some of the little towns around here are pretty jealous. We even had Miss America."

Miss America, whose four sponsors include the Pepsi-Cola Company, had consented to come to Taylorville as part of the preliminary celebrations. She received a gilded Key to the City and a serenade by a high-school band, which, as it turned out, had not learned how to play *Here She Comes, Miss America.*

"Those kids will probably never have an honor as great as welcoming Miss America," the mayor said.

Miss America had passed out autographed photographs of herself during a luncheon for local businessmen and neighboring mayors. One of the mayors confessed he needed a tranquilizer. After estimating that the Millers' grocery bill would hit $10,000, Miss America praised them as "the kind of people who preserve our American democracy."

The mayor said, "I think her visit, this whole shebang, will make Taylorville the Pepsi-Cola Capital of the World. Of course, we're already the Soybean Capital."

A short, ruddy man with a broad grin and a large tie clasp shaped like a paper clip emerged from the store. In a Brooklyn accent, he announced that he was Bob Windt, Director of Publicity for Pepsi.

"I just got back from a promotion thing in the Far East. The boss told me I wouldn't like this next assignment, Taylorville. But he was wrong. This is more fun than the time I took a horse into the Conrad Hilton Hotel in Chicago or when I had a guy box a kangaroo in 'Frisco. This is really my country down here." He looked down Pepsi Boulevard and smiled. "These are my people." The mayor smiled back.

"Inside the supermarket," Windt said, "there's a real human-interest drama." In honor of Mrs. Miller's winning and the attendant publicity, the store manager was financing a telephone call to the Millers' married daughter who was quartered on an Army base in Germany. The daughter was having a particularly difficult third pregnancy, and Mrs. Miller had hoped that Miss America might ease things by saying hello. But Miss A's chaperone had pointed out that the Queen's contract expressly forbade her to enter grocery stores. Windt explained: "Grocery stores downgrade the Miss America image." So Mr. and Mrs. Miller were placing the call sans celebrity, while a cameraman from nearby Springfield recorded the scene.

Windt had hoped for something more than a cameraman from Springfield. When he had walked away from the mayor, he said: "Frankly, the negative thing about all this is having it in central Illinois. If the winner had only been from Henderson, Nevada [twenty miles from Las Vegas], we'd have planned a three-day weekend and you'd have had to beat the news guys off with a club. Well, maybe the adrenalin will start flowing yet."

The store manager was having trouble completing the Millers' call; neither the daughter nor her spouse seemed to be at home. Mrs. Miller and her husband, who looked like the man in Grant Wood's "American Gothic," were busy in the manager's office figuring the transatlantic time difference and wondering where their daughter could be at so late an hour. (It was nine p.m. in Germany.) Finally Windt suggested they fake the call to accommodate the cameraman, and adjusted the receiver between them.

"Now, *action!*" he ordered. "Mrs. Miller, say something." Mrs. Miller stared blankly at the camera. "Anything . . . 'Hello, how are you?' "

"Hellohowareya," Mrs. Miller said.

"Mr. Miller, say something."

"Hellohowareya," Mr. Miller said.

"No biz like show biz," Windt muttered.

When the camera stopped whirring, Windt left to track down "a police whistle that blows with authority" to signal the start of the race the next morning, and the Millers followed the store manager back to the meat counter. A staff of butchers was stacking up nearly two tons of choice meats and double-checking a list of the Millers' preferences: 125 sirloins, seventy hams, seventy-five roasts, 250 porterhouses, twenty turkeys, etc. The manager predicted that more than $5,000 worth of meat would be brimming over the top when the Millers raced down the aisles. Mr. Miller whistled appreciatively.

"Don't waste time trying to compare cuts," the manager told them. "Just grab whatever you see. Remember, seconds are dollars."

Mrs. Miller nodded. "Can we keep whatever we got in our hands when the final bell rings, or do we hafta drop it?"

"Keep it," the manager said. The Millers smiled at each other. "Now if you happen to drop or break anything when you're running, just leave it on the floor and grab more. We'll have boys stationed in the aisles to sweep up."

Much of the merchandise, the manager pointed out, was stocked on the shelves and stacked in aisles in shipping cartons, the tops of which had been cut off diagonally. "Take the whole thing. Don't waste time picking out individual items. We've got salmon, canned chickens, vegetables, everything stacked like that. If you're in doubt, just grab. Whatever you do, don't stop."

"Oh, we won't!" Mrs. Miller promised. "This is gonna be *marvelous*! But wouldn't it be wonderful if all nine kids was still at home and could be in on this?"

Even with only three offspring eligible to run, if Miss America's $10,000 estimate proved accurate, their grocery haul, plus the value of the 1964 Mercury station wagon which they were being given, would nearly double their combined yearly income, thereby raising them to a much higher tax bracket. The Millers were asked how they felt about that aspect of their windfall.

"We got the tax bite licked," Mr. Miller said.

"We're borrowin' money," Mrs. Miller added. "The Pepsi people have been just wonderful. They told us this was the smart thing to do rather than give up a once-in-a-lifetime opportunity for something like taxes."

Mr. Miller had spent several evenings with a diagram of the store, mapping out an elaborate battle attack. He and two of the three eligible sons—nineteen-year-old Jackie, a motorcycle buff, and thirteen-year-old Ronnie, a Little League catcher—would run relays to clean out the meat counter, while Mrs. Miller and nine-year-old David went for frozen foods, coffee and other light items. David, however, would need a mother's guiding hand. "A boy that young don't understand and might take just anything. Something nice but cheap, like candy or potato chips."

"Of course, we're going to take some Pepsi," Mr. Miller added. "Pepsi first and last." Mrs. Miller gave a thoughtful nod.

Both remarked that they were delighted with the store's compactness. Normally they shopped at a rangier supermarket, but lately had been boycotting it because it was being struck and they were opposed to crossing union picket lines. Now they were seeing the importance of a social conscience first-hand. "The meat counter over at that place is lots farther from the check-out stands," Mrs. Miller said. "We wouldn't be able to get near as much."

The store manager said he, too, was glad things worked out as they did. "This will bring in new customers, even from out of town. It'll be a status symbol to shop where Mrs. Miller shopped."

On Pepsi Boulevard, outside the store, the mayor was staring apprehensively at storm clouds overhead. He suggested a tour of the special displays in the downtown store windows. "Our businessmen used their inventive genius to honor the Millers and Pepsi. Miss America herself judged the windows."

Around the courthouse square, Taylorville's inventive genius was everywhere apparent. Most of the displays had been designed with promotional material supplied by the local Pepsi bottler. They featured mannequins (some wearing only bras and girdles) capped with paper Pepsi hats, alternating rows of Diet and Regular Pepsi cartons, corrugated paper Pepsi signs, glossy prints of Miss America holding a Pepsi, and hand-lettered posters congratulating Opal Miller—all before backdrops of gigantic red-white-and-blue Pepsi bottle caps. Reportedly, it had been extremely difficult for Miss America to narrow the field to *the* most outstanding display from among so many competitors. Down the street, a deliveryman, with furtive caution, toted a case of Coca-Cola into a drugstore just as the heavens opened up. A downpour.

Bob Windt was slouched in a chair in the hotel lobby, toying with a foot-long red-and-yellow plastic whistle and staring at the rain. A Pepsi photographer from New York was trying to cheer him: "I saw a woman drinking a Coke downtown, so I smashed her in the face." Windt said nothing.

He looked at the latest copy of the Taylorville *Breeze-Courier* which had kept on top of the story ever since Mrs. Miller's entry was drawn. Now, on the eve of the running, its twelve pages were filled with fifty-four display ads, praising the Millers and Pepsi-Cola under such headlines as: "Another milestone in Taylorville's history"; "Taylorville's bowled 'em over again"; "Congratulations for making such an unforgettable experience possible"! The advertisers included the county sheriff and a local pest-control firm. The copy revealed that the shopping event was touching off a number of related contests. One tavern, for instance, was offering a "free thirty-minute eating-and-drinking spree for the customer who comes closest to guessing the dollar value of the Millers' total take."

Windt was still brooding. "This contest was too honest, so we came up with Taylorville. Hell, in Henderson we'd have even had Telstar."

Mr. Miller was partly to blame for the lack of journalistic enthusiasm, Windt decided, because he had not taken more days off from his job to join in preliminary promotional activities. "He could have asked for his vacation now," Windt said. "But he just sat there with his nose out of joint and didn't say anything."

The phone rang. ABC-TV was on the line from Chicago. Windt's face brightened. "That old adrenalin. Before this is over, *Time* and *Life* will be begging for stills!"

The rain was over by evening. Pepsi Boulevard had been blocked off in front of the store, and a dozen city laborers were there, noisily throwing together sets of wooden bleachers from the high-school football field. The choice center seats were to be roped off for the Miller kin and other dignitaries. The other seats were to be on a first-come first-served basis. "People will be here early," a worker said. "They know the TV cameras will sweep across the crowd." To assure *some* visibility for all, glaziers were removing the supermarket's large plate-glass front windows.

Inside, electricians were checking the efficiency of the wiring. Extra lines had been added. An independent moviemaker, hired by Pepsi, crammed a camera and a cameraman into a shopping cart and careened it up and down the aisles, rehearsing camera angles. The ABC crew, freshly arrived from Chicago, scanned the scene and declared that things weren't commercial enough. They suggested that prominent Pepsi signs be pasted atop cash registers directly in front of the TV camera platform. Stock boys, some of whom would work all night, were corraling one hundred extra shopping carts, three thousand paper bags and mountains of S&H Green Stamps, while other employees dismantled display cases of cigarettes, phonograph records, kitchen utensils and other non-foodstuffs which the Millers would not be permitted to grab during the race. "We decided to get these things out of the way rather than have Mrs. Miller get excited and grab something she can't have," the manager explained.

Near the check-out counter, Bob Windt was in a rage over the cans of Jewel Mixed Nuts and the boxes of Chef Boy-Ar-Dee Pizza mix flanking a Pepsi display. "Terrible, terrible!" he bellowed to Tony Becker, a hulking Pepsi troubleshooter from Chicago who would be master of ceremonies for the running. "Our stake in this is to promote Pepsi. I don't give a damn about mixed nuts. Get 'em outa here or cover 'em up with Pepsi!"

Becker tried to explain that nuts and pizza could be considered "related food items" and that Pepsi "often ties in with related food items promotion-wise," but a fresh crisis was already pushing Windt's blood pressure to new heights. The wall clock Becker had chosen as "official timer" was imprinted only with the name of the supermarket. "When the cameras flash to the clock for the time, we want PEPSI to come out on the screen. I've had a hard enough time getting some of these news guys down here without blowing it like this," Windt said. In a hasty conference, he and Becker decided that a Pepsi clock would be designated "official," but to avoid hard feelings from the store staff, the first clock would be kept in reserve "in case of emergency."

Two aisles over, another important conference was underway. Two Pepsi promotion experts from New York had cornered the store manager and were informing him that the Millers would not be permitted to carry food in the pasteboard shipping cartons, despite the fact that their briefings and battle plans had been built around this stratagem. "We're mostly interested in something exciting, something *visual,*" one of them explained in a confidential tone. "We might have a prism lens, say, that'll make Mrs. Miller suddenly be eight Mrs. Millers to the camera's eye. Basically, it will be better if they just carry what they can in their arms."

"Besides," said the other man, "we don't want to take a bath on this."

"Without the cartons," the first expert added, "the unexpected is more likely to happen. Why, we may be dragging those people up off the floor by the time thirty minutes is over."

All evening, a steady stream of townsfolk filed down to the store to watch the preparations—mothers with babes in arms, grizzled old men, housewives in slacks and hair curlers, kids with baseball gloves and bubble gum, young farmers with sun-leathered faces, businessmen with cigars. Some sat on the bleachers for hours, staring at the activity inside the store or plotting their own imaginary assault on the shelves or ruminating over the tragic fact that six of the Miller brood had already flown the nest and thus they were ineligible for the spree.

The editor of the *Breeze-Courier* had just returned from a country-club banquet honoring the Millers for all they'd done for Taylorville.

"You know, Pepsi has hit on a real fine idea. We're a gluttonous race, I guess, but the idea of the supermarket, the grocery-store phenomenon and all, really thrills people. It's like the hunt. You get to sack the game yourself."

A husband and wife walked past, carrying youngsters in pajamas. "At least there's five of 'em," the man was saying. "They'll be able to get something. If some guy had won who was taking care of a seventy-five-year-old mother or something, hell, she wouldn't be able to grab nothing."

Miller Day (so designated by mayoral proclamation) dawned. On an early morning radio interview, a Pepsi executive said: "Out of all forty-eight states, the national spotlight is focused today on Taylorville." The bleachers were already filling (some local shops had given employees time off to attend) and inside the manager was assuring a group of nervous pink-smocked checkers that each of them would have a chance to handle the Millers' groceries and that there would be extra checkers standing by in case anyone got overly excited and had to quit. Two empty semi-trailers had been jockeyed into the parking lot; whatever couldn't be crammed into the station wagon the semi-trailers would carry to storage lockers the Millers had rented in the next town, and a uniformed cop was on hand to direct shopping-cart traffic. The festival crowd swigged free cups of Pepsi, tapped time to the Sousa marches blaring from a loudspeaker, and waved eagerly at TV cameramen and press photographers. Then, when a woman in black slacks and sneakers entered the store, followed by three sneakered boys and a man, someone shouted: "Is that *her*?"

It was. Taylorville's queen for a day walked directly to the manager's office and opened her purse. "I'm going to take off my rings and my watch and anything that might hamper me in any way," Mrs. Miller announced. Her hair had been set gratuitously by a local beauty operator. Her sneakers were donated by J. C. Penney. She joined the rest of her family for a final reconnaissance of the battlefield. Women in the crowd looked on with unveiled envy as Mrs. Miller experimentally wrapped her arms around a tall stack of canned chickens. The store manager said, "Don't worry about being neat at the checkout counters, just dump the stuff and *go!*"

Finally, just before the zero hour of nine-thirty, Tony Becker got on top of a sturdy safe at the front of the store, grabbed a microphone, and said: "It's almost spree time! Millers, get on your marks!" As one, the five Millers dropped to a crouch at the check-out counters, their eyes on the twentieth-century cornucopia arrayed before them. "Awright, folks, let's count 'em down like a Sa-turn rocket. *Ten . . . nine . . . eight . . . .*"

Four thousand voices thundered in unison. In a second-story window across the street, an American Legion volunteer pressed the official bugle to his lips. At the base of the safe, Bob Windt put the police whistle to his lips. Alongside the Millers, the store manager raised a pearl-handled starter's pistol.

" . . . three . . . two . . . one . . . GO!"

Bugle blast, whistle shrill, revolver crack. The crowd shrieked as the Millers sprinted down the aisles, followed closely by the movie man in the shopping cart. In a blur of flying legs and snatching hands, they swarmed over the shelves like locusts through a cornfield. "Go! Go! Go!" the crowd chanted. Becker turned the march music double volume, and the bugler blared a cavalry charge.

Cash registers began to ring as Jackie dumped two dozen steaks on the counter. His mother staggered up with three huge frozen turkeys, and someone yelled: "Atta boy, Mrs. Miller!" Little David, momentarily bewildered, finally got his bearings and began heaving boxes of chocolate milk flavoring into the check-out aisles, where adult store employees scrambled frantically to pick them up. At the brimming meat counter, Mr. Miller loaded Ronnie to the chin with rib roasts. A sympathetic butcher, seeing sweat pouring down the boy's face, held a cup of water to his lips. "Not too much now," his father said. Alarmed Pepsi officials, noting that only the youngest of the Millers had remembered the "Pepsi first" pledge, rushed to a Pepsi display and grabbed a dozen cartons for them. The first shopping cart was loaded now, but in the frenzy the sacker rammed it through a glass door enroute to the parking lot, then kicked the broken glass aside and raced on. Becker called on the crowd to give him the old Taylorville yell.

Bob Windt surveyed the scene with rapture. "This is great. We're in the greatest business in the world—*philanthropy!*"

For thirty minutes, the scream of the crowd, the blare of the music, the clang of the cash registers, the steady avalanche of steaks, bananas, sugar, shortening, coffee, cake mixes, frozen shrimp, fish, tea, honey-glazed hams in champagne sauce never slackened. Then suddenly, moments after the meat counter was stripped bare and Mrs. Miller dumped an armload of Metrecal on the counter, Becker bellowed: "We're coming down to the wire now! Pandemonium—*let it break loose!*" The crowd went out of control. People jumped up and down on the bleachers. They threw their paper Pepsi cups into the air. And as the sound of their voices reached the pitch of hysteria, there was a general movement, a surge toward the ravaged store. The final gun sounded.

Each panting Miller was handed a Pepsi. Flashbulbs popped. Jubilantly, the store manager announced the grand-total food value: $6,274.64, plus Green Stamps.

The Millers stopped smiling. "That's not as much as we'd planned on," Mrs. Miller said. She looked around to see what they had missed.

"Well, we don't wanna be big hogs. Just little ones," said her husband.

Then the crowd closed in and well-wishers smothered the winners with hugs and kisses.

Out in the parking lot people were inspecting the seventy-five loaded carts stretched under the boiling sun, and those fortunate enough to be neighbors or friends of the Millers were letting everyone else know about it. Someone shouted that the grocery grabbers had gotten twenty-eight twenty-five-pound bags of sugar. Someone else counted sixty one-pound cans of coffee. Another spotted a dozen bags of charcoal briquettes.

"Charcoal briquettes!" a woman said. "That's not foodstuffs! I thought they were only supposed to get foodstuffs!"

Windt was pushing through the crowd now, trying to get the truck loading started. He was asked what his next promotional idea might be.

"Well, I'll just sit back, study the elements and see what develops. Something will come up. I've been foolin' 'em since I was twelve, so what the hell?"

A man wearing a Pepsi-Cola shirt came past, and he was holding a radio shaped like a Pepsi dispenser. The volume was turned up to the limit, and a commercial that had made its debut that day came booming out:

"Come alive, Come alive, You're in the Pepsi generation."

As the Saints Go Marching By: Modern Jokelore Concerning Mormons

Jan Harold Brunvand

When Mark Twain journeyed to Nevada in 1861 the stage stopped at Salt Lake City, the stronghold of the Mormon community in America. In Roughing It Twain records the mixture of fascination, hatred, and fear with which he and his fellow travelers studied the Mormons. Their reactions were typical of nineteenth-century Americans who were aghast at Mormon customs and doctrines, especially polygamy. Eventually polygamy was ended because of the widespread sentiment against it, which led to the Edmunds Act of 1882 providing for fines and imprisonment for polygamy. In 1890 the church directed all members to "refrain from contracting any marriage forbidden by the law of the land." Today Mormons continue to be viewed as a peculiar people by many Americans. Nationwide attention has been focused upon them by the assertion of blacks that the church is racist.

The Mormon joke has been popular ever since the founding of the church. Representative of early witticisms is Mark Twain's remark that Mormon women were so "homely" that "the man that marries sixty of them has done a deed of open-handed generosity so sublime that the nations should stand uncovered in his presence and worship in silence." Generally the jokes told about Mormons are related from the point of view of a Gentile (non-Mormon) majority. Jan Harold Brunvand provides a unique perspective on the contemporary Mormon joke in his collection of those told by the Gentile minority in Salt Lake City.

Thomas F. O'Dea's The Mormons is the best introduction to their history. The record Folklore of the Mormon Country, told by Hector Lee, is an excellent collection of humor.

For the student of Mormon affairs, the streets
of Salt Lake City are filled with fascination.
    —Wallace Turner, *The Mormon Establishment* (1966)

Members of the Church of Jesus Christ of Latter-day Saints, popularly
known as Mormons (to themselves as LDS), have long been recognized as
constituting a folk group in the sense that they share a common body of
oral traditions and are the subject of oral traditions circulated by non-
Mormons, known among Mormons as Gentiles.[1] Utah Mormons are regarded as a folk group comparable in the homogeneity and strength of
their traditions to other regional groups such as the Pennsylvania Ger-
mans, Louisiana Cajuns, southern Illinois "Egyptians," and southwestern
Spanish-Americans.[2] A large body of Utah Mormon folklore has been collected, and some of it has been published. The emphasis in the printed
material (and probably the unpublished as well) has been upon the old
historical-legendary-anecdotal ingroup Mormon lore that has served
largely to strengthen the sense of group solidarity, especially for the
young.[3] Typical examples of this lore—familiar to all students of American
folklore—include the "Handcart Song," the legends of the Three Nephites,
and the stories about J. Golden Kimball.[4]

    Studies of Utah Mormon folklore have been almost exclusively de-
voted to analyzing survivals, with some attention to adaptations of survivals in later circulation and to the traditional functions of these survivals
and adaptations.[5] Conspicuously absent has been any collecting of recent
Mormon folklore or any study of the functions of current traditions known
among or told about Mormons. Even a straightforward allusion to these
interesting subjects in a recent and excellent anthology is phrased in
terms of survivals and greatly oversimplifies the situation. Richard M. Dorson remarks in his introduction to Utah Mormon folklore in *Buying the
Wind,* "Some relics of the earlier phase [of anti-Mormon lore] still endure,
and can be found in good-natured jokes and songs which caricature the
Mormon's supposed libidinous tendencies."[6]

    In this article I want to break some new ground in the study of mod-
ern traditions surrounding Utah Mormons in order to demonstrate as a
basis for further studies that this folklore is not made up just of surviving
"relics," that not all of it is "good-natured," that some comes from within
the group as well as from outside, and that other themes than the sexual
predominate. My emphasis will be on the neglected area of contemporary
jokelore concerning Mormons; by "jokelore" I mean all kinds of modern

From *Journal of American Folklore,* 83 (327), January–March 1970, 53–60. Reprinted by permission
of the author and the editors. (Footnotes have been placed at the end of the text.)

jesting lore that have become traditional, whatever their form or type. My examples were collected largely in Salt Lake City within the past two years, partly by my students.

To begin with, let us contrast the rare printing of a piece of contemporary anti-Mormon folklore with what circulates in oral tradition. The fine study of Mormon lore by Austin and Alta Fife contains the following quatrain collected from the well-known Mormon scholar Juanita Brooks of St. George, Utah, in 1947:

> I can tell you're a Mormon by the clothes that you wear,
> I can tell you're a Mormon by the color of your hair.
> You left your own country to marry a squaw,
> You're a Mormon, you're a Mormon, go back to Utah.[7]

This song, usually rendered as a chanted rhyme, still circulates in Mormon country (at least in Idaho and Utah), and my most recent student collector to submit it heard it in the Union Building snack bar at the University of Utah. But the third line usually contains some expression like "bangin' a squaw" or "humpin' a squaw," and the last line replaces the repetitive formula, "You're a Mormon, you're a Mormon" with "You're a Mormon God damn you" (or "God damn it") or "You son of a bitch." Several versions replace the vague phrase "clothes that you wear" with "long underwear," a clear reference to the Temple Garments (sacred underwear) that the devout LDS faithful may wear. Pressures for propriety are discussed by Austin Fife who admits to self-censorship in his article "Myth Formation in the Creative Process" (*Western Folklore,* 23, 1964, 229–239). The point is not just that previous collectors or informants felt obliged to suppress rough language. Only through full verbatim collection of these kinds of texts—with their contexts—may we hope to understand how such lore circulates and how it functions at the present time.

To pose an analogy, if we attempted to characterize Mormon folklore today without collecting such materials, it would be like describing Negro folklore after reading *Uncle Remus* but not Roger Abrahams' *Deep Down in the Jungle.*[8] Understanding current Mormon folklore does not command the same degree of sociological urgency perhaps as does understanding current Negro folklore, but in a theoretical sense it is an extremely interesting project. Utah—the Mormons' Zion—especially Salt Lake City, is a virtual modern folklore laboratory situation where several distinct and easily identified groups and subgroups intermingle or avoid one another, and share or secretly harbor traditional lore about the other groups or about themselves, lore that is partly unique and partly common to other groups. Every condition described by William Hugh Jansen as contributing to the esoteric-exoteric factor in folklore is present in Salt Lake City.[9]

Complicating the picture is the fact that, whereas other groups for which comparable studies might be made are usually minorities, in Utah the Mormons are still a powerful majority, and even outside Utah, prominent Mormons are often highly respected public figures, such as Secretary of Housing and Urban Development George Romney, former Secretary of the Interior Stewart Udall, and golf professional Billy Casper. Stuart Gallacher of Michigan State University has shared with me a piece of modern folklore about Romney. "What's the surest way to contact God?" ("Let George do it! He has a direct pipeline." Or, "Leave it to George, his pipeline is always open.") This refers to remarks Romney made in press conferences before he decided to run for office, alluding to his meditating over the question and listening for the still, small voice to advise him. He told reporters that the same pipeline was open to them and to anybody.

In such a new, wide-open, and untilled field, I can do little more now than offer a rough survey; however, several broad generalizations may be made and easily documented. First, it is obvious that the old stereotypes of anti-Mormonism have largely disappeared. One study distinguished seven images of the Mormon in nineteenth-century fiction: the drunken and abusive husband, the white-slave procurer, the seducer, the sinister secret-society member, the dweller in the sinful fallen city, the lustful Turk, and the cruel, lustful Southern slaveholder.[10] If one were to draw up a list of Mormon stereotypes from modern folklore, it would be most likely in terms such as these: the naive Mormon bishop, the skeptical elder, the hypocritical Saint, the devoted missionary, the rigid church official, the emancipated intellectual Mormon youth, and so forth. In other words, Mormon folklore keeps up to date, so much so that I have met native Utah adolescents who do not know of the Three Nephites except through formal indoctrination, and who have never heard a J. Golden Kimball story except on Hector Lee's Folk-Legacy recording,[11] but who do know the right answer to the question, "What's the difference between LSD and LDS?" (LSD you take on a cube of sugar, LDS you take with a grain of salt.) Furthermore, they are well aware (perhaps partly from reading *Dialogue,* the liberal and unofficial "Journal of Mormon Thought" founded in 1966) that many "good Mormons" nowadays may take their "Articles of Faith" with a grain of salt. In fact, a traditional parody of this doctrinal manifesto begins each statement with, "Would you believe . . ." instead of the correct, "We believe that. . . ." An indication of an even more lax and sacrilegious attitude is found in a folk parody of a favorite Mormon hymn, played in every Tabernacle organ concert.

> Come, come, ye Saints; no toil nor labor fear.
> But with joy wend your way.

Some Utah youngsters sing the following instead:

> Come, come, ye Saints; no toilet paper here.
> But with grass wipe your ass.

Another parody rhyme is more modest and merely comments on the demanding set of religious and social obligations any active Mormon performs.

> Mary had a little lamb,
> It grew to be a sheep.
> Then it joined the Mormon church,
> And died from lack of sleep.

Such parodies are familiar in modern folk tradition, where they fulfill a common function of folklore, to provide an outlet for tabooed topics and terms.[12]

Many other general American religious joke themes circulate in Utah in such forms as folk speech, nicknames, proverbial sayings, wisecracks, daffy definitions, parodies, jokes, riddle-jokes, rhymes, and graffiti. For instance, a cycle of priest–minister–Mormon bishop stories is almost identical to the priest–minister–rabbi stories of other regions. The little Catholic child who tells a Mormon bishop that his newborn puppies are "Mormon puppies," but later says they are "Catholic puppies now that their eyes are open," is a familiar character from other joke cycles.[13]

Riddle-jokes provide good examples of adapted or original content in widely known forms of modern folklore. The moron joke becomes a Mormon joke in, "Why did the little moron take a ladder to church?" (So he could become a Latter-day Saint.) The fruit joke—such as, "What's red and bumpy and rides a white horse?" (The Lone Raspberry)—emerges as, "What's purple and has twenty-seven wives?" (Brigham Plum.) More complex is the variant, popular among Gentiles, "What's yellow and has a long gray beard?" (David O. Banana.) David O. McKay, the president and prophet of the church since 1951, died on January 18, 1970, at the age of ninety-six; he did not wear a beard. This is a lingering stereotype of the nineteenth-century church leaders. Calling McKay "yellow" via a nonsense joke may suggest a feeling that the church leadership avoids innovation, a charge frequently made in letters to the editor in Salt Lake City. A riddle-joke usually collected from LDS members is, "Did you hear about the hippy who didn't know LSD from LDS?" (He went on a mission instead of a trip.) Here the natural confusion the similar initials lead to is the foreground of the joke, and the background probably is the attitude that it would be a far, far better thing to go on a mission for the church than to indulge in a drug trip. Mormons would like to channel the hippies' search for spiritual integrity and their energy for love and goodwill into some constructive social activity.

Specialized jokelore of Utah depends on esoteric understandings about Mormons gained only by some exposure to their traditions. An outsider's first few months in Salt Lake City constitute his initiation period, during which he acquires by means of misunderstandings, errors, corrections, repetition, and experience the requisite terms and facts for a sociable residence in the new culture. Through these initial rites of passage he enters a folk group of his own, that of the Utah Gentile, the major distinguishing quality of which is knowing all the best and newest Mormon jokes. Only much later—and more gradually, depending upon his personal contacts—does the settler begin to learn some of the most guarded Mormon lore.

The very initials LDS often require explanation for the Gentile newcomer, as may the cryptic initials naming the largest Utah department store, ZCMI ("Zion's Cooperative Mercantile Institute"). Having mastered these terms, one is ready for the satiric explanation of ZCMI as "Zion's Collection of Morons and Idiots" or of LDS/ZCMI as "Lay down sister, Zion's children must increase," which refers to the Mormon emphasis on early marriage and large families and is phrased in the conventional Mormon manner, encouraging members to address each other as brothers and sisters. Similarly, only after the newcomer understands the term "Jack Mormon" (roughly, a backslider), as well as the miracle of the seagulls and crickets, is he prepared to appreciate the question, "What's a Jack Seagull?" (One that won't eat crickets.)

Many a new arrival to Utah has heard an explanation of "Jack Mormon" such as that given recently to a reporter by the Los Angeles lawyer Russell E. Parsons when he became chief counsel for Sirhan Sirhan. Parsons was quoted as saying, "I'm a jack Mormon, which means not a very good one. I don't smoke, I don't swear much, and I drink not at all."[14] In Utah, however, the explanation would likely be reinforced by a traditional joke or anecdote, such as the story about a newly inducted Utah serviceman who stated his religion as Jack Mormon because "You have to be something! You can't just be a God damned atheist!" One of the most esoteric Mormon jokes that I have collected has St. Peter quizzing a new arrival in heaven (usually a pope) about the progress of the various religious sects. When his informant confesses that he doesn't know much about Mormonism, St. Peter asks, "Would you like to learn more?" While this may seem funny enough on the surface, Mormons are aware of the reference to the "Golden Questions," traditionally used by Mormon missionaries when they approach Gentiles with the intention of converting them: "What do you know about Mormonism? Would you like to learn more?"

Wallace Turner, a Gentile writing about Mormons, rightly observed that "words have special meanings in Salt Lake City, and one for a time feels the need of a translator."[15] He listed several of the formal, technical terms of the faith that Utahans freely use in conversation: "ward," "stake," "primary," "MIA," "relief society," "Deseret Industries," "quorum," "council," "first presidency," and so forth. He did not, of course, list the informal, usually impolite, folk terms that circulate, often as clichés, expressing the Utah culture's stereotypes.[16] Brigham Young University (BYU) in Provo, for instance, in popular speech is called "The Y" (distinguished from "The U," or the University of Utah); but in uninhibited folk speech BYU may be referred to as "Jesus Tech" or "Purity Playhouse" because of the supposed tendencies of students and faculty to be excessively religious and moral. "Jesus Tech" is a common *blason populaire* for sectarian colleges everywhere. More localized nicknames are "Matrimony Tech" or "B Y Woo," referring to BYU's supposed emphasis on marriage, but even here we can recognize adaptation of a pattern traditional elsewhere—witness NYU, sometimes dubbed "N Y Jew." An indigenous nickname is "Miriam Young University" ("Marry 'em young"); Miriam supposedly was the name of Brigham Young's favorite wife. All of the terms mentioned so far are well known and fairly acceptable for use in mixed—that is, Mormon-Gentile—groups, but I lived in Salt Lake City for about a year and one half before I learned that Temple Garments (sacred underwear) have nicknames in use among young Mormons. Some call them "Rocky Mountain Surfing Shorts," others refer to them as "Angel Chaps."

Folklore is often used in the strategies by means of which various groups cope with one another and with each other's stereotypes. For instance, middle-aged and older Mormons cling to traditional "faith-promoting stories"—accounts of miracles and providences—and to pioneer historical experiences. These are circulated in print, in testimony meetings, and in casual oral transmission or handwritten family records. Modern Mormon youths, however, tend to reject these hoary tales, and they express their distaste for them by such remarks as, "Let's go down to Temple Square and throw rocks at the seagulls." Others may sneeringly claim that Brigham Young really said, "Piss on this place" instead of "This is the place." LDS informants have also pointed out with obvious glee that the statue of Brigham Young, standing in the intersection of South Temple and Main streets just off the corner of Temple Square, "has his back to the temple and one hand outstretched to Zion's First National Bank."

As one replacement for the faith-promoting stories, young Mormons may believe in stories about Famous Church Members, well-known show business personalities (and always wholesome exemplary types) who supposedly are LDS members and tithe faithfully, but do not publicly admit their affiliation for fear of losing their appeal to Gentiles. The list includes Charlton Heston, Pat Boone, Gene Autrey, Roy Rogers and Dale Evans, Tennessee Ernie Ford, and Walt Disney. An excellent clue to group relationships is found in the implication of "LDS only" in classified advertising by such phrases as "no smokers or drinkers wanted," or "returned missionary preferred." A Gentile's rebuttal to this is a claim that he has seen an invitation for a lewd or homosexual encounter written as a bathroom graffito with the special requirement stated, "LDS only."

One of the best ways through which to pursue these attitudes is to explore what we might call the "clean living" theme, or the "Word of Wisdom." This is the name of the Church injunction against use of coffee, tea, alcohol (most would include Coke), and tobacco. Responses to this theme in modern folklore are considerably varied and often combined with the marriage-childbearing theme, perhaps because of supposed indulgence on one side to balance asceticism on the other. In children's folklore these ideas are reflected in the local variant of the jump-rope rhyme that begins,

> I love coffee, I love tea,
> How many boys are stuck on me?

Salt Lake children have been heard chanting,

> I hate coffee, I hate tea,
> How many boys are stuck on me?

Obviously the whole rhyme fits perfectly with the group ethic. Some older Mormons, especially if they were converted out of families where much coffee was drunk (for instance, Scandinavians), have devised a substitute drink of hot water with cream and sugar added. The term for this, Mormon coffee (or Mormon tea), is reminiscent of phrases like Mennonite lipstick, a little bit of chapstick used to brighten the lips without artificial color. Commonly circulating among Mormons are stories that make gentle little jokes out of the Word of Wisdom taboos—at least of coffee and alcohol, though seldom of smoking. Three Mormons go on a spree; one drinks coffee, one orders Coke, and the third takes milk. The first two tease the third one about how timid he is, and he replies, "Yes, maybe so, but somebody has to drive home." A similar story collected from Gentiles tells of a Mormon bishop invited to a Gentile household. He is offered Irish coffee after dinner and asks what that is. "Oh, just coffee with whisky added and whipped cream on top." "Well, perhaps just this once, but could you make it with Postum?"

This idea of not tolerating one vice while allowing an apparently worse one comes up in many jokes, almost always in the Utah Gentile tradition. A coed comes home pregnant from BYU, and her father says, "Why don't you just marry the young man who did this to you?" She replies, "Oh, but I can't. He drinks coffee and smokes cigarettes." A riddle-joke asks, "How can you tell if you're in a Mormon whorehouse?" ("No Smoking" signs. Variant, "No ashtrays.") In another story about St. Peter in heaven, the new arrivals are invited to sit down in the vestibule and have a cup of coffee while their papers are being processed. To a Mormon, St. Peter snaps (as the Gentile storyteller might like to do himself), "You can go to hell; I haven't got time to make hot chocolate today."

Coffee drinking in Utah serves as a fairly reliable indicator of Church affiliation. One can usually spot the Mormons at a banquet or luncheon because as soon as they are seated they invert their coffee cups on the saucers, while Gentiles and Jack Mormons will add an extra flourish, as a gesture of retaliation, when they adjust their cups for the pouring. Aware of the Mormon attitude toward coffee, other church groups in Utah may overreact and emphasize their use of the beverage. A result is the new riddle-joke, "What's a Jack Unitarian?" (One that won't drink coffee.) Terms like "coffee break" are heard in Salt Lake City, but often with a slight hesitation, especially if one is with a new acquaintance. Colleagues of mine, though non-Mormon, may refer to going out for coffee as "going out for some dissipation." Or they may even ask, "What's your poison?" (That is, coffee, tea, hot chocolate, milk, or soda.)

To a great extent, then, we can see in all these items how a visible, nonsensitive quality differentiating Mormon and non-Mormon serves as a safety valve for releasing pressures built up over other matters. It is one thing to joke with a Mormon neighbor or co-worker about coffee or smoking, but it would be quite another thing to make light of Temple Garments or of the visions of Joseph Smith. It seems clear that non-Mormon Americans have learned to tolerate some fairly exotic doctrinal matters as long as they may poke fun at some minor, and really quite praiseworthy, matters of simple social and personal behavior.

In conclusion, we may take a glance at another especially fascinating avenue for study. This is the lore of the Gentile tourist in Utah, who is the victim of his own misconceptions and of some of his guides' hoaxes. Many visitors seem to expect that Mormons will wear some distinctive old-fashioned garb, perhaps like that of an Amish or Mennonite sect. Others swallow tall tales about fish in the Great Salt Lake, Jackelopes or Salt Bears on the deserts, vestal virgins in the Mormon Temple, and polygamy in the suburbs. Many ask whether Mormons are Christians, or how visitors may be admitted to the Temple. One eager tourist actually wrote to the Utah State Tourist Council asking when she could hear the

"Mormon Luboff Choir" sing. One of the best stories of this kind is an eloquent little pageant of exoteric expectations met by esoteric wit and
might well epitomize our subject. A tourist in Salt Lake City asks her
tour guide on the Grey Lines bus, "Will you point out one of those awful
Mormons to me?" The guide looks about furtively, and then he silently
points an index finger at himself.

NOTES

1. Paper read at the annual meeting of the American Folklore Society, Bloomington, Indiana, 1968.

2. Richard M. Dorson, *Buying the Wind* (Chicago, 1964).

3. Wilfrid Bailey, "Folklore Aspects in Mormon Culture," *Western Folklore*, 10 (1951), 217–
225.

4. These items appear in every general survey of Mormon folklore, such as in Richard M.
Dorson, *American Folklore* (Chicago, 1959), 112–121.

5. Representative studies are Hector Lee, *The Three Nephites: The Substance and Significance of the Legend in Folklore* (Albuquerque, New Mexico, 1949), and Austin E. Fife, "Folk Belief
and Mormon Cultural Autonomy," *Journal of American Folklore*, 61 (1948), 19–30.

6. Dorson, *Buying the Wind*, 499.

7. Austin E. and Alta Fife, *Saints of Sage and Saddle* (Bloomington, Indiana, 1956), 124.

8. Roger D. Abrahams, *Deep Down in the Jungle* (Hatboro, Pennsylvania, 1964).

9. Wm. Hugh Jansen, "The Esoteric-Exoteric Factor in Folklore," *Fabula*, 2 (1959), 205–211;
reprinted in Alan Dundes, *The Study of Folklore* (Englewood Cliffs, New Jersey, 1965), 43–51.

10. Leonard Arrington and Jon Haupt, "Intolerable Zion: The Image of Mormonism in Nineteenth Century American Literature," *Western Humanities Review*, 22 (1968), 243–260.

11. *"Folklore of the Mormon Country," J. Golden Kimball Stories Together With the Brother
Petersen Yarns.* FTA–25 (Huntington, Vermont, 1964).

12. Compare items in my note "Jokes about Misunderstood Religious Texts," *Western Folklore*, 24 (1965), 199–200; see also Joseph Hickerson and Alan Dundes, "Mother Goose Vice Verse,"
Journal of American Folklore, 75 (1962), 249–259.

13. A variant appears in Elizabeth Tokar, "Humorous Anecdotes Collected from a Methodist
Minister," *Western Folklore*, 26 (1967), 98.

14. Reported in *The National Observer*, June 24, 1968.

15. Wallace Turner, *The Mormon Establishment* (Boston, 1966), 7.

16. See Wm. Hugh Jansen, "A Culture's Stereotypes and their Expression in Folk Clichés,"
Southwestern Journal of Anthropology, 13 (1957), 184–200.

"Woodstock,"
A Nation at War

Lawrence J. Dessner

As early as 1944 Walter Oakes wrote of a "permanent war economy" in the United States. However, the thesis that preparation for war (through "defense" industries) was essential to the American economy did not become popular until the sixties when American aggression in Southeast Asia fueled a debate over the "military-industrial complex." "What would happen if peace broke out?" asked opponents of the Vietnam war; they received a lurid answer in the satirical Report from Iron Mountain on the Possibility and Desirability of Peace. *The report, purportedly a government study, suggested that permanent peace would be inexpedient: "If it were necessary at this moment to opt irrevocably for the retention or dissolution of the war system, common prudence would dictate the former course." More frightening, several members of the defense establishment were quoted as believing the report was authentic since they had read similar studies.*

Cultural historians are beginning to move beyond the economic argument to examine the wider effects of war on America. No study better illustrates the promise of such an undertaking than Lawrence J. Dessner's essay on "Woodstock." Valuable starting points for an exploration of this general subject are Ralph E. Lapp's The Weapons Culture, *and Tristram P. Coffin's* Armed Society: Militarism in Modern America; *Roy Bongartz's "Remember Bomb Shelters?" and Susan Sontag's "The Imagination of Disaster," both in this book.*

The people who assembled at the Woodstock music festival, the entrepreneurs who produced the film based on it, and the audience for whom both film and festival were undertaken would vigorously describe themselves, with no doubt some minority in dissent, as against American involvement in the Vietnamese war. Performers at the festival demonstrated such opposition with unrelenting conviction. The festival itself was described by its promoters and participants first as a great experiment in peaceful living, then as a successful demonstration of how a nation, the "Woodstock nation," could live in peaceful harmony.

One can hardly doubt the sincerity with which participants and moviegoers celebrated the life-style and moral imperatives of peace. They displayed peacefulness, gentleness, in much of their behavior. The combativeness in which youthful peace protesters often indulge was deliberately and consciously avoided by the Woodstock audience, and even more scrupulously avoided by the producers of the film. Yet war is an inseparable strand in the fabric of modern American culture. For many young people it is at least a temporary career; for most it is known through motion pictures, television fiction, and television news. Most of these young people, generally but not exclusively under thirty, played as children with guns and the forms and paraphernalia of war—or watched, perhaps with envy, as their brothers did so. Their fathers, uncles, and older brothers served in the military. Many of their earliest memories are of these men in uniform. Many of their earliest forays into the attics and storage closets of their homes culminated in the discovery of military uniforms, medals, insignia, even rifles and souvenir weapons. They heard, with unvarying reverence and with low-voiced seriousness, of those of the family circle who died at war. They thrilled to military parades. They learned that no matter how much military activities seemed like their own play, it had an adult aspect of unfailing seriousness and significance. Their early images of patriotism were influenced by motion pictures celebrating military heroism. They saluted the flag, while, on the screen, machinery of war, guns, planes, stoic or sad-faced dogfaces, passed to martial trumpets. Outside their schools, as outside the most imposing buildings in their community, their flag flew above monuments to warriors: honor rolls, outsize sculpture of men in battle. They wore scout uniforms, and drilled and marched and paraded. They envied their peers who got to carry the silvered rifles at the head of the file. They saw military men on their postage stamps, on their saving stamps, in their coloring books. The most noticeable college students were those in the uniform of the Reserve Officers Training Corps.

From *Journal of Popular Culture*, 4 (3), Winter 1971, 769–776. Reprinted by permission of the author and the editors.

The people of Woodstock have repudiated war. They have undergone a moral revulsion that expands from a commitment to peace to a disdain of militarism as it appears in civilian life in the guises of regimentation, authoritative control, and ideals of physical prowess and bravery. (Doubtless the revulsion is not always simply or uniquely moral or idealistic, nor untouched by the social dynamics of group and family relationships.) They have created their own society, collected its members physically at Woodstock, and recreated that community at movie theaters. By assembling their nation in one place, they have had to invent forms of group behavior and administration. In so doing they have drawn on their culture, its norms, ideals, attitudes, and technologies. They have, for the first time, produced a nation in which they play the roles of adults.

This nation, whose existence is predicated on moral disapproval of American involvement in Vietnam, invents new styles of individual and group life which are mirror images of the very war they oppose, or, more accurately, of that war as it is comprehended through television newsfilm superimposed on the previously imbibed war culture of past decades. To describe Woodstock, as it strikes the senses, ignoring its underlying moral postures, is, in a surprising number of instances, to describe the war in Vietnam. It is not a case of conscious critical parody but, although Woodstock's life style derives from a refusal to imitate, of imitation of, and initiation into, the learned culture of the nation at large.

The number of those who made the trip to Woodstock, and who brought their own culture into the alien, rural, agricultural countryside is on the same order of magnitude, 400,000, as the number of Americans who did the same in South Vietnam. (There is no reason to assume simply that this is a gratuitous likeness unrelated to modern logistical technologies or concepts of social groupings.) The attitudes of the natives to the invaders was in both cases mixed: they represented at once economic relief or opportunity, for some the chance of a windfall, yet also the potential for unrest and danger, not only to person and property, but to the social mores and moral values of the community. For the public relations men of both armies this relationship with the host community represented both a problem and an opportunity. The same solutions were found by each group, and with equally limited success: television camera teams filmed interviews with selected natives who described their early fears about the invaders and their new-found convictions that such fears were unreasonable.

Despite such forced evidence of shared values, a self-conscious tolerance was the limit of rapport. Native and invader do not merge. The native becomes a valuable adjunct—"Woodstock" shows a native good-humoredly, even devotedly, cleaning portable lavatories—but he has no relationship at all to the central missions of the festival: music, drugs, community. The native supplies water in an emergency, allows the pitching of tents on a lawn, but he does not enter the festival grounds nor respond to the special cultural characteristics of the invading warriors. Another set of outsiders have a place in the consciousness of the invaders: the worried folks back home. These appear, by implication, in scenes found on all military bases, as soldiers line up to use the telephone center.

With these outsiders too there is an unbridgeable gap, but a gap that can be ignored as long as the invaders are not subject to outsiders' pressure. A tolerant even submissive gentleness is made possible by the native pretense that the invaders have no special role, no important enterprise. That enterprise is indeed kept secret from the natives, not by keeping it hidden, but by refusing to make it public, by refusing to attempt to proselytize. It is the expression of the invaders' elitism, of their disdain for the native, his culture, his pretensions. The invader treats the natives as children, beneath serious indoctrination. They are not invited to participate because they are children, not because they are, or might be, naughty children. The invader assumes that the natives' business is not business at all, only play. They are given a pacifier—and pacified. The invader assumes that pacification works—it is unthinkable that it should not.

In many aspects of style, posture, gesture, as well as in verbalized sentiment, the invader is self-consciously aware of the merit of his moral behavior and that of his group. He knows that his group is under surveillance and that he himself is apt to be filmed and interviewed without notice. Natives too, and less dedicated invaders, need his example of self-confidence. The invader mutters about the hardships of bivouac life, often he exclaims with disbelief at the degree of his inconvenience, but both invader and spectator know this is but modesty masking speechless pride.

The Woodstock nation is given to military paraphernalia. Surplus webbed belts support khaki-clad canteens and first-aid kits. As in the army, these hold a variety of irregular supplies. Bull horns, commands, dog tags, shoulder patches, marching boots, mess kits, are in plain sight. Ragged military uniforms and other clothes in shreds, and shredding, are popular too. Those who have guitars never seem to put them down or to become accustomed to their burden. The instrument, like the soldier's rifle, is held, petted, caressed, even pointed, and kept always at hand like the "best-friend" it is said to be. The guitar *is* their weapon, and it is carried with the secret care and excitement with which one totes a machine-gun in a violin case. So armed and with a stupified gaze and a gingerly movement through the littered camp, one gives the impression of a soldier just, and barely, escaped from a holocaust.

A sense of being in the eye of the storm, just returned from or just about to re-enter the disaster area or combat zone, colors the mundane activities of the invaders. There is an earnestness, a careful scrupulosity, in the way tents are set, food prepared and served. Each invader has, in addition to his primary role before the music stage, a secondary but formal social function to fulfill. He may be on a feeding team (K.P.), assistant to a roving medic, or engaged in some chore of sanitation. He may wear a special armband and have special authority to keep peace and order among the troops (M.P.). We are in a disaster area. Roads are closed to all but emergency vehicles. Even so, the terrain being what it is, helicopter evacuation of the wounded is essential. The invaders take the sight of helicopters in their stride—in affairs of great danger and moment, one does not gape at one's tools however exotic.

Most all of the invaders are engaged in the same danger-filled endeavor, yet only a few, by the blindest chance, become casualties. We keep a stiff upper lip, use understatement and clipped, almost professional jargon to describe it: a bad trip, KIA, POW, LSD. Sleep and meals are irregular, unpredictable, for the large emergency spawns minor calamities. But the confusion of crowded and makeshift quarters, of random and separated movements, congeals into machine-like order and competence when it must. A walkie-talkie sputters. Lights are focused on an important installation. The invaders cannot wait for new struts and couplings, or for a team of specialists. Tools are hung from belts, the tower scaled, the grid repaired—all with a convincingly assumed professionalism. Hand signals alert a hovering 'copter. Unseen eyes respond and the tower throws down light like artillery on the stage where invaders return to their carpentry and wiring. Repairs are jury-rigged. One makes do because one has to. Only in extreme emergencies does a chopper bring supplies or reinforcements from the outside. It lands among the blase.

It is a time of constant sacrifice. Cooperation is a necessity, not a virtue. One does not show pride in his valor, skill, or passing acts of love and kindness. The pride is in one's participation, in the larger sacrifice. Only when prodded does it come out: "I hitchhiked 3,000 miles, got no sleep, spent all my money, got sick on bad grass." If sacrifice is an assumption, compensations are also assumed. The proprieties of the quotidian are inappropriate here. One need not shave. Shelter for the night is freely given. Sex is a trivial consideration when safety, or at least health, is at stake. Race too is irrelevant in battle. The freedom of spontaneous nudity can be more easily attained under fire, in crowded quarters, and where there are no special places for medical treatment, no bathrooms, no dressing rooms. The ambiance of danger and possible catastrophe makes the courting of new levels of sensation or risk almost mandatory. The Woodstock nation invades in order to do what they need not invade to do.

But the aura of the battlefield provides an unspoken supportive sanction, even an injunction.

The discomforts and privileges of the bivouac are not suffered merely for the sake of "togetherness." The invaders come together to hear the music, although their role is not merely a passive one. They respond to it, emotionally and physically. They know they are in fact responsible for its presence and its nature. The performers assume this intimate relationship with their patrons. The applause of recognition greets familiar numbers and well-known trade-mark mannerisms. The performers acknowledge the recognition, even prompt it.

The prelude to performance is a hushed silence. The onset is prodigiously and unexpectedly swift and loud. The volume would be painful were it not for the special nature of the occasion. The performer's kleiglit violence is in extreme contrast to the gentle stupefaction of the darkened audience. The words and the melodic line are torn, wrenched, hurled, distorted to incoherence. An explosion, a barrage of shells in a quiet night. A psychedelic spatter bursting in the neon-acrylic color of a frenzied lightshow. The bursts are of unpredictable duration. The listener is stunned; he listens and cannot act. The volume and the beat subside as suddenly and unexpectedly as they accelerated. Obscenities in the lyric are like grace notes, for their audience is shocked by the music well beyond usual thresholds. The performer gyrates with sudden and grotesque violence. Legs, arms, heads, snap out not as gesture but as response to invisible stimulus—a frog under galvanic spell. No pattern of grimace or contortion can be traced. There are shouts, moans, yells, the looks and sounds of some ultimate desperation, some final anguish. There seems to be neither control nor coordination of elements. It is like a demonic possession. It is the reaction of a man shot in the stomach. One watches in awe. He is one of us; it might have been me. But we are all helpless beyond volition. It is the ultimate heroic sacrifice, our century's version of the slow-dying tenor in an Italian opera, or of the primordial rite of the scape-goat. The senselessly selective thunderbolt of the bad trip is its daily analogue. It is chaos made conventional, ordered, and meaningful, although its larger structure is that of a spot on a television variety show. There are sententious introductions and commercials, though of a self-congratulatory and public service nature. It is the format in which war films reach us— moments of chaos regularly interspersed with profitably gentle, if bland, order.

On the last day, the immense business of breaking camp. Much grass has been trampled, much defoliation, but squads of volunteers "police the area." There is a sense of accomplishment of a well-ordered maneuver. The technologies, from helicopters to electric amplification of sound, have been mastered, as have modern administrative technologies: the division of labor and the American knack of make-do ingenuity. Military discipline—not that of the parade ground, but the harder and less obvious silent exigencies of the battlefield—has been maintained. There have been no cowards or malingerers. Snafus have been overcome and made comic. An exhausted invader stretches out on a blanket. His nurse, looking toward the horizon, lights a cigarette, draws, exhales. She puts it in his mouth, barely looking at him. His smile is scarcely apparent through his stolid grimness. A camera's long lens finds a couple strolling in the distance, knee-deep in soft-focus grass. Suddenly they embrace and fall beneath the grass line. Lovers. But the scene lacks only the sound of sniper-fire to be a news department's favorite Vietnam footage.

The Woodstock invaders do not march off, they trudge—emptied. But there will be more battles elsewhere, and the elan will return. They will polish their armor and oil their guns. The Woodstock nation that has morally repudiated the war of its decade, unable to legislate or to otherwise control events, reacts through style: life-style and counter-culture. Their festival is a paradigm of the military culture of their youth: a ready peacefulness punctuated with orgies of release through the accepted chaos of purposeful war on foreign soil. Their symbol is not the flag, but to their symbols they are sternly and deeply patriotic. Their forms are contemporary: modern technologies, including the technology and programming of television, are carelessly, proudly, assimilated. They have the war they were brought up for. It is a child's war; it is play. Who are more serious, and more proud of that seriousness, than children at play? Their game is a success. They demonstrate their moral superiority to the father by an irrefutable idealism while they replace the father in his most cherished public role, that of the warrior. By the lottery of drugs, with their random revenges, and by the communal selection and adulation of the sacrificial performer, they mitigate their violence.

The Imagination of Disaster

Susan Sontag

Science fiction became popular when late nineteenth-century thinkers began to replace or supplement their faith in God with a belief in science. Jules Verne and H. G. Wells pioneered the genre and developed the now-classic themes of space and time travel and invasion by aliens. The first memorable American science-fiction author was Edgar Rice Burroughs— better known today as the creator of Tarzan. As science fiction matured, the writers became more knowledgeable about science, but most of them continued to exhibit a serene assurance in a simplistic idea of progress (two robots in every home equals happiness) and thus were rudely jolted by the horrors of World War II. Since that time they have been wary of technological utopias; much science fiction is now devoted to speculation about the impact of scientific knowledge on humanistic values.

Futuristic stories have been adopted for use on radio and television and for the movies. Rarely have these media utilized the most imaginative stories; they have been content to repeat certain formulas. Perhaps, as Susan Sontag notes in her study of science-fiction movies, this tendency casts light on the obsessions of contemporary America. Or, it may only indicate the desire of those in control of the media to imitate successful plots.

Dick Allen's Science Fiction: The Future *is the best introduction to science fiction. Brian Murphy's "Monster Movies: They Came from Beneath the Fifties" contains intriguing speculations about the function of monster movies.*

The typical science fiction film has a form as predictable as a Western, and is made up of elements which, to a practiced eye, are as classic as the saloon brawl, the blonde schoolteacher from the East, and the gun duel on the deserted main street.

One model scenario proceeds through five phases.

(1) The arrival of the thing. (Emergence of the monsters, landing of the alien spaceship, etc.) This is usually witnessed or suspected by just one person, a young scientist on a field trip. Nobody, neither his neighbors nor his colleagues, will believe him for some time. The hero is not married, but has a sympathetic though also incredulous girl friend.

(2) Confirmation of the hero's report by a host of witnesses to a great act of destruction. (If the invaders are beings from another planet, a fruitless attempt to parley with them and get them to leave peacefully.) The local police are summoned to deal with the situation and massacred.

(3) In the capital of the country, conferences between scientists and the military take place, with the hero lecturing before a chart, map, or blackboard. A national emergency is declared. Reports of further destruction. Authorities from other countries arrive in black limousines. All international tensions are suspended in view of the planetary emergency. This stage often includes a rapid montage of news broadcasts in various languages, a meeting at the UN, and more conferences between the military and the scientists. Plans are made for destroying the enemy.

(4) Further atrocities. At some point the hero's girl friend is in grave danger. Massive counter-attacks by international forces, with brilliant displays of rocketry, rays, and other advanced weapons, are all unsuccessful. Enormous military casualties, usually by incineration. Cities are destroyed and/or evacuated. There is an obligatory scene here of panicked crowds stampeding along a highway or a big bridge, being waved on by numerous policemen who, if the film is Japanese, are immaculately white-gloved, preternaturally calm, and call out in dubbed English, "Keep moving. There is no need to be alarmed."

(5) More conferences, whose motif is: "They must be vulnerable to something." Throughout the hero has been working in his lab to this end. The final strategy, upon which all hopes depend, is drawn up; the ultimate weapon—often a super-powerful, as yet untested, nuclear device—is mounted. Countdown. Final repulse of the monster or invaders. Mutual congratulations, while the hero and girl friend embrace cheek to cheek and scan the skies sturdily. "But have we seen the last of them?"

From Susan Sontag, *Against Interpretation and Other Essays* (New York: Farrar, Straus & Giroux), pp. 209–225. Copyright © 1965, 1966 by Susan Sontag. Reprinted by permission of the author and Farrar, Straus & Giroux, Inc.

The film I have just described should be in color and on a wide screen. Another typical scenario, which follows, is simpler and suited to black-and-white films with a lower budget. It has four phases.

(1) The hero (usually, but not always, a scientist) and his girl friend, or his wife and two children, are disporting themselves in some innocent ultra-normal middle-class surroundings—their house in a small town, or on vacation (camping, boating). Suddenly, someone starts behaving strangely; or some innocent form of vegetation becomes monstrously enlarged and ambulatory. If a character is pictured driving an automobile, something gruesome looms up in the middle of the road. If it is night, strange lights hurtle across the sky.

(2) After following the thing's tracks, or determining that It is radioactive, or poking around a huge crater—in short, conducting some sort of crude investigation—the hero tries to warn the local authorities, without effect; nobody believes anything is amiss. The hero knows better. If the thing is tangible, the house is elaborately barricaded. If the invading alien is an invisible parasite, a doctor or friend is called in, who is himself rather quickly killed or "taken possession of" by the thing.

(3) The advice of whoever further is consulted proves useless. Meanwhile, It continues to claim other victims in the town, which remains implausibly isolated from the rest of the world. General helplessness.

(4) One of two possibilities. Either the hero prepares to do battle alone, accidentally discovers the thing's one vulnerable point, and destroys it. Or, he somehow manages to get out of town and succeeds in laying his case before competent authorities. They, along the lines of the first script but abridged, deploy a complex technology which (after initial setbacks) finally prevails against the invaders.

Another version of the second script opens with the scientist-hero in his laboratory, which is located in the basement or on the grounds of his tasteful, prosperous house. Through his experiments, he unwittingly causes a frightful metamorphosis in some class of plants or animals which turn carnivorous and go on a rampage. Or else, his experiments have caused him to be injured (sometimes irrevocably) or "invaded" himself. Perhaps he has been experimenting with radiation, or has built a machine to communicate with beings from other planets or transport him to other places or times.

Another version of the first script involves the discovery of some fundamental alteration in the conditions of existence of our planet, brought about by nuclear testing, which will lead to the extinction in a few months of all human life. For example: the temperature of the earth is becoming too high or too low to support life, or the earth is cracking in two, or it is gradually being blanketed by lethal fallout.

A third script, somewhat but not altogether different from the first two, concerns a journey through space—to the moon, or some other planet. What the space-voyagers discover commonly is that the alien terrain is in a state of dire emergency, itself threatened by extra-planetary invaders or nearing extinction through the practice of nuclear warfare. The terminal dramas of the first and second scripts are played out there, to which is added the problem of getting away from the doomed and/or hostile planet and back to Earth.

I am aware, of course, that there are thousands of science fiction novels (their heyday was the late 1940s), not to mention the transcriptions of science fiction themes which, more and more, provide the principal subject-matter of comic books. But I propose to discuss science fiction films (the present period began in 1950 and continues, considerably abated, to this day) as an independent sub-genre, without reference to other media—and, most particularly, without reference to the novels from which, in many cases, they were adapted. For, while novel and film may share the same plot, the fundamental difference between the resources of the novel and the film makes them quite dissimilar.

Certainly, compared with the science fiction novels, their film counterparts have unique strengths, one of which is the immediate representation of the extraordinary: physical deformity and mutation, missile and rocket combat, toppling skyscrapers. The movies are, naturally, weak just where the science fiction novels (some of them) are strong—on science. But in place of an intellectual workout, they can supply something the novels can never provide—sensuous elaboration. In the films it is by means of images and sounds, not words that have to be translated by the imagination, that one can participate in the fantasy of living through one's own death and more, the death of cities, the destruction of humanity itself.

Science fiction films are not about science. They are about disaster, which is one of the oldest subjects of art. In science fiction films disaster is rarely viewed intensively; it is always extensive. It is a matter of quantity and ingenuity. If you will, it is a question of scale. But the scale, particularly in the wide-screen color films (of which the ones by the Japanese director Inoshiro Honda and the American director George Pal are technically the most convincing and visually the most exciting), does raise the matter to another level.

Thus, the science fiction film (like that of a very different contemporary genre, the Happening) is concerned with the aesthetics of destruction, with the peculiar beauties to be found in wreaking havoc, making a mess. And it is in the imagery of destruction that the core of a good science fiction film lies. Hence, the disadvantage of the cheap film—in which the monster appears or the rocket lands in a small dull-looking town. (Hollywood budget needs usually dictate that the town be in the Arizona or California desert. In *The Thing From Another World* [1951] the rather sleazy and confined set is supposed to be an encampment near the North Pole.) Still, good black-and-white science fiction films have been made. But a bigger budget, which usually means color, allows a much greater play back and forth among several model environments. There is the populous city. There is the lavish but ascetic interior of the spaceship—either the invaders' or ours—replete with streamlined chromium fixtures and dials and machines whose complexity is indicated by the number of colored lights they flash and strange noises they emit. There is the laboratory crowded with formidable boxes and scientific apparatus. There is a comparatively old-fashioned-looking conference room, where the scientists unfurl charts to explain the desperate state of things to the military. And each of these standard locales or backgrounds is subject to two modalities—intact and destroyed. We may, if we are lucky, be treated to a panorama of melting tanks, flying bodies, crashing walls, awesome craters and fissures in the earth, plummeting spacecraft, colorful deadly rays; and to a symphony of screams, weird electronic signals, the noisiest military hardware going, and the leaden tones of the laconic denizens of alien planets and their subjugated earthlings.

Certain of the primitive gratifications of science fiction films—for instance, the depiction of urban disaster on a colossally magnified scale —are shared with other types of films. Visually there is little difference between mass havoc as represented in the old horror and monster films and what we find in science fiction films, except (again) scale. In the old monster films, the monster always headed for the great city, where he had to do a fair bit of rampaging, hurling busses off bridges, crumpling trains in his bare hands, toppling buildings, and so forth. The archetype is King Kong, in Schoedsack and Cooper's great film of 1933, running amok, first in the native village (trampling babies, a bit of footage excised from most prints), then in New York. This is really no different in spirit from the scene in Inoshiro Honda's *Rodan* (1957) in which two giant reptiles—with a wingspan of 500 feet and supersonic speeds—by flapping their wings whip up a cyclone that blows most of Tokyo to smithereens. Or the destruction of half of Japan by the gigantic robot with the great incinerating ray that shoots forth from his eyes, at the beginning of Honda's *The Mysterians* (1959). Or, the devastation by the rays from a fleet of flying saucers of New York, Paris, and Tokyo, in *Battle in Outer Space*

(1960). Or, the inundation of New York in *When Worlds Collide* (1951). Or, the end of London in 1966 depicted in George Pal's *The Time Machine* (1960). Neither do these sequences differ in aesthetic intention from the destruction scenes in the big sword, sandal, and orgy color spectaculars set in Biblical and Roman times—the end of Sodom in Aldrich's *Sodom and Gomorrah,* of Gaza in De Mille's *Samson and Delilah,* of Rhodes in *The Colossus of Rhodes,* and of Rome in a dozen Nero movies. Griffith began it with the Babylon sequence in *Intolerance,* and to this day there is nothing like the thrill of watching all those expensive sets come tumbling down.

In other respects as well, the science fiction films of the 1950s take up familiar themes. The famous 1930s movie serials and comics of the adventures of Flash Gordon and Buck Rogers, as well as the more recent spate of comic book super-heroes with extraterrestrial origins (the most famous is Superman, a foundling from the planet Krypton, currently described as having been exploded by a nuclear blast), share motifs with more recent science fiction movies. But there is an important difference. The old science fiction films, and most of the comics, still have an essentially innocent relation to disaster. Mainly they offer new versions of the oldest romance of all—of the strong invulnerable hero with a mysterious lineage come to do battle on behalf of good and against evil. Recent science fiction films have a decided grimness, bolstered by their much greater degree of visual credibility, which contrasts strongly with the older films. Modern historical reality has greatly enlarged the imagination of disaster, and the protagonists—perhaps by the very nature of what is visited upon them—no longer seem wholly innocent.

The lure of such generalized disaster as a fantasy is that it releases one from normal obligations. The trump card of the end-of-the-world movies—like *The Day the Earth Caught Fire* (1962)—is that great scene with New York or London or Tokyo discovered empty, its entire population annihilated. Or, as in *The World, The Flesh, and The Devil* (1957), the whole movie can be devoted to the fantasy of occupying the deserted metropolis and starting all over again, a world Robinson Crusoe.

Another kind of satisfaction these films supply is extreme moral simplification—that is to say, a morally acceptable fantasy where one can give outlet to cruel or at least amoral feelings. In this respect, science fiction films partly overlap with horror films. This is the undeniable pleasure we derive from looking at freaks, beings excluded from the category of the human. The sense of superiority over the freak conjoined in varying proportions with the titillation of fear and aversion makes it possible for moral scruples to be lifted, for cruelty to be enjoyed. The same thing happens in science fiction films. In the figure of the monster from outer space, the freakish, the ugly, and the predatory all converge—and provide a fantasy target for righteous bellicosity to discharge itself, and for the aesthetic enjoyment of suffering and disaster. Science fiction films are one of the purest forms of spectacle; that is, we are rarely inside anyone's feelings. (An exception is Jack Arnold's *The Incredible Shrinking Man* [1957].) We are merely spectators; we watch.

But in science fiction films, unlike horror films, there is not much horror. Suspense, shocks, surprises are mostly abjured in favor of a steady, inexorable plot. Science fiction films invite a dispassionate, aesthetic view of destruction and violence—a *technological* view. Things, objects, machinery play a major role in these films. A greater range of ethical values is embodied in the décor of these films than in the people. Things, rather than the helpless humans, are the locus of values because we experience them, rather than people, as the sources of power. According to science fiction films, man is naked without his artifacts. *They* stand for different values, they are potent, they are what get destroyed, and they are the indispensable tools for the repulse of the alien invaders or the repair of the damaged environment.

The science fiction films are strongly moralistic. The standard message is the one about the proper, or humane, use of science, versus the mad, obsessional use of science. This message the science fiction films share in common with the classic horror films of the 1930s, like *Frankenstein, The Mummy, Island of Lost Souls, Dr. Jekyll and Mr. Hyde.* (Georges Franju's brilliant *Les Yeux Sans Visage* [1959], called here *The Horror Chamber of Doctor Faustus,* is a more recent example.) In the horror films, we have the mad or obsessed or misguided scientist who pursues his experiments against good advice to the contrary, creates a monster or monsters, and is himself destroyed—often recognizing his folly himself, and dying in the successful effort to destroy his own creation. One science fiction equivalent of this is the scientist, usually a member of a team, who defects to the planetary invaders because "their" science is more advanced than "ours."

This is the case in *The Mysterians,* and, true to form, the renegade sees his error in the end, and from within the Mysterian space ship destroys it and himself. In *This Island Earth* (1955), the inhabitants of the beleaguered planet Metaluna propose to conquer earth, but their project is foiled by a Metalunan scientist named Exeter who, having lived on earth a while and learned to love Mozart, cannot abide such viciousness. Exeter plunges his spaceship into the ocean after returning a glamorous pair (male and female) of American physicists to earth. Metaluna dies. In *The Fly* (1958), the hero, engrossed in his basement-laboratory experiments on a matter-transmitting machine, uses himself as a subject, exchanges head and one arm with a housefly which had accidentally gotten into the machine, becomes a monster, and with his last shred of human will destroys his laboratory and orders his wife to kill him. His discovery, for the good of mankind, is lost.

Being a clearly labeled species of intellectual, scientists in science fiction films are always liable to crack up or go off the deep end. In *Conquest of Space* (1955), the scientist-commander of an international expedition to Mars suddenly acquires scruples about the blasphemy involved in the undertaking, and begins reading the Bible mid-journey instead of attending to his duties. The commander's son, who is his junior officer and always addresses his father as "General," is forced to kill the old man when he tries to prevent the ship from landing on Mars. In this film, both sides of the ambivalence toward scientists are given voice. Generally, for a scientific enterprise to be treated entirely sympathetically in these films, it needs the certificate of utility. Science, viewed without ambivalence, means an efficacious response to danger. Disinterested intellectual curiosity rarely appears in any form other than caricature, as a maniacal dementia that cuts one off from normal human relations. But this suspicion is usually directed at the scientist rather than his work. The creative scientist may become a martyr to his own discovery, through an accident or by pushing things too far. But the implication remains that other men, less imaginative—in short, technicians—could have administered the same discovery better and more safely. The most ingrained contemporary mistrust of the intellect is visited, in these movies, upon the scientist-as-intellectual.

The message that the scientist is one who releases forces which, if not controlled for good, could destroy man himself seems innocuous enough. One of the oldest images of the scientist is Shakespeare's Prospero, the overdetached scholar forcibly retired from society to a desert island, only partly in control of the magic forces in which he dabbles. Equally classic is the figure of the scientist as satanist (*Doctor Faustus,* and stories of Poe and Hawthorne). Science is magic, and man has always known that there is black magic as well as white. But it is not enough to remark that contemporary attitudes—as reflected in science fiction films—remain ambivalent, that the scientist is treated as both satanist and savior. The proportions have changed, because of the new context in which the old admiration and fear of the scientist are located. For his sphere of influence is no longer local, himself or his immediate community. It is planetary, cosmic.

One gets the feeling, particularly in the Japanese films but not only there, that a mass trauma exists over the use of nuclear weapons and the possibility of future nuclear wars. Most of the science fiction films bear witness to this trauma, and, in a way, attempt to exorcise it.

The accidental awakening of the super-destructive monster who has slept in the earth since prehistory is, often, an obvious metaphor for the Bomb. But there are many explicit references as well. In *The Mysterians,* a probe ship from the planet Mysteroid has landed on earth, near Tokyo. Nuclear warfare having been practiced on Mysteroid for centuries (their civilization is "more advanced than ours"), ninety percent of those now born on the planet have to be destroyed at birth, because of defects caused by the huge amounts of Strontium 90 in their diet. The Mysterians have come to earth to marry earth women, and possibly to take over our relatively uncontaminated planet. . . . In *The Incredible Shrinking Man,* the John Doe hero is the victim of a gust of radiation which blows over the water, while he is out boating with his wife; the radiation causes him to grow smaller and smaller, until at the end of the movie he steps through the fine mesh of a window screen to become "the infinitely small." . . . In *Rodan,* a horde of monstrous carnivorous prehistoric insects, and finally a pair of giant flying reptiles (the prehistoric Archeopteryx), are hatched from dormant eggs in the depths of a mine shaft by the impact of nuclear test explosions, and go on to destroy a good part of the world before they are felled by the molten lava of a volcanic eruption. . . . In the English film, *The Day the Earth Caught Fire,* two simultaneous hydrogen bomb tests by the United States and Russia change by 11 degrees the tilt of the earth on its axis and alter the earth's orbit so that it begins to approach the sun.

Radiation casualties—ultimately, the conception of the whole world as a casualty of nuclear testing and nuclear warfare—is the most ominous of all the notions with which science fiction films deal. Universes become expendable. Worlds become contaminated, burnt out, exhausted, obsolete. In *Rocketship X-M* (1950) explorers from the earth land on Mars, where they learn that atomic warfare has destroyed Martian civilization. In George Pal's *The War of the Worlds* (1953), reddish spindly alligator-skinned creatures from Mars invade the earth because their planet is becoming too cold to be inhabitable. In *This Island Earth,* also American, the planet Metaluna, whose population has long ago been driven underground by warfare, is dying under the missile attacks of an enemy planet. Stocks of uranium, which power the force field shielding Metaluna, have been used up; and an unsuccessful expedition is sent to earth to enlist earth scientists to devise new sources for nuclear power. In Joseph Losey's *The Damned* (1961), nine icy-cold radioactive children are being reared by a fanatical scientist in a dark cave on the English coast to be the only survivors of the inevitable nuclear Armageddon.

There is a vast amount of wishful thinking in science fiction films, some of it touching, some of it depressing. Again and again, one detects the hunger for a "good war," which poses no moral problems, admits of no moral qualifications. The imagery of science fiction films will satisfy the most bellicose addict of war films, for a lot of the satisfactions of war films pass, untransformed, into science fiction films. Examples: the dogfights between earth "fighter rockets" and alien spacecraft in the *Battle in Outer Space* (1960); the escalating firepower in the successive assaults upon the invaders in *The Mysterians,* which Dan Talbot correctly described as a non-stop holocaust; the spectacular bombardment of the underground fortress of Metaluna in *This Island Earth.*

Yet at the same time the bellicosity of science fiction films is neatly channeled into the yearning for peace, or for at least peaceful coexistence. Some scientist generally takes sententious note of the fact that it took the planetary invasion to make the warring nations of the earth come to their senses and suspend their own conflicts. One of the main themes of many science fiction films—the color ones usually, because they have the budget and resources to develop the military spectacle—is this UN fantasy, a fantasy of united warfare. (The same wishful UN theme cropped up in a recent spectacular which is not science fiction, *Fifty-Five Days in Peking* [1963]. There, topically enough, the Chinese, the Boxers, play the role of Martian invaders who unite the earthmen, in this case the United States, England, Russia, France, Germany, Italy, and Japan.) A great enough disaster cancels all enmities and calls upon the utmost concentration of earth resources.

Science—technology—is conceived of as the great unifier. Thus the science fiction films also project a Utopian fantasy. In the classic models of Utopian thinking—Plato's Republic, Campanella's City of the Sun, More's Utopia, Swift's land of the Houyhnhnms, Voltaire's Eldorado—society had worked out a perfect consensus. In these societies reasonableness had achieved an unbreakable supremacy over the emotions. Since no disagreement or social conflict was intellectually plausible, none was possible. As in Melville's *Typee,* "they all think the same." The universal rule of reason meant universal agreement. It is interesting, too, that societies in which reason was pictured as totally ascendant were also traditionally pictured as having an ascetic or materially frugal and economically simple mode of life. But in the Utopian world community projected by science fiction films, totally pacified and ruled by scientific consensus, the demand for simplicity of material existence would be absurd.

Yet alongside the hopeful fantasy of moral simplification and international unity embodied in the science fiction films lurk the deepest anxieties about contemporary existence. I don't mean only the very real trauma of the Bomb—that it has been used, that there are enough now to kill everyone on earth many times over, that those new bombs may very well be used. Besides these new anxieties about physical disaster, the prospect of universal mutilation and even annihilation, the science fiction films reflect powerful anxieties about the condition of the individual psyche.

For science fiction films may also be described as a popular mythology for the contemporary *negative* imagination about the impersonal. The other-world creatures that seek to take "us" over are an "it," not a "they." The planetary invaders are usually zombie-like. Their movements are either cool, mechanical, or lumbering, blobby. But it amounts to the same thing. If they are non-human in form, they proceed with an absolutely regular, unalterable movement (unalterable save by destruction). If they are human in form—dressed in space suits, etc.—then they obey the most rigid military discipline, and display no personal characteristics whatsoever. And it is this regime of emotionlessness, of impersonality, of regimentation, which they will impose on the earth if they are successful. "No more love, no more beauty, no more pain," boasts a converted earthling in *The Invasion of the Body Snatchers* (1956). The half-earthling, half-alien children in *The Children of the Damned* (1960) are absolutely emotionless, move as a group and understand each others' thoughts, and are all prodigious intellects. They are the wave of the future, man in his next stage of development.

These alien invaders practice a crime which is worse than murder. They do not simply kill the person. They obliterate him. In *The War of the Worlds,* the ray which issues from the rocket ship disintegrates all persons and objects in its path, leaving no trace of them but a light ash. In Honda's *The H-Man* (1959), the creeping blob melts all flesh with which it comes in contact. If the blob, which looks like a huge hunk of red Jello and can crawl across floors and up and down walls, so much as touches your bare foot, all that is left of you is a heap of clothes on the floor. (A more articulated, size-multiplying blob is the villain in the English film *The Creeping Unknown* [1956].) In another version of this fantasy, the body is preserved but the person is entirely reconstituted as the automatized servant or agent of the alien powers. This is, of course, the vampire fantasy in new dress. The person is really dead, but he doesn't know it. He is "undead," he has become an "unperson." It happens to a whole California town in *The Invasion of the Body Snatchers,* to several earth scientists in *This Island Earth,* and to assorted innocents in *It Came From Outer Space, Attack of the Puppet People* (1958), and *The Brain Eaters* (1958). As the victim always backs away from the vampire's horrifying embrace, so in science fiction films the person always fights being "taken over"; he wants to retain his humanity. But once the deed has been done, the victim is eminently satisfied with his condition. He has not been converted from human amiability to monstrous "animal" bloodlust (a metaphoric exaggeration of sexual desire), as in the old vampire fantasy. No, he has simply become far more efficient—the very model of technocratic man, purged of emotions, volitionless, tranquil, obedient to all orders. (The dark secret behind human nature used to be the upsurge of the animal—as in *King Kong*. The threat to man, his availability to dehumanization, lay in his own animality. Now the danger is understood as residing in man's ability to be turned into a machine.)

The rule, of course, is that this horrible and irremediable form of murder can strike anyone in the film except the hero. The hero and his family, while greatly threatened, always escape this fate and by the end of the film the invaders have been repulsed or destroyed. I know of only one exception, *The Day That Mars Invaded Earth* (1963), in which after all the standard struggles the scientist-hero, his wife, and their two children are "taken over" by the alien invaders—and that's that. (The last minutes of the film show them being incinerated by the Martians' rays and their ash silhouettes flushed down their empty swimming pool, while their simulacra drive off in the family car.) Another variant but upbeat switch on the rule occurs in *The Creation of the Humanoids* (1964), where the hero discovers at the end of the film that he, too, has been turned into a metal robot, complete with highly efficient and virtually indestructible mechanical insides, although he didn't know it and detected no difference in himself. He learns, however, that he will shortly be upgraded into a "humanoid" having all the properties of a real man.

Of all the standard motifs of science fiction films, this theme of dehumanization is perhaps the most fascinating. For, as I have indicated, it is scarcely a black-and-white situation, as in the old vampire films. The attitude of the science fiction films toward depersonalization is mixed. On the one hand, they deplore it as the ultimate horror. On the other hand, certain characteristics of the dehumanized invaders, modulated and disguised—such as the ascendancy of reason over feelings, the idealization of teamwork and the consensus-creating activities of science, a marked degree of moral simplification—are precisely traits of the savior-scientist. It is interesting that when the scientist in these films is treated negatively, it is usually done through the portrayal of an individual scientist who holes up in his laboratory and neglects his fiancée or his loving wife and children, obsessed by his daring and dangerous experiments. The scientist as a loyal member of a team, and therefore considerably less individualized, is treated quite respectfully

There is absolutely no social criticism, of even the most implicit kind, in science fiction films. No criticism, for example, of the conditions of our society which create the impersonality and dehumanization which science

fiction fantasies displace onto the influence of an alien It. Also, the notion of science as a social activity, interlocking with social and political
interests, is unacknowledged. Science is simply either adventure (for good
or evil) or a technical response to danger. And, typically, when the fear of
science is paramount—when science is conceived of as black magic
rather than white—the evil has no attribution beyond that of the perverse
will of an individual scientist. In science fiction films the antithesis of black
magic and white is drawn as a split between technology, which is bene-
ficent, and the errant individual will of a lone intellectual.

Thus, science fiction films can be looked at as thematically central
allegory, replete with standard modern attitudes. The theme of depersonalization (being "taken over") which I have been talking about is a new
allegory reflecting the age-old awareness of man that, sane, he is always
perilously close to insanity and unreason. But there is something more
here than just a recent, popular image which expresses man's perennial,
but largely unconscious, anxiety about his sanity. The image derives most
of its power from a supplementary and historical anxiety, also not experienced *consciously* by most people, about the depersonalizing conditions
of modern urban life. Similarly, it is not enough to note that science fiction
allegories are one of the new myths about—that is, one of the ways of
accommodating to and negating—the perennial human anxiety about
death. (Myths of heaven and hell, and of ghosts, had the same function.)
For, again, there is a historically specifiable twist which intensifies the
anxiety. I mean, the trauma suffered by everyone in the middle of the 20th
century when it became clear that, from now on to the end of human history, every person would spend his individual life under the threat not only
of individual death, which is certain, but of something almost insupporta-
ble psychologically—collective incineration and extinction which could
come at any time, virtually without warning.

From a psychological point of view, the imagination of disaster does
not greatly differ from one period in history to another. But from a political
and moral point of view, it does. The expectation of the apocalypse may
be the occasion for a radical disaffiliation from society, as when thousands
of Eastern European Jews in the 17th century, hearing that Sabbatai
Zevi had been proclaimed the Messiah and that the end of the world
was imminent, gave up their homes and businesses and began the
trek to Palestine. But people take the news of their doom in diverse ways.
It is reported that in 1945 the populace of Berlin received without great
agitation the news that Hitler had decided to kill them all, before the Allies
arrived, because they had not been worthy enough to win the war. We are,
alas, more in the position of the Berliners of 1945 than of the Jews of 17th
century Eastern Europe; and our response is closer to theirs, too. What I

am suggesting is that the imagery of disaster in science fiction is above all the emblem of an *inadequate response.* I don't mean to bear down on the films for this. They themselves are only a sampling, stripped of sophistication, of the inadequacy of most people's response to the unassimilable terrors that infect their consciousness. The interest of the films, aside from their considerable amount of cinematic charm, consists in this intersection between a naïve and largely debased commercial art product and the most profound dilemmas of the contemporary situation.

Ours is indeed an age of extremity. For we live under continual threat of two equally fearful, but seemingly opposed, destinies: unremitting banality and inconceivable terror. It is fantasy, served out in large rations by the popular arts, which allows most people to cope with these twin specters. For one job that fantasy can do is to lift us out of the unbearably humdrum and to distract us from terrors—real or anticipated—by an escape into exotic, dangerous situations which have last-minute happy endings. But another of the things that fantasy can do is to normalize what is psychologically unbearable, thereby inuring us to it. In one case, fantasy beautifies the world. In the other, it neutralizes it.

The fantasy in science fiction films does both jobs. The films reflect world-wide anxieties, and they serve to allay them. They inculcate a strange apathy concerning the processes of radiation, contamination, and destruction which I for one find haunting and depressing. The naïve level of the films neatly tempers the sense of otherness, of alien-ness, with the grossly familiar. In particular, the dialogue of most science fiction films, which is of a monumental but often touching banality, makes them wonderfully, unintentionally funny. Lines like "Come quickly, there's a monster in my bathtub," "We must do something about this," "Wait, Professor. There's someone on the telephone," "But that's incredible," and the old American stand-by, "I hope it works!" are hilarious in the context of picturesque and deafening holocaust. Yet the films also contain something that is painful and in deadly earnest.

There is a sense in which all these movies are in complicity with the abhorrent. They neutralize it, as I have said. It is no more, perhaps, than the way all art draws its audience into a circle of complicity with the thing represented. But in these films we have to do with things which are (quite literally) unthinkable. Here, "thinking about the unthinkable"—not in the way of Herman Kahn, as a subject for calculation, but as a subject for fantasy—becomes, however inadvertently, itself a somewhat questionable act from a moral point of view. The films perpetuate clichés about identity, volition, power, knowledge, happiness, social consensus, guilt, responsibility which are, to say the leas* not serviceable in our present extremity. But collective nightmares cannot be banished by demonstrating that they are, intellectually and morally, fallacious. This nightmare—the one reflected, in various registers, in the science fiction films—is too close to our reality.

References

Allen, Dick (ed.). *Science Fiction: The Future.* New York: Harcourt Brace Jovanovich, 1971.

Allport, Gordon, and Cantril, Hadley. *The Psychology of Radio.* New York: Peter Smith, 1941.

Atherton, Lewis. *Main Street on the Middle Border.* Bloomington: University of Indiana Press, 1954.

Barnouw, Erik. *The Image Empire: A History of Broadcasting in the United States.* 3 vols. New York: Oxford University Press, 1970.

Barthel, Joan. "The World Has Turned More Than 3,200 Times." *The New York Times Magazine* (September 8, 1968), 67, 142, 144, 147, 152, 154.

Baum, Lyman Frank. *The Wizard of Oz.* Chicago: Rand McNally, 1971.

Bell, Daniel. "Crime as an American Way of Life." *Antioch Review,* 13, 1953, 131–154.

Berger, Arthur. *Li'l Abner: A Study of American Satire.* New York: Twayne Publishers, 1969.

Booth, Stanley. "A Hound Dog, To the Manor Born." *Esquire,* 69 (2), February 1968, 106–108, 48, 50, 52.

Cawelti, John G. "The Spillane Phenomenon." *University of Chicago Magazine,* 61, 1969, 18–25.

Cleaver, Eldridge. *Soul on Ice.* New York: Dell, 1968.

Coffin, Tristram P. *Armed Society: Militarism in Modern America.* Baltimore: Penguin Books, 1964.

Daniels, Les, and Peck, John. *Comix: A History of Comic Books in America.* New York: Outerbridge & Dienstfrey, 1971.

Deloria Vine. *Custer Died For Your Sins· An Indian Manifesto.* New York: Macmillan 1969.

————. *We Talk, You Listen: New Tribes, New Turf.* New York: Macmillan, 1970.

Douglas, George William. *The American Book of Days.* Revised by Helen Douglas Compton. New York: H. W. Wilson, 1937.

Dreiser, Theodore. *Sister Carrie.* New York: World Publishing Co., 1927.

Dulles, Foster Rhea. *America Learns to Play.* New York: Appleton-Century, 1940.

Easy Rider (Columbia, 1969). Director, Dennis Hopper.

Everson, William K. *Pictorial History of the Western Film.* New York: Citadel Press, 1971.

Feather, Leonard. *Inside Be-Bop.* New York: J. J. Robbins & Sons, 1949.

Feiffer, Jules (ed.). *The Great Comic Book Heroes.* New York: Bonanza Books, n.d.

Fiedler, Leslie. *An End to Innocence: Essays on Culture and Politics.* Boston: Beacon Press, 1955.

Fishwick, Marshall, and Browne, Ray B. (eds.). *Icons of Popular Culture.* Bowling Green: Bowling Green University Popular Press, 1970.

Folklore of the Mormon Country: J. Golden Kimball Stories, Together with the Brother Petersen Yarns, Told by Hector Lee (Folk Legacy Records, Inc., FTA-25: Huntington, Vt., 1964).

Gardiner, Martin, and Nye, Russel B. *The Wizard of Oz and Who He Was.* East Lansing: Michigan State University Press, 1957.

Goodman, Ezra. "Delirium Over Dead Star." *Life,* 61 (13), September 24, 1956, 75–76, 79–80, 85–86, 88.

The Graduate (Embassy, 1967). Director, Mike Nichols.

The Grapes of Wrath (Twentieth Century-Fox, 1940). Director, John Ford.

Griffith, Richard, and Mayer, Arthur. *The Movies.* Revised edition. New York: Simon & Schuster, 1970.

Higby, Mary Jane. *Tune in Tomorrow.* New York: Cowles Education Corp., 1968.

Hopkins, Jerry (ed.). *The Hippie Papers: Notes From the Underground Press.* New York: New American Library, 1968.

————. *The Rock Story.* New York: New American Library, 1970.

Hud (Paramount, 1963). Director, Martin Ritt.

Kael, Pauline. *Kiss Kiss Bang Bang.* Boston: Little, Brown, 1968.

Landau, Jon. "In Praise of Elvis Presley." *Rolling Stone,* No. 98, December 23, 1971, 72.

Lapp, Ralph E. *The Weapons Culture.* New York: Norton and Co., 1968.

Lasch, Christopher. "The Cultural Cold War: A Short History of the Congress for Cultural Freedom." In *Towards A New Past: Dissenting Essays in American History,* ed. Barton J. Bernstein. New York: Vintage Books, 1969. Pp. 322–359.

The Last Picture-Show (Columbia, 1971). Director, Peter Bogdanovich.

McLuhan, Marshall. *Understanding Media: The Extensions of Man.* New York: McGraw-Hill, 1964.

McMurtry, Larry. *Horseman, Pass By.* New York: Harper & Row, 1961.

———. *The Last Picture-Show.* New York: Dial Press, 1966.

Madden, David (ed.). *Tough Guy Writers of the Thirties.* Carbondale: Southern Illinois University Press, 1968.

Mailer, Norman. "The White Negro." In *Advertisements for Myself.* New York: New American Library, 1959. Pp. 302–322.

Miller, Henry. *Tropic of Capricorn.* New York: Grove Press, 1961.

Modern Times (United Artists, 1936). Director, Charlie Chaplin.

Murphy, Brian. "Monster Movies: They Came From Beneath the Fifties." *Journal of Popular Film,* 1 (1), Winter 1972, 31–44.

Nuttall, Jeff. *Bomb Culture.* New York: Dell, 1968.

Nye, Russel B. *The Unembarrassed Muse: The Popular Arts in America.* New York: Dial Press, 1970.

O'Dea, Thomas F. *The Mormons.* Chicago: University of Chicago Press, 1957.

Peters, Harry T. *Currier and Ives, Printmakers to the American People.* Garden City: Doubleday, Doran & Co., 1942.

Peterson, Robert W. *Only the Ball Was White.* Englewood Cliffs: Prentice-Hall, 1970.

Pitkin, Walter B. *Life Begins at Forty.* New York: McGraw-Hill, 1932.

Powdermaker, Hortense. "The Channeling of Negro Aggression by the Cultural Process." *American Journal of Sociology,* 48, May 1943, 750–758.

Purdy, Ken W. *Wonderful World of the Automobile.* New York: Crowell, 1960.

Report from Iron Mountain on the Possibility and Desirability of Peace. Introductory material by Leonard C. Lewin. New York: Dial Press, 1967.

Rowsome, Frank. *They Laughed When I Sat Down: An Informal History of Advertising in Words and Pictures.* New York: McGraw-Hill, 1959.

Seldes, Gilbert. *The Seven Lively Arts.* New York: Harper & Row, 1924.

Simkin, Colin (ed.). *Currier and Ives' America.* New York: Crown Publishers, 1952.

Stearns, Marshall. *The Story of Jazz.* New York: Oxford University Press, 1956.

Steinbeck, John. *The Grapes of Wrath.* New York: Viking Press, 1939.

Steiner, Stan. *The New Indians.* New York: Dell, 1970.

Steranko, Jim. *A History of Comics.* Reading, Pa.: A Supergraphics Publication, 1970.

Stewart, George R. *American Ways of Life.* Garden City: Doubleday, 1954.

Thurber, James. *The Thurber Carnival.* New York: Harper & Bros., 1945.

Twain, Mark. *The Adventures of Huckleberry Finn.* New York: New American Library, 1971.

Voigt, David Q. *American Baseball: From Gentleman's Sport to the Commissioner System.* Norman: University of Oklahoma Press, 1966.

Wakefield, Dan. *Going All the Way.* New York: Dell, 1970.

Warshow, Robert. *The Immediate Experience.* New York: Doubleday, 1962.

The Wizard of Oz (MGM, 1939). Director, Victor Fleming.

Printed in U.S.A.